Tales of an American
Culture Vulture

Tales of an American Culture Vulture

Bill McGuire

iUniverse, Inc.

New York Lincoln Shanghai

Tales of an American Culture Vulture

iUniverse, Inc.

For information address:
iUniverse, Inc.
2021 Pine Lake Road, Suite 100
Lincoln, NE 68512
www.iuniverse.com

ISBN: 0-595-27097-2 (pbk)
ISBN: 0-595-65650-1 (cloth)

Printed in the United States of America

I dedicate this book to my beloved maternal grandparents, Lewis and Anne Boppel, who so successfully passed on their high moral, ethical and cultural standards to their children and grandchildren. As they often reminded me, "If you do not know from where you are coming, you'll never know where you are going."

Contents

ACKNOWLEDGMENTS

I would like to express my eternal gratitude to my friend of many years, John L. Aldriedge—as his Russian-speaking friends call him "Dzhon Vasilyevich"—for all his help and encouragement in writing this book. He is an important figure in the events I describe and without his excellent knowledge of computers, there would be no book.

The idea for the cover came from my talented and devoted friend Alex Rosales. No words can express my gratitude for all he has done for me and my family over the years.

INTRODUCTION

What was it like to be a young American working on a US Government-sponsored cultural exchange exhibition in Soviet cities where the inhabitants had never seen an American before? What kinds of questions did they ask? How did they treat us? How did Soviet authorities treat us? What was it like to be among the first native-born Americans of non-Russian origin to broadcast to the Soviet Union on the Voice of America? What was it like to travel around the USA with high-level Soviet delegations or with American groups in the Soviet Union? What juicy tales can now be told that never reached the newspapers about both Soviet and American stupidities? Why did the Voice of America stop hiring Americans and replace them with recent émigrés from the USSR? These are some of the questions I try to answer in this autobiography. It is the story of my life working on American exhibitions in the former USSR, acting as an escort-interpreter for Soviet delegations visiting the USA, working eighteen years as a Russian-language broadcaster on the Voice of America and also, my second and final career, working with electronic programming in Spain and Latin America. I was very fortunate to have had two such different careers, at least geographically speaking. Nevertheless, for me both positions had American culture as the focal point.

During the height of the Vietnam war, as a guide on American exhibits in the USSR, I was often asked if I were a hawk or a dove in respect to the war. I would usually answer that I was more of a vulture, a culture vulture to be exact. I considered culture to be more important than politics in my life. I still do. Now I will go into a few reasons that prompted me to write this book. In August 1998 my dear friend of many years, with whom I studied at Georgetown University and worked with at the Voice of America, the lovely Marina Levitzky Oeltjen, gave me a copy of an article she had translated into English from the Russian journal *Tefi* from the July8, 1998 issue. I'll only quote the first paragraph.

> "VOA has been well known to us for a long time. And although the times when we called it hostile are well behind us, we still haven n t begun calling it friendly. Back in the days when we, with a fisherman's persistence, were catching it on the hooks of our receivers while floundering on the airways, and bumping into the reefs of the jammers, it was for us a unique, singular, sophis-

ticated guest with the voices of Bill McGuire or Enver Safir. Now it's lost in the choir of other voices. And yet, an old friend, however hostile, is better than two new ones."

I left the Russian Service in 1984. Yet, Russians still remember me. Several VOA employees have asked me for interviews, based on letters from their listeners, asking where I am and what became of me. Whenever I meet people over forty from today's Russia, they know my name. I am deeply honored by this.

In the summer of 1997 I attended a party at the home of my friend and neighbor, Dr. Ludmila Foster. She was entertaining a group of members of the Russian Duma (parliament). Dr. Foster invited some of her close friends from academia, the Congress of Russian Americans and a few of her Russian-speaking American friends. We three "token Gringos" (John Aldriedge, his wife Margot, and I) are often invited by the gracious Ludmila whenever she entertains guests from Russia. One of the female members remembered attending an American exhibition in 1966 and talking to a young American from Philadelphia who "had a wonderful command of the Russian language and an unforgettable sense of humor." Well, there was but one Philadelphian on that show and it was yours truly. We both agreed that the American exhibits were a real eye-opener to the average Soviet citizen. Who would ever dream in 1966 that this young Soviet visitor to the American exhibition would one day represent her city in the Russian parliament and would one day meet the young guide that impressed her so much. I knew about whom she was speaking, but I did not tell her she was speaking with him in Dr. Foster's home. More than likely I did not want her to say—as other Russians I have met since the collapse of Communism—"Oh, YOU'RE Bill McGuire? But you're no longer young!" What I considered more important than announcing myself was the significance of our American exhibitions in the former USSR. I served on three of them between the years 1966 and 1971. Few Americans even know about them. Fewer know what it was like to work on these cultural exchanges. After speaking with the Parliamentarian, I began to think seriously about writing a book.

Perhaps I was even more inspired by a meeting with seven young Russian Radio and TV journalists at USIA's Worldnet studio shortly after the collapse of the Soviet system in 1989. Worldnet Director Steve Murphy invited me to join them for a reception and a luncheon because I could speak to them in their native tongue. At first I spoke English until I realized that two of them spoke no English. When I switched to Russian, one of the men came up to me and said: "I recognize that voice. Please say the words: You are listening to the Voice of America." I repeated his words. He then continued: "This is Bill McGuire at the microphone." They all knew me from my Voice of America programs. In fact, they astounded me with their memory. They remembered things that I had said in my VOA Russian programs as long as twenty years ago. Then came the compliment of my lifetime. Another of the journalists asked if he could pose a "ticklish" question to me. I said sure. The question was: "Will you please tell us what your own social and political persuasions are? After having listened to you all these years, we could never figure out if you are a Democrat or a Republican, a liberal or a conservative, an atheist or a religious zealot…(pause) or whatever. You always seemed to give both sides to any story. In short, you never told us what YOU think." I repeat. This was the greatest compliment given to me in my life. It convinced me that my eighteen years on the Voice of America were not in vain. I had accomplished my goal. I believe that the audience of a good, professional journalist does not know these things about him or her. A second reason for writing this book.

However, the final impetus for my decision to jot down my memoirs took place on May 1, 1998. It was y birthday. I had gone home to Philadelphia to celebrate it with my uncle Charles, the last of my immediate family, most of whom passed away within the past few years. After a magnificent meal, my uncle said the following words to me: "Bill, your uncle is getting old. I have a favor to ask you before I close my eyes. Please, please write a book about your life, your career, your travels, the people you met, the things you did. You owe it to history. I want to read that book before I die." How could I say no?

I hope I have made some small contribution to spreading the good, American culture around the world while at the same time never failing to admit what is wrong with us Americans. I do not pass myself off as an expert on any subject. This book is not a history book nor a textbook. My thoughts and opinions are my own. But, as an American, I feel my thoughts and opinions are as valid as anyone else's. This book is aimed at the average American reader, not the so-called Russian expert. But, at the same time, it is also meant to inform those loyal listeners in the former USSR. While we were broadcasting how wonderful it is in the USA, they had no idea of the horrible things that were going on, and are still going on, at the Voice of America. For those who thought that the cultural exchange with the USSR was a piece of cake, this will open their eyes. Nevertheless, this book is not an expose. It is a collection of my stories and observations. I took copious notes of the happenings. There are many witnesses to back up what

I write. Some will be displeased by reading the painful truth. Others will say: Thank God someone finally is telling the truth. So here it is, the tales of this American culture vulture. Happy reading!

A MISSION BABY…OR A BABY WITH A MISSION?

It was an unusually hot, muggy evening that August 1939 as my mother and her younger sister Louise were walking up to Saint Joseph's Church in Ashland, Pennsylvania to hear the sermon of one of the Maryknoll priests who visited the parish from such far away places as China, Brazil, and the Congo to talk about the starving children the Maryknolls were caring for. Needless to say, every year the members of the parish opened up their hearts and pocketbooks to the good fathers. However, this particular sermon was different and unexpected.

Fifteen years later I was having afternoon tea with my grandmother at her home in Philadelphia. I happened to remark that I was confused why nearly half of my classmates had birthdays within a few days of my own. I hated birthday parties, especially my own. At this time of year I was forced by my parents to attend all those parties of their friends' children whom I did not particularly care for. My grandmother burst into laughter. "You are the Mission Babies," she howled. "What?" said I. Then she proceeded to recount the memorable evening in 1939 when—instead of discussing the missions—the Maryknoll priest spoke for an hour about the evils of birth control. Within a few months several of the women in the parish were "with child." I was one of the fruits of the harvest. My parents had been married for two years and were in no hurry to make babies…that is until the young Maryknoll priest put the fear of God in my mother.

While my mother was six months' pregnant, she attended a county fair, again with her sister Louise, who was always interested in the occult, the supernatural and the powers of gypsies. When Aunt Louise discovered a gypsy lady on the scene, she rushed to ask her what the future held for the young, attractive and unmarried blonde. The gypsy told her that her sister was expecting a baby, the baby would be a boy, who would resemble his Aunt Louise, and that this child would grow up to "speak many tongues," would travel far and wide and—above

1

all—his voice would be heard on the opposite end of the Earth. "Good," said Aunt Louise to my Mother. "Your son will be a Maryknoll priest."

I was born on May 1, 1940. On the opposite end of the Earth Joe Stalin and his fellow Communists were celebrating the International Day of the Proletariat.

THE EARLY YEARS, THE POST-WAR YEARS

For the United States World War II broke out in December of 1941. I was 19 months old, had all my teeth, loved to sing and was the pride and joy of my grandparents—the "first" grandchild, mind you. Within three months my father and two uncles were serving in the military. Mother and I were living in the big, old four-story house up in Ashland with the grandparents and their three unmarried daughters. The house was high up on a hill overlooking the town of Ashland. The beautiful Broad Mountain rose in front and an unnamed mountain behind our house. The cellar was huge and stored the anthracite coal, which everybody burned to keep warm and which was the main industry of the region. The mines were thriving in those days.

Our cellar also had huge vats in which my grandfather made sauerkraut (such a stench!) and wine. All this was protected by a ferocious cat named Tiger. The second floor had a living room, dining room and large kitchen, which opened out to the first of three yards. Yard number one was made of cement. A stairway of about twelve steps led to the second level, which was mainly the flower garden. Roses of every color, lilies, petunias, sunflowers and others adorned this place where I played as a child. After ascending four more short steps, one found oneself in the upper yard, the largest of the three. That was also surrounded by flowers and was the play area for our dog Boots. It also served as a place where clothes were hung out to dry in the sun. A huge gate protected us from stray dogs or strangers—not that there were strangers in a town of about 5,000 people.

The third floor of the house consisted of bedrooms and one bathroom. However, our favorite was the fourth floor, which we referred to as Comforts Cottage. It was the length of the house and had on one side a bedroom with the bedroom furniture of my great-grandmother: marble-top tables, oil lamps, a sewing machine and a trunk containing the belongings of my maternal forefathers when they left Germany for the United States. It had a huge bay window filled with my grandmother's flowers (especially gardenias) and looked out on the mountain. We always looked forward to the first snowfall. The scene from that window was superior to any Christmas card I've ever seen. However, the other part of the floor was our culture center. It had big, comfortable chairs, lovely pictures on the wall and a huge Victrola. I had the honor of winding the phonograph nightly as we listened to the music of the Dorsey Brothers (born in the nearby town of Shenandoah), the Andrews Sisters, Bing Crosby, Vera Lynn and John McCormack. The room also had a big bay window with a spectacular view of the town and Broad Mountain. Every night after dinner the entire family gathered to chat, listen to music, read and play with "the Baby."

The town of Ashland was populated by three main ethnic groups: German, Irish, English, with a few representatives of the Welsh, Italian and Jewish communities. There were several churches, mainly Protestant. The two Catholic churches (St. Joseph's and St. Mauritius) were better known as the "Irish" church and the "German" church. Each had its own school and order of nuns. Both parishes were headed by feisty, older and severely strict priests who used the whip as quickly as the tongue. Whenever a family fought with the Irish priest they would register with the German parish, and vice versa. In addition there was a lot of intermarrying between these two groups. There were less fraternal attitudes between the Protestants and Catholics and even among the Protestants. Nevertheless, the town was more homogeneous than the surrounding towns of Girardville, Shenandoah and Frackville, all of which had (God forbid!) Poles, Lithuanians, Slovaks, Ukrainians, Italians and Greeks.

In the nearby town of Lakewood each of these ethnic groups organized their national festivals during the summer months. Surprisingly enough, they were attended by everyone, mainly because the food and the music were always so good! There was no serious animosity among the residents of Schuylkill County, just some foolish ethnic pride and ignorance that existed everywhere in the 40's (and beyond).

Lakewood was also an amusement park, surrounded by a beautiful lake, and it had a huge dance pavilion. In the 30's and 40's the best of the Big Bands appeared here. It's probably where the Dorsey Brothers got their start. My Aunt Louise—still unmarried in 1944—often took me with her on dates (much to the chagrin of her beaus!!) and I was often entertained by the music of Paul Whiteman, Sammy Kaye, Glen Miller, Harry James and others.

Several local events of the 40's stand out in my memory to this day. For instance, sugar was rationed. I remember going to the local bakery to order my—and others'—birthday cakes and we had to bring sugar for the cake. Butter was also in short supply. I enjoyed watching my grandmother making oleomargarine in the electric mixer. I participated by putting the food coloring in at the very end. We were more fortunate than some families because my grandfather's sister-in-law, Aunt Katie Boppel, had a grocery store a few blocks from our home. Through her we often had access to rare commodities.

One of my earliest recollections was when the first Ashland boy killed in the War was brought home for burial. His name was O'Donnell, and he arrived one evening at dusk by train. The entire town, including all my family, went down to the station to welcome our local hero. As the flag-draped coffin was unloaded from the train everybody burst into tears. I asked my grandfather, "What's in the box that makes people cry?" His response—"The body of our Ashland son killed in the war"—made no sense to me. But I knew it was serious when grandfather lost control and wept bitterly.

A second encounter with death, this time much more vivid, came about a year later when a local seven-year old boy died of poliomyelitis. His family was too poor for a funeral parlor, so the manager of the local Kresge store allowed the body to be viewed in the display window of the store. My Aunt Mary told the story that when I saw the coffin in the window with her, I asked: "Is that dummy in the box for sale? How much?"

The War ended, but not until every family in America, mine included, had its share of sorrow. My cousin Tommy was killed on Christmas day near the town in Germany from which his ancestors came. My father was a Naval officer whose ship was torpedoed by the Japanese in the Pacific in 1944. He almost lost his right arm and suffered from that injury until the day he died. I remember the day he arrived home in uniform in 1945. My grandmother reminded me that he was my father and that soon I would be going to live with my mother and him. I ran into the kitchen and made him an American cheese sandwich with a lot of mustard. Later that day, grandmom said she was impressed with my "hospitality," but she also asked why I made a cheese sandwich? We had other things and she knew I HATED cheese. "Yes, I hate cheese," I replied, "and I hope he does too. Maybe that will make him return to the Navy and leave me in peace with my real mommy and daddy." Going to live with my parents was traumatic. However, I managed to spend every weekend with the grandparents. I would take an overnight bag to school on Fridays and go directly to the "folks" after school. My parents had a rich social life, so my absence was not felt that much. They were smart enough to realize that nobody could give me the love, affection and support I got from my grandparents.

Perhaps my grandparents spoiled me in that whatever I wanted I got. But I was loving, respectful and grateful to them at all times. They never had to chastise me with harsh words or a strap. Instead they had a way of looking at me with eyebrows raised. I knew it meant "be good." In addition, they always took my part against everyone, especially my parents, and on one occasion against the nun that taught me in third grade. We were studying Bible History one day and the nun was quoting Jesus Chris, "Let he who is without sin cast the first stone." I raised my hand and asked, "Why didn't the Virgin Mary pick up a rock and let him have it?" Sister flew into a rage and gave me a hard one—right in the kisser! I had never been hit. I threw my catechism book in her face, called her a wicked witch and ran out. I found a cab and had him take me the nine-mile trip to my grandparents. Grandpop was a bit shocked (especially at the cab fare!!). However, when I told him what happened, he called the Mother Superior and informed her that if any nun in that school ever laid her hand on his grandson, he'd break the hand of the nun. She said she would discuss the matter with Mr. McGuire. "Don't worry about him, Mother. If he allows a nun to touch our Billy, I'll break BOTH of his hands."

After that no nun had the nerve to touch me. I was a good student, studied hard, respected everybody. I did not, however, like my classmates. I was much more comfortable with older people. Kids bored me. I had neither the time nor desire to play with my classmates. By age ten I was taking art, piano and dancing lessons. After a while I gave up the art and piano to concentrate on dance. I wanted to be a choreographer, a famous one. I'd spend hours in front of the mirror inventing new steps. My teacher, who had studied ballet in London with Tamara Karsavina, encouraged me. But, at the same time, she agreed with my family that an education is necessary…just in case.

Growing up I had the best of two worlds. I am grateful to have spent the first five years of my life in a small, American town like Ashland, Pennsylvania. Everyone knew everyone, helped and cared for everyone (knew everyone else's business!!) Doors were not locked at night. Crime was limited to some guy getting drunk and punching his old lady. Profanity was not heard. Girls did not have babies out of wedlock and children knew who their father was. Holidays were very special, especially Memorial Day, July 4th, Labor Day and Thanksgiving. Religious holidays like Christmas and Easter were just that. No memory is more inspirational for me than the entire family walking up a snow-covered hill for midnight mass on Christmas eve and coming home to sing Christmas carols before going to bed. The next day family and friends joined forces to celebrate this joyous day. At the same time, I had the luxury—if one would call it so—to have a family home in Philadelphia. My grandmother and I would often take the morning King Coal train down to Philadelphia to spend a few days with my aunts in West Philly. We soaked up all the culture there was. Life was a series of shopping at Wanamakers, seeing movies at the Mastbaum, the Fox or the Earle, plays and concerts, visiting family and friends. We called Philadelphia "the City," and we enjoyed all it had to offer; but we also were delighted to take the 5:30 pm train back to Comforts Cottage.

PREPARING FOR
THE MISSION

Whatever I have been and am today I owe to the combined efforts of my family and my Catholic education. The family instilled in me a sense of pride in who I am, where I come from and where I want to go. But I owe even more to the Sisters of the Immaculate Heart of Mary, who taught me in elementary school. Thanks to them I survived the U.S. Army, the Soviet Union, the Voice of America and all tragedies in my personal life. In addition to the three R's, they taught us to be good, honest, truthful, patriotic, charitable, tolerant and self-disciplined human beings. Needless to say, not all of us are the perfect products the nuns tried to form. The system worked for centuries and it works today. The problem is not the system, but the flawed few in it, be they nuns, priests or students. Nothing irritates me more than those who attack religion and religious education. It is the church—and not just the Catholic Church—that cares for unwanted children, for the sick and the infirm, the elderly and abandoned. I have yet to see an orphanage, a hospital or an old age home operated by any liberal group. Their endeavors to place women on the same level as alley cats, to abort the seed in the womb, to give clean needles to drug addicts and to do whatever feels good at the moment are hardly in the interest of humanity. While I agree with many who fight for equal rights for everybody, equal pay and opportunities for all and—above all—for respect for human dignity, I see the breakdown of the civilization it took us centuries to build.

As I reflect on my early school days (I never really liked school until I got to college) I realize how important it was to learn not only the three R's, but penmanship, geography, spelling, history, languages. My fifth grade nun in Annunciation school was excellent at geography. I remember how she made us study not only the capital of the countries, but we each had to do research on a second major city of the country. When we studied the Soviet Union, I chose Novosibirsk (I have no reason why. Probably because I could not pronounce it.) We prayed daily to the Virgin Mary that the USSR would return to God and to the civilized society from which it came. Seeing pictures of Lenin and Stalin frightened me. They had such cruel, demonic faces. I was fascinated by the history of Siberia, the birch forests, the rich mineral wealth, the folk costumes and above all the history and traditions of the Russian Orthodox Church. When I visited Novosibirsk in 1971, it was like revisiting a place I had already known.

Another lesson I learned very early in my schooling was tolerance. I never remember the nuns making a cruel or biased statement about anybody. Above all I remember Sister Mary Martha chastising the entire class one day when a new boy arrived to study with us. By the way, he was not a Catholic. In the middle of the morning he had an epileptic seizure. It scared all of us half to death and he was sent home. One boy remarked, "I'm never going to play with Joseph, Sister. What if I catch his disease?" Sister spent nearly an hour lecturing us about "people who were different from us." Any of us could be afflicted with epilepsy or any other disease, for that matter. In the eyes of God Joseph was equal to any of us. We must love him, respect him and help him. She ended with a statement that made no sense to me at the time. Now I realize the wisdom of her words. "Whenever you see anybody that is different from you, instead of making fun of him or her, imagine that person was in the majority and you in the minority. How would you want that person to treat you? Look at all other human beings as flowers in the garden of God and be grateful that we are part of that garden."

I was very good at spelling, history, catechism, geography and, later, languages; however, to this day I cannot make two and two come out four. Science was interesting, but I never devoted much effort to it because I thought most scientists were crazy. I happened to be at Princeton University (where my father taught for a while) in the late 40's and ran into Albert Einstein on the campus. I asked my father if they also had an insane asylum on the grounds. He said, "No, why?" I was certain that man had escaped from the loony bin. Dad said he was the most important scientist of the 20th century and a genius who suffered greatly at the hands of the Nazis. My response, "So that's why he looks that way?"

My father later went on to teach at La Salle in Philadelphia. He was a professor of Latin and Ancient Greek. These guys were rarely known for their sense of humor. However, I remember two times in his life when he cracked a joke and both incidents occurred at La Salle. Once we were chatting with some exchange professors from die Freie Universitaet of Berlin. A Jewish colleague brought up the war. Their immediate answer was that among the population nobody had any idea of what was going on. Dad then asked them, "Didn't you suspect anything when your gas bills rocketed?" No response. The second gem came a few years later when a Soviet basketball team played the La Salle team. It was the first time in my life I ever saw Russians in person. They walked out onto the court looking as if they had just seen a ghost. Not a smile on any of them. When they lost the game they looked fearful and depressed. Later there was a reception for the Soviet athletes. I could not help but notice the steel teeth, the body odor and the horrible stench that came from their cigarettes. My father took my comments lightly and merely said, "What can you expect from a country that does not have Lucky Strike or Camels?"

By the time I was a junior I was seriously thinking about college. I had aready had Latin and German. In both courses I was always first in the class. German was and always will remain my favorite language. I think this is partially because of my own German and Irish roots. Regardless, never have I felt more American than during my two trips to the Emerald Isle and dozens of trips to Germany. This "roots" fascination can be carried too far. If one is born, raised and educated in the USA, one IS an American. Period. We must all be proud of our ancestors and heritage, but let us never forget that the United States is one country where you can be an Italian and an American at the same time. I also believe it is up to the family, not the government, to preserve our languages and cultures. I have seen with my own eyes the disastrous results of bilingual education. It usually produces illiterates in two languages.

By age sixteen I gave up the notion of becoming a famous choreographer and knew I wanted to work with foreign languages. The thought of becoming an interpreter for the United Nations appealed to me. My junior class visited the UN one day, and I listened to the voice of Mr. Nicholas Orloff translate from Russian into English. I wrote him a letter, which—to my surprise—he answered. First he suggested that I finish high school (a marvelous idea!) and then study Russian at a major American institution. He explained that UN interpreters were trained in Moscow at a special school subsidized by the UN. Nevertheless, I also wanted to pursue the German language, literature and culture. I never wanted to become a stuffy college professor like so many I knew through my father. No, not I. I had other interests, mainly watching the American Bandstand, which I never missed, and listening to Bill Haley and the Comets, Elvis Presley, Buddy Holly, Georgia Gibbs, Bobby Rydel, Frankie Avalon, Fabian Forte and Connie Francis. Oh, yes, I liked the Rhythm and Blues artists as well, especially Ruth Brown.

Two events, however, impressed me greatly and began to steer me into the direction of Russian. The first was the launching of Sputnik. What American was not impressed that those dirty Commies could send a satellite into space and later sew two heads on a dog? Little did we know that they could not make decent toilet paper or chewing gum...or that they were continuing to send people to concentration camps, normal people to insane asylums, dissidents to jail. Wasn't this the same country that brutally suppressed the uprisings in East Germany and Hungary? Was this not the land that persecuted all religions, that turned children into informers on their parents, that sent residents of the Baltics to Siberia to starve and/or freeze to death? No, suddenly this was the new Mecca of science and technology, the country of the future, possibly the language of the future.

The second influence was to read Doctor Zhivago and become totally mesmerized by the events in that book. I was confused by the various nicknames one person could have (Larisa, Lara, Larochka, etc.) but also mesmerized by the magnificent poetry of Pasternak. I thought to myself that I must learn more about this distant land. In fact, I bought a Russian pocket dictionary. Then I wrote a letter to Boris Pasternak in English, but wrote the envelope in Russian from the alphabet I found on page one of the dictionary. Little did I realize that Russian had declension, conjugation and that the country goes first, followed by the city, street and name of the addressee in the dative case. In spite of my errors, the letter must have reached him in Peredelkino. About four months later I received a letter (with a Soviet stamp—Wow!!) and a small note in English saying, "Receive this unsigned greeting from a person that was pleased to read your letter. Glad you liked the novel. Best wishes for the future." Why wouldn't anyone sign his name? I decided it was written by the KGB and threw it away. However, that book—much later the film—convinced me I must be in some way connected with Mother Russia, even if she now called herself the Soviet Union.

THE GEORGETOWN
UNIVERSITY YEARS

My years at Georgetown University were perhaps the happiest and most rewarding of my life. I was exposed to people from all over the world, people of stature
and grace, money and influence, people of different religions and philosophies,
people who were there to learn and not just to have fun. The fun seekers did not
survive long, though. Even though many thought of Georgetown as a party
school, one had to study hard to graduate. Many of the teachers taught for one
dollar a year. To me it showed their love and devotion to education. Then there
were the Jesuits. Ah, the Jesuits! They were there too. I learned to both respect
them and like them. I was shocked to hear my theology professor begin the class
one day by saying that if Christ did not want us to drink, the first miracle would
not have been turning water into wine. I remembered his words but waited until
I was twenty-one before ever tasting wine. In a later class devoted to marriage,
Father Belwoar (a Philadelphian) gave an impressive answer to a student who
asked why celibate priests should be teaching a class on marriage. Father
reminded him that you need not be the best wrestler to be the best referee.

One of the first classmates I met was Sadeh Ghotzbadeh, a young Iranian (he
usually called himself a Persian) with a huge emerald ring on his finger. Obviously a man of means, or a family of means. We worked part-time together in the
language laboratory of the Institute of Languages and Linguistics. Sadeh taught
me to write my name in Persian and I, in turn, taught him how to write his name
in Cyrillic. We got along well, although he was very critical of the United States
government and people, not to mention the Jesuits! Sadeh talked incessantly
about the "Old Man" who would save Iran from "that terrible Shah." One
evening Sadeh arrived at the lab with his hand all bandaged up. When people
asked him what happened, he replied that day he had gone down to the Iranian
Embassy to kill the ambassador and someone shut the door on his hand. Sadeh
was not known as the perfect Muslim. Although he spoke a lot about Allah, he
drank, smoked, had passions for women and men and had some really wild par-

ties at his home. Finally Sadeh was thrown out of Georgetown for missing too many classes. I thought I would never see nor hear from him again. But I was wrong. Years later, after the Shah fled Iran, our American TV stations showed Ayatollah Khomeni leaving Paris to take control of the Iranian government. Who was right by his side? My Georgetown buddy, Sadeh Ghotzbabeh, dressed, as always, in a finely-tailored suit, even wearing the ring. He was appointed Minister of Foreign Affairs, but most likely could not resist the "good life" on the side. He was later executed. I wonder who got the ring?

I shall never forget my first day of Introductory Russian. On that day I learned the most important guideline for dealing with that world. The class of about fifteen was seated when our professor walked into the room. He was a short man (about 5'7") with a mustache, an enchanting smile, too much cologne—who seemed to walk, talk and act on double speed. His choppy gestures made us wonder if this man were for real. Would we really learn anything from this puppet? Actually Dr. Mikhail Georgievich Krupensky turned out to be the best teacher I have ever had. He was born in St. Petersburg in an aristocratic family. His father served in the Duma under Tsar Nicholas II. He was brought up with private tutors and studied in St. Petersburg, Prague, Bucharest, Paris and Berlin. When Dr. Krupensky taught us a new word, for instance, he would not only give us the entomology of the word but would compare it to the same word in other languages. For example. "Today you will learn the word for 'watermelon' in Russian. It is 'arbuz' and has Turkish origins. Yes, notice that it is different from the Greek 'karpuzi' or the Spanish 'sandia' or the Dutch word 'watermelon.'"

But let's get back to the first lesson. After looking around the room to see who was in his class, he sat down at his desk and said with a very thick but charming accent: "Ladies and gentlemen, I am your teacher this semester. My name is Krupensky, Mikhail Georgievich. Born in Imperial St. Petersburg. God save the Tsar! (He bowed his head.) As you begin your study of things Russian, I want you to ALWAYS keep one important thing in mind. Whenever you have two Russians, you have three opinions." How true those words turned out to be!

Mikhail Georgievich was of the old school. He was a strict grammarian and expected his students to put as much effort into the course as he did. Although he had been teaching for years, he acted like every class was the first, and he gave it the same attention and enthusiasm of a new teacher on the first day of the school year. You had to love him. He reminded me a lot of my grandfather. For whatever reason, he liked me too. Perhaps he sensed my deep interest in what he was teaching. We had weekly tests for which I usually got a perfect score. The first time I did not, he delivered the test to my desk and exclaimed, "Oops poops!" (his favorite expression for everything, good or bad). He grabbed my green necktie and commented, "Well, green is the color of hope. I hope next time you will do better. You CAN do better." I could feel the blood drain from my head. I almost shook with fear. Then I looked at my disgraceful paper to discover that I had made only one mistake. That comment forced me to study ever harder. I wanted him to be proud of me.

We continued to learn what seemed to be an impossible language, with more exceptions than rules, countless numbers of declensions, conjugations...in what other language would the word for man (muzhchina) have a feminine ending?...where every verb has two aspects...where verbs of motion depend on the mode of motion...where numerals can be declined in the middle and the end...what a language!!! I began to feel I would never be able to make a sentence using the instrumental case or to use the command form of the verbs. Dr. Krupensky used to say that one night we would dream in Russian and then the language would become easier. To this day I have never dreamed in Russian There were two especially memorable classes. The first was the day we heard that every Russian has a first name and a patronymic (the father's name) and that in polite society one addressed a Russian using both names. Dr. Krupensky gave all of us a Russian name and patronymic based on our father's first name. Since I was one of about four named William in the class, he did not want all of us to be called Vasilii. Knowing of my German roots, he christened me Vilgelm Ivanovich (after the German name Wilhelm), and to this day my colleagues in the Russian world call me by that name. The funniest name, by the way, was that of an elderly lady who was taking the course in preparation for an upcoming trip to the USSR with her husband. She was Ekaterina Archibaldovna and was like a child with a new toy when she was given her new identity. Dr. K became so accustomed to calling me by my Russian name that I believe he forgot my real one. Two years later my mother was visiting me. We ran into Dr. Krupensky in the corridor and I told Mother she must meet my first Russian professor, about whom I spoke so much. "Dr. Krupensky, I want you to meet my Mother, Juel McGuire." He clicked his heels, kissed her hand and exclaimed: "Delighted to meet you, Mrs....Mrs....Mother of Vilgelm Ivanovich!" Mother smiled and replied, "Nice to meet you too, Dostoyevsky. You obviously know my son by another name than I do. It sounds very un-American." The second class was for men only. The film "Quiet Flows the Don," based on the novel (later found to be plagiarized) by

Nobel prize winner Mikhail Sholokhov, was showing in Washington. The class was going to go with our teacher to see it. Certainly our Russian was not yet at the level that we would understand the film without subtitles, but Mikhail Georgievich wanted us to understand certain words that he could not teach in class, mainly profanity. Russian is very rich in profanity. So, the good professor took all the men across the street to Teehan's restaurant, ordered beer and proceeded to shock all of us with the wealth of vulgar words in the Russian language. I was so impressed that I began to invite Dr. K for other one-on-one sessions at Teehan's (the beer was on me) to learn more. At the time I had no idea that knowing and using these words in future trips to the USSR would help me in my work. For example, in 1975 in Moscow I was conversing with a very high-ranking Soviet official, a woman no less, and she was handing me the usual Soviet crap about the glorious USSR. When I exclaimed, "That is a bunch of…kh" she hugged me and replied: "Darling, you speak Russian so well." It endeared me to her forever! Unfortunately for me and the rest of the Russian majors, we lost Dr. K After the first semester. The other professors were not of his quality; and the Russian department was far behind the French, German, Spanish and Arabic chairs. Twenty-two of us began as Russian majors, and only two actually graduated with a degree. Georgetown made the same mistake that was made all over the country in those days—they thought that to teach Russian, you had to be a native speaker. Ridiculous. As a result, we had "native speakers" who were biologists, former Soviet Air Force pilots, sculptors, etc. Most of them expected us to leap from Introductory Russian to reading Tolstoy and Dostoyevsky with nothing in between. The courses taught about these great writers were first-class, but we were not prepared to do the readings. For instance, one day I complained to Dr. Marianna Poltoratzky, the department head, that I knew I was not ready for these courses; but she said to me, "Darling, you are speaking Russian to me, whether you realize it or not. Come take my course." And that was that. I began to lose interest in the language. In fact, I took all my electives in German and not one in Russian. I refused to even sing in the Russian choir during the yearly Christmas concerts at the Institute of Languages and Linguistics. The German Department was excellent, and I found myself going back to my original love. I took every course Prof. Herta Mueller taught. She was a strict, hard-line, no-nonsense teacher of the European school with little or no sense of humor. Her love of her native language, literature and history—and her ability to pass it on to her students—more than compensated for her nasty side, of which we were all well aware. I was one of the few students to whom she gave an A. Just before I graduated in 1963 I ran into her in the corridor of the Walsh building. She stopped me to say: Herr McGuire, I want you to know that you were one of the most talented and dedicated students ever to attend my classes. I admire your work, your ability and your strange sense of humor. As a student I have to like you. As a human being, I find you distasteful." What a boost for my ego! I had to reply, right? "Frau Mueller, you are one of the finest teachers at Georgetown…after Dr. Krupensky (whom she hated). As a professor of the great German language, you have my utmost respect. You know I took every course you teach. As a person, however, I cannot stand you. You are as close to a witch as I've ever come. Zum Nimmerwiedersehen!"

Another driving force took place my first year at Georgetown. One of my friends once told me that if I wanted to have a great social life at Georgetown, I should befriend the many Latin American students there. I did not speak a word of Spanish, nor was I interested in beginning a third language until I mastered Russian. Quite by accident I met a group of young Mexican students studying English as a second language (for which Georgetown had become famous). Among them was Luis Rafael Macedo of Colima. The following year we roomed together and through him I met several other Latinos. They sure did know how to party! Yet the parties were dignified. There was no use of drugs, limited alcohol, complete respect for the Latin girls (less for the Gringuitas) and wonderful music to dance to. Little by little I began to pick up individual words in Spanish. I also got to know a Mexican Jesuit, Padre Acevez, and the beautiful daughter of the Mexican ambassador, Lupita Carrillo Flores.

All of us teamed up in December of 1961 to organize the first Guadalupe Day celebration at Georgetown. The Virgin of Guadalupe, although she appeared in Mexico, was named Patroness of All the Americas by the Vatican. Our group decided to include everybody in the celebration. So, on December 12 we began by attending a mass in Dahlgren Chapel, marched together to the School of Foreign Service three blocks away, where we dined on Mexican food catered by el Sombrero Cordobes and later were entertained by other students from throughout the Americas. There were songs and dances from Mexico, Argentina, Colombia, Venezuela, Cuba, Nicaragua, the United States and a real show-stopper from the Brazilians. This event became a tradition at Georgetown, at least until after I graduated.

It was at one of the Guadalupe celebrations that one of the Spanish professors, Conchita Paddock, took me aside and said the following words: "Bill, my dearest, when are you going to open your eyes? What ARE you doing in the Russian department? You do not have a Russian soul, you have a Latin soul. The Russians have no soul; they only think they do. Drop all that nonsense and come study Spanish with me and all your favorite American friends. You were meant to be with us. That's why your best friends are studying Spanish, your girlfriend is a Mexican, you dance the guaguanco like a Cuban, and God sent you to begin the Guadalupe Day celebration at our university." I was touched beyond words. Nevertheless I reminded the sweet Prof. Paddock that I had spent much time and money to learn Russian. I was first in the class. I felt after graduation I had a better chance of employment with Russian than with Spanish. She became very irate and—while shaking her finger at my nose—decried: "One day you will see the light. You will forget that awful language and you will work with your brothers and sisters throughout the Americas. And, at last, YOU will be happy." I kissed her hand and thanked her for her confidence in me.

Several years later (1984 to be exact) when I finally left the Voice of America after eighteen years with complete burnout, I went over to USIA's Office of Satellite Speakers as Program Officer for Spain and Latin America. My first transmission from our TV studio was a program to Venezuela. When I entered the studio a man with gray hair was standing there. He asked me if that was the correct studio for the program to Venezuela. I reminded him it would be in Spanish. "No problem," he answered, "I spoke it all my life." After the show I asked him how he enjoyed the program. He did. "By the way, my name is Bill McGuire. And yours?" "Kit Paddock of the USIA International Visitors Bureau." Paddock? I suddenly heard the voice of Conchita Paddock of many years ago making her prediction. "Are you any relation to Prof. Conchita Paddock who taught Spanish at Georgetown University in the '60's?" "Yes, that's my mother." I almost fainted. "Well, tell her she was right about me. She might not remember me, but I remember her. She predicted that one day I would work with Latin America and finally find peace of mind." "Mother passed away a few years ago while visiting me in Peru," said Mr. Paddock.

I had many Cuban friends as well at Georgetown. From day one I was impressed with Cuban culture, the fantastic music, the beauty of the Cuban girls, their sincerity and openness. About the same time, many of their families had to leave Cuba after Fidel Castro came to power. The only time in my life I ever participated in a political demonstration was in the early '60's when I joined other students, both Cuban and American, to condemn Fidel Castro. We marched in front of the White House. I felt like I was becoming politically mature.

Washington was becoming a haven for many Cuban refugees, who fled their homeland with nothing but the clothes on their backs. Georgetown was looking for volunteer English teachers to train these doctors, lawyers, educators, scientists and other professionals in English. It was one of the most rewarding periods of my life. Most of my students went on to make it here in the USA, and for years I received Christmas cards from them. These people had lost everything and lived from hand to mouth. Yet, their generosity was amazing. They often came to class with maduros, ropa vieja or Cuban pastries for me. I weighed 145 pounds at the time. Maybe they thought I needed the food more than they did! At the time I was sharing an apartment on Harvard Street, NW with my buddy Barrie Ciliberti. One of my neighbors was a concert pianist from Havana named America Suarez. The building had a baby grand piano in the lobby, and almost nightly Senora Suarez played for us. She had two beautiful daughters younger than myself. We all spent many happy hours together. About twenty years later my mother and I were shopping at Tysons Corner in Virginia. A woman with a teenage daughter began to stare at me. She finally approached me and asked if my name was Bill something or other. It was one of the daughters. Her daughter asked Miriam: "Who is that man, Mommy?" The reply: "He used to teach English to your grandmother."

One of the first people I met when arriving at Georgetown was a girl from Wilmington, Delaware named Marie Delikat, affectionately called Manya by family and friends. She was also studying Russian but in graduate school. Since I was born on May 1 and Manya on November 7 (Russian Revolution Day), we decided that we were put on the Earth to save Mother Russia from Communism. Dr. Krupensky agreed. Many a night we burned midnight oil discussing how we would do it. There was no answer. But she helped me with my Russian and years later—after she married my roommate, Barrie Ciliberti,—we both wound up at the Voice of America, and we actually lived to see the collapse of Communism. Unfortunately, our friendship did not last because of the terrible atmosphere at the VOA in the '70's, which helped break up friendships of many years.

One friendship that has lasted all these years—and just gets stronger—is my relationship with a Russian-American girl from New York City named Tamara Azarova, who arrived in my junior year but was immediately placed in the Advanced Russian class. She had all the good traits of both cultures. She admired both while acknowledging—like myself—that we were Americans. She was stunning, but I was rather shy in those days. I watched her in class but never spoke. Finally, one evening in the cafeteria I saw her sitting alone at a table. As I passed,

I suddenly decided to break the ice. "What is a nice Jewish girl like you doing eating pork?" "I'm not Jewish." I saw the pork on her plate and should have thought of a better opening line. At any rate, the night we celebrated thirty years of friendship, we dined on pork to commemorate my stupid question that led to an eternal friendship. She, too, wound up at the Voice of America as part of the Georgetown "mafia" a few years later.

I was not politically concerned nor active in my early years, but I did support Richard Nixon in his race against John F. Kennedy. Kennedy lived a few yards from the University and attended mass at Holy Trinity most Sundays. I did too until I got sick of seeing the adoring crowds around Kennedy and returned to our chapel on campus. The first time I showed up with my big I LIKE NIXON button, I was almost tarred and feathered. Even my theology professor asked me how could I, a Philadelphia Irish Catholic, be against Senator Kennedy? I reminded him that the man gave me bad vibes. I did not think he was sincere nor good for the country. "If it's any consolation to you, Father, the rest of my family supports Kennedy. Besides, I am too young to vote but never too young to have an opinion. I thought that our Church supported individuality."

One morning—completely unexpectedly—our Russian class was visited by a group of Soviet teachers of English from Moscow. They wanted to see how Russian was taught in the USA. They could not have come to a worse class. The teacher, although a kind, elderly gentleman—the scientist I mentioned earlier—was using a Soviet textbook called "Russian as We Speak It" by Nina Potapova. He was probably unaware that our own Georgetown Professor Michael Zarechnak's Russian textbook was already out and was probably used more outside of Georgetown U. than within. Our Soviet textbook, full of typical Communist propaganda, was what the Soviets saw and were shocked. We were learning dialogues that were absurd. An example: "Hello. My name is Misha. My father, Oleg, is a miner. He and his coworkers overfulfilled their plan this month and were awarded the Outstanding Red Banner by the local committee. My mother works in Factory Number 46, and my sister is studying physics through a correspondence course." Need I say more? The teachers began to speak to us in Russian and were not very impressed. They suggested we all spend a year in Moscow at Moscow State University, and we would come home speaking flawless Russian. To me the teachers did not come across as sincere. They smelled a bit. Above all, they seemed to take their cue from a dumpy, older man with two gold front teeth. That evening there was a reception for the Soviet teachers at Georgetown, and all the department students were invited. What made this evening so special was that it was the evening that President Kennedy gave his famous Cuban missile crisis speech. Someone brought a radio for us to hear the President's words. I could hardly keep from laughing. Our guests had absolutely no reaction. The evening ended on a sour note.

Georgetown University had an impressive Junior Year Abroad program, and most of our students took advantage of it. The remaining Russian majors asked for a meeting with our new department head, Father Frank Fadner, after Dr. Poltoratzky left for greener pastures. We expressed our frustrations to the good Jesuit, and he listened attentively (at least we thought he did). Finally he announced his decision. "As long as I am in charge of the Russian department, not one soul from this school will have anything to do with the Soviet Union. Case dismissed." About three months later Father Fadner called another meeting with us. He gleefully announced: "Ladies and gentlemen (there were only gentlemen), I have a solution to your problem. I have found an institution of higher learning where you may go for your junior year." "Where is it, Father?," we asked. "It's called Collegio do San Vladimiro in the south of Brazil run by Russian Jesuits." Was he joking? Unfortunately not. We might have considered it, had Portuguese been our minor, but going to Brazil (in the jungle, no less) did not turn any of us on.

I have to admit that Georgetown realized its mistakes and, after I graduated, brought in an American to teach Russian. Dr. Robert Lager (whom I've never met) produced some of the finest speakers of Russian and even began an exchange program with Leningrad University.

Visitors from the Soviet Union in the early '60's were few and far between. Only the most trusted comrades were allowed out and, even then, had to leave loved ones behind as hostages. One exception was the infamous Minister of Culture, Ekaterina Furtseva, who always traveled with her interpreter-bodyguard and KGB "nyanka" Alla Butrova. Furtseva was here to open up a Soviet cultural exchange program and to see the sights of Washington. Marjorie Merriweather Post held a reception for the Minister at her Hillwood estate, which was adorned with icons and other Russian treasures that Mrs. Post's husband bought for pennies back in the '20's when the USSR needed hard currency. Mrs. Post invited Jacqueline Bouvier Kennedy, as well as some of the Russian majors from Georgetown, to act as hosts. At the given time Furtseva arrived in a huge black limo. Pleasantries were exchanged at the door and then the ladies entered the home. Instantly the Minister of Culture could not contain herself upon seeing the treasures. "These items should be in the Soviet Union!!!!," she yelled like a mad-woman. "Return them!" Everyone was shocked by the behavior of the Minister. Those who knew more about the USSR and her personally were aware that this Communist peasant was not capable of any other reaction, much less able to hide it. First Khrushchev pounding the podium at the UN. Now Furtseva bursting into a fit of rage at a formal reception. Just what was with these Soviet officials, I thought? I remembered a favorite phrase of my grandfather, "What can one expect from a pig but a grunt?"

I must here tell a joke that was floating around the USSR after Furtseva's death. It seems that Pablo Picasso died and arrived at the Golden Gate. He announced that he was Pablo Picasso and deserved a place in eternity. St. Peter told him that from now on people had to prove who they were, not just give a name. Picasso grabbed a sheet of paper and made a drawing. "Indeed you are Pablo Picasso," said St. Peter…"Go on in." A few minutes later Ekaterina Furtseva arrived at the gate. "I am Ekaterina Alekseevna Furtseva, Minister of Culture of Soviet Union. Let me in!." "Just a minute," replied St. Peter. "You say you are the Soviet Minis-ter of Culture, but you have to prove it." Furtseva flew into a rage. "Look…said Peter…Nothing against you personally. We are just checking IDs. Five minutes ago even Pablo Picasso had to prove who he was." "Pablo Picasso???"—asked Furtseva—"Who is he??" "Oh, this is definitely the Minister of Culture of the Soviet Union," replied St. Peter.

At Georgetown I had other opportunities to meet very cultured Russians. There were several Russian-Americans in my class. Two of them went on to interpret for several American presidents. Others had distinguished careers in government and the private sector. But we were also fortunate to have contact with Russian emigres. The most impressive lecturer in my days there was Countess Alexandra Tolstoy, daughter of the writer. She filled the room of the Walsh auditorium one Friday evening. Among the attendees were four diplomats from the Soviet Embassy. Alexandra Lvovna recounted touching stories about her father, their life on the Yasnaya Polyana estate, the "good, old days." Then she began to speak about the Tolstoy Foundation, which she founded, to help refugees from Com-munism. Her diatribe against the Soviet system—especially when she called the Kremlin leaders thugs and butchers—angered the diplomats, who quickly left the room. I was honored to have met her and later in my career her niece Vera Tol-stoy, who befriended me and whom I love and admire to this day.

I graduated from Georgetown University in June 1963. It was one of the hottest days I can remember. It was a also bitter-sweet day for me. During the commencement I was the surprised recipient of the Regent's Award for 1963, a great honor indeed. But, after accepting the citation, I looked into the audience and was overcome with sadness. It was the day my grandparents always wanted to see. They were not there. My grandfather had died with me by his side in 1952, and my beloved grandmother was bedridden after a series of strokes.

THE YEARS 1963–1966

I am not going to go into much detail of my life after I graduated from Georgetown. I knew military service was catching up with me and, unlike many of my colleagues and one family member, I did not become a "Kennedy husband" to avoid the draft. No private companies would consider me. On the other hand, the Cyrillic Bibliographic Project of the Library of Congress needed Russian speakers (actually readers) for a certain program, which I suspected was funded by the CIA. Maybe not. It paid well, and I enjoyed the work. Our section had its share of deranged people, but they were neither vicious nor threatening to me and the few American-born coworkers. They gave me a very nice good-bye party when I finally received my draft notice. I was to report on November 27, 1963.

Many people remember what they were doing when they heard that President Kennedy had been shot. In my case I was breaking up my small apartment on 42nd Street NW, selling some items, putting others in storage. The phone rang. It was my dear friend from my Georgetown years, Fran Barbour, to tell me the horrible news. Although I was not a fan of John F. Kennedy, I did not want to see him, or anybody else, shot to death. I grieved with the rest of the country. As scheduled, I was inducted into the U.S. Army on November 27 and sent to Fort Dix, New Jersey for basic training. I often refer to my military service as my two-year course in humility, which I flunked. Basic Training was a real eye-opener for me. For the first time in my life I had to eat, sleep and train with guys who had raped their girlfriends, family members, spent time in prison, had little or no education, had a chip on their shoulders and resented college graduates.

Rarely did I mention that I had a degree in Russian. I did, however, take the language test for Russian and German and received a very high score. My testing officer assured me I would probably be sent to Monterey to teach or become a translator. It took the Army thirteen months to finally make me an offer, actually two. Either I could attend the Army Language School to learn Vietnamese (they had to be joking, right?) or go to a Russian listening post in Korea. All I had to do was volunteer to spend one more year in the Army. To me it was not one year but 365 days. I said no.

I lucked out three times in my Army career. After basic training most of my unit was sent to Vietnam. I and just a few others were shipped off to Signal School in Ft. Gordon, Ga. After I completed the course in Morse code and other radio-affiliated work, I was told that I was going to the 69th Signal Battalion in Ft. Eustis, Va. as a Radio Operator. Most of the class was sent to Vietnam. Finally, just as I was about to be granted an "early out" to attend school in Germany, my unit came down on orders for Vietnam. The day they arrived in Saigon, the convoy was attacked by the Viet Cong, and thirty of my buddies lost their lives.

One might ask, "Just what did I do for Uncle Sam?" Once I was in possession of a typewriter I used to say "I'm a Remington raider; I never retreat, I just backspace!" I arrived in Ft. Eustis in early 1964. They had no need for me, so I was assigned to the Motor Pool. Keep in mind I still do not know a spark plug from a muffler. The sergeant was so appalled with my lack of knowledge and enthusiasm for the work that he simply told me to disappear. By that time I made friends with another college grad from New York named Don Masco. He was a clerk of some kind—also with little to do. So, every morning around 10am Don and I would take off for the canteen, drink several cups of coffee, listen to the Beach Boys on the juke box, and discuss what we'd do when we got out of the Army. We referred to these trips to the canteen as "Masco-bating."

One hot April morning I was reading a book under a large Army truck when I saw two well-polished shoes. A voice called, "Who is under there?" So I crawled out to see who was interrupting my reading. As my eyes moved upward from the shoes, I saw a cross on the shoulder. Immediately I snapped to attention and saluted. "Hi, I'm Bob Gushwa, the new battalion chaplain." We chatted a bit. I asked him from where he came. "Indiana." "Oh," said I, "I have a lot of friends that studied Russian at Indiana U. They have a great Russian program." "What is your interest in Russian?" When I told him I had a degree in Russian from Georgetown, he laughed hysterically. The Reverend said he was looking for an assistant—a good man who could type and drive the Jeep. I could do neither, but life under an Army truck was getting to me and the thought of an air-conditioned office with no extra duties (like KP and guard duty) appealed to me. I assured Rev. Chaplain Gushwa I was his man. There was one slight misunderstanding. I thought he was a priest, and he assumed I was a Protestant. Wrong! A Presbyterian. It was the beginning of a wonderful friendship that lasted up to his death in

1988. I do not think he ever learned that I typed with two fingers. As for the Jeep, that was a real disaster. We were given a new Jeep. The first evening I begged my buddy Masco to teach me to drive the Jeep. He did his best. I took him back to the barracks and decided to do some practicing on my own. I drove for several minutes when I smelled something burning. In short, I had forgotten to take off the break handle. The story must end here rather than provoke a bill from the U.S. Army at this late stage. Chaplain Gushwa and I had to make several trips to Washington on business and also to see some of our men at Walter Reed Hospital. When that was necessary, I always called the motor pool and ordered a car with a driver for the Reverend. I insisted on going along for the ride. After all, I had many friends in Washington. He was fresh out of some small parish in Indiana and was enchanted with Bill McGuire's Washington.

Rev. Gushwa came into the Army as a First Lieutenant with a wife and three young children. They lived from hand to mouth. Nevertheless, the Gushwas opened their hearts and their home to me. Sharon Gushwa was a fantastic cook, although the food at Ft. Eustis was surprisingly tasty. I'll never forget May 1, 1964. It was not only my birthday, but the first birthday in my life that I did not celebrate with my family. I was depressed and looking out my office window feeling sorry for myself. Suddenly Sharon Gushwa's car pulled up. She was carrying a homemade German chocolate birthday cake for me. It made me feel so much better. It turned out that her birthday was May 2. To show my appreciation for the cake I insisted on treating the two Gushwas (I always called them the "Gushwazzie") to dinner at Nick's Seafood Pavilion in nearby Yorktown. For the first time in her life Sharon drank several glasses of Liebfraumilch wine I had ordered. All three of us were half-crocked, but for those few hours we were celebrating good friendships. Many an evening I used to insist on watching their three (extremely well-behaved) children so that Bob and Sharon could go to a movie or wherever. Robert Lee Gushwa was not only an exemplary husband, father and friend, he was the most popular man in the battalion. His monthly lectures on Army morality were so witty and well-delivered that none dared to sleep through them.

A year later Rev. Gushwa and the 69th Signal Battalion were in Vietnam. Yours truly was in Moscow. We corresponded on a regular basis. I always began my letters with, "Greetings from the center of the Cold War." He began his with, "Greetings from the center of the Hot War."

When I was released from the Army in September 1965, I headed to fulfill a life's dream of studying in Munich, Germany. There were so many things I respected and enjoyed in Germany, especially the student discount rates for cultural events and student tours. I did not like the food, however. I lived with a very well-bred, sophisticated family (Sven and Alexandra Jarolimek) on Nietzestrasse. Most of the time I took my meals with them, but, by Thursday my non-German friends and I would go to an Italian restaurant in downtown Munich and gorge ourselves.

Among my most vivid memories of Germany was my first trip to Berlin and seeing the Berlin Wall. As I mentioned earlier, never did I feel more American than in Germany and Ireland. Nevertheless, when I saw the Wall, I said to a German friend, "What have these Communist barbarians done to OUR people?" For one minute I felt like a German. We crossed Checkpoint Charlie and—for the first time in my life—I was behind the Iron Curtain. It was weird. With my American passport I simply walked across. My German friends had to endure all kinds of harassment and delay to get in. In 1965 many parts of East Berlin were still in ruins. I assume the Russians did not want to let Germans forget a war for which people my age had not been responsible. We had to exchange "x" amount of West German Marks, and there was nothing to buy. So we went to a restaurant for a sandwich and a beer (both were awful!) around 7 in the evening. I went into a state of shock when I saw two female East German military officers dancing with each other. My colleagues and I came to the conclusion that we were seeing the worst of the Communist empire. The Soviet Union wouldbe much better. A year later I would find out for myself.

TO RUSSIA WITH LOVE...

✦

[WELL, AT LEAST WITH ENTHUSIASM!]

One Spring day in 1966 I was having lunch with an old friend, a Russian-American named Masha Grekova, who was working as an announcer in the Russian Service of the Voice of America. Masha asked me what my plans were. I had been thinking about returning to Georgetown University to begin work on a Ph.D., but something told me that was not really what I should do. In those days Russian majors had basically two options: teach or work for the government. I had so many friends with MA's and Ph.D's who were working as waiters or secretaries. I also had friends who were teaching and hated it. So I asked Masha what she thought I should do. She suggested I apply for the upcoming American exhibition in the Soviet Union. I remembered that she had worked on one of these shows, and I was interested to learn more about it. Masha thought it was the perfect way for me to earn some money, get back into speaking Russian, learn more about the country, make some useful contacts and, above all, decide what I wanted to do with my life. "There are few distractions," she remarked. "You'll have plenty of time to reflect and to plan." I had just seen the movie Dr. Zhivago for about the fourth time, and suddenly I had a burning desire to finally see the Soviet Union.

Masha's family friend, Dr. Yuri Elagin, was in charge of testing the candidates' Russian capabilities for the U.S. Information Agency, the organizer of the exhibits. She said she would call him and put in a good word for me. When I went for the test, it was as if Dr. Elagin owed Zinovieva a favor. He spoke "baby-Russian" to me and pronounced each syllable distinctly so that I would understand and pass the test. He seemed surprised that my Russian was that fluent. He had assumed that I spoke Russian poorly and he had to pass me as a favor to Masha. All the paper work was in, I passed the test and now it was just a matter of receiving my security clearance. A few months later I was informed that I was hired to begin training at USIA in mid-June for a six month position in the Soviet Union at $5100 per year (GS-5), salary plus per diem.

For the benefit of the majority who know little about these programs, I would like to devote just one paragraph to US-USSR Cultural Exchanges. They were started in the late '50s under President Eisenhower and included not only yearly exhibitions depicting life in the two countries but also exchanges of teachers, scientists, performing artists and a monthly magazine (*America Illustrated* from our side and *Soviet Life* from theirs). Finding *America Illustrated* in the USSR was like finding gold. It was beautifully illustrated and well written. Soviets would beg, borrow or steal to get a copy. In the USA you got *Soviet Life* easily. The Soviet government was disappointed with the sales of their propaganda journal in the USA, so every month they returned thousands of our *America Illustrated* (most wound up in the basement of the American Embassy in Moscow) saying that the magazine was not selling well—one of the many Soviet lies we heard over the years. The academic and scientific exchanges were popular (mainly because the Soviets could learn important facts about American research) and rarely gave us any information we did not already have. Soviet participants were carefully screened and had to leave wives and children at home as hostages. They were well prepared by the KGB as to what to say, how to act, etc. We later learned that they even had access to special clothing stores for their trips abroad so that they did not look like the average, poorly-dressed Russian man-on-the-street.

The exhibits were extraordinary. For us they were the most important way of reaching the average Soviet citizen. The first exhibit opened in Moscow in 1959. It is also the most famous because of the spirited exchange between Richard Nixon and Nikita Khrushchev known as the "Kitchen Debate." Pepsi Cola gave out free drinks and several other American firms gladly donated all kinds of their products with an eye on future sales. By the way, I attended the first Soviet exhibit in New York. These exhibits were staffed by young English (or Russian) speaking guides whose task it was to answer any question about life in the USA or USSR. As I remember, the Soviet guides in NYC were not that young, spoke rather artificial English and told everybody, "Hope to see you soon in Moscow." Unfortunately, any American that ever looked up the guide in Moscow was told that he or she was either ill or out of the country. I also remember seeing a mock-up of a "typical" Soviet apartment, which I never saw in all my trips to the Soviet Union. Their exhibits were not very popular in the USA, even though USIA did its best to promote them. Our shows, on the other hand, were amazing successes. People stood in line for hours just to spend fifteen minutes inspecting just what

America was all about. We sent exhibits about Education in the USA, Architecture in the USA, Medicine in the USA, Graphics, Leisure, Design, Communications and many more. My first exhibition was called "Hand Tools USA."

As I said, these exhibits were coordinated and managed by the U.S. Information Agency but were built by private companies. Without intending to be overly critical, I must say that most of us who were connected with exhibits agree that, at best, they were mediocre. It was obvious that whoever designed them had little or no idea about life in the Soviet Union. They had more glitz than substance and were rightfully attacked in the Soviet press as "American propaganda and a distortion of American life." When we participants returned from an exhibit, we were always asked what themes we would suggest for future exhibits; but nobody ever paid attention to our suggestions. For instance, I personally pushed for an exhibition on "Children in the USA" to include clothing, toys, pre-schooling, children's health, etc. Russians love children. What little they have, they give to their children. This was one aspect of Soviet reality that I truly admired. Such an exhibit would be impressive, non-controversial and informative, not to mention a pleasure to put together. In all my years with the Agency, nobody ever picked up on my idea. As the quality of our exhibits went down, we added insult to injury by having them built in Italy. Soviet visitors would see the panels marked "Made in Italy" and wonder why we could not produce them in America. On a more positive note, I must say how impressive our exhibit brochures and buttons were. The brochures were of magazine size, colorful, and, of course, in Russian. The buttons *(znachki)* were similar to our political ones ("I like Ike"), but stamped with the emblem of the exhibit. Soviets collected them and loved them.

But, it's time to return to my training for my first mission in the Soviet Union. The guides assembled one Monday morning in the old USIA building at 1776 Pennsylvania Ave NW. I was the second to arrive. When I entered the room, I saw a rather tall, broad-shouldered man with a Cheshire cat smile on his face and horn-rimmed glassed. "Hi, I'm Charlie Trumbull," said the guy. By the time I gave my name and asked from where he came, the room was filling up with other guides. Everybody was a bit nervous and apprehensive. Our nerves and concerns, however, were soon calmed by the pleasant smile and voice of Mary Hourrigan, our hostess. The training lasted about two weeks. We had lectures on the Soviet Union, on the tools we would be demonstrating, on frequently asked questions from previous exhibits, about protocol, about security.

Let me say a few unkind words about USIA Security. Perhaps they were, in reality, patriotic, dedicated Americans who wanted to do their part in the "war against Communism." But, in my opinion, they were a bunch of zealots, pitifully uninformed about the USSR, overly absorbed in their own power to make or break careers and overly delighted to dig up dirt on their fellow Americans. They decided who was and was not suitable to receive a security clearance. Many of the best candidates for these exhibit positions were turned down by Security. One woman I knew almost did not make it because her uncle was a Communist in the '20s. Several candidates were turned down because they smoked pot in college, were homosexuals, belonged to leftist organizations or gave the wrong answers during the interview. Many of these security men were from former military security units and were now on their second career. Indeed, they tried to frighten us about the consequences if we misbehaved in the USSR. When we returned we were "interviewed" by the same group of buffoons. The most despicable thing they did in the second briefing was to try to get us to say negative things about our fellow guides. I shall relate more about my dealings with USIA Security later in the book. It gets juicier!!!

I want to make one thing very clear. I have never had any dealings with the CIA, FBI or any other intelligence (not even the KGB!!) network. I know these institutions are necessary for the security of the USA. If I ever felt I had information to help them, I would have given it. Also, there are people who can do intelligence work well. They are trained and interested in the profession. I was interested strictly in cultural exchange. Someone had to do that work, too, right? I also knew well that, if I were involved in intelligence work in the USSR and were caught, I'd be left to rot in a Soviet jail. In almost every American exhibit in the USSR at least one guide was sent home (PNG'd) after being accused of espionage. In most cases the charges were trumped up (at least I hope so), but in other cases it may have been true. Most of the earlier exhibits were staffed by Americans of Russian origin who spoke native Russian and were obviously rabid anti-Communists. On Hand Tools USA, we had only one guide of Russian extraction. I sincerely believe the Soviets knew who was clean and who was suspicious. At any rate, I never had a problem getting my visas.

Speaking of getting a visa, we had already finished our training and were ready to head for Mother Russia. Airline tickets had been ordered, other reservations made. In those days the Soviet Embassy was infamous for waiting until the last minute (or even later) to issue visas. We waited at least a week before Mary Hourigan announced one morning, "They're here! You're leaving tomorrow." That

week of waiting was hard on our nerves but gave us a chance to spend more leisure time together and to get to know each other better. Most of us were staying
at a hotel behind USIA. Some had kitchenettes and some of the girls were very
good cooks. Some of us were real party people; others were "too intellectual" for
such rubbish. One evening at one of these parties Charlie Trumbull asked me if I
wanted to room with him in the USSR. I agreed but asked why he asked me over
others with a personality more like his own. "Because, the first day you walked
into the guide room, I said to myself, 'This guy is a fun seeker; he'll be fun to
room with in the dismal USSR.'" I hope I did not disappoint him!

Most of the guides were intelligent, easy-going, reasonable, spoke Russian from
fair to excellent and came from various parts of the country. Charlie was from
New Mexico. A beautiful blonde gal that studied Russian with me at Georgetown, Marlyn Lebedzinski, was from Texas, Alex Koltsov-Mosalsky from California, Elliot Gilmore from Connecticut, John Aldriedge from Oklahoma. Other
states were represented as well. One thing that separated us were our views on the
Vietnam war. There were the hawks and the doves, the liberals and conservatives,
the religious and the anti-religious. But this was good. It showed the Soviets what
diversity really means. We could disagree, but we were all Americans at heart.

Another quick digression. I constantly use the word Soviet instead of Russian.
Keep in mind that not all residents of the Soviet Union were Russians. There
were fifteen republics, and many of the so-called Fraternity of Socialist Brothers
were not there because they wanted to be, nor did they want to be referred to as
brothers. I admit to my own prejudice of calling Russians the ones who left,
escaped or were born outside of the USSR. It is these Russians that have main-
tained the Russian soul, the literature, the culture and the religion. I knew Russians here in Washington, New York, San Francisco, Paris, Madrid, Munich,
Buenos Aires, Rio de Janeiro and London. What I encountered in the Soviet
Union had nothing to do with the Russians I knew in the diaspora. Even the
food did not taste the same.

Our little group departed Washington for New York early one afternoon. In
those days there were no direct flights to Moscow and no American carriers going
there. We were scheduled to take Lufthansa to Frankfurt and Pakistani Air Lines
from Frankfurt to Moscow. Most of us decided to have one, good, last American
meal in Kennedy airport before boarding the 9:00 pm flight. Most of us of us
stuffed ourselves on steak and, of course, dessert. After dinner I was walking
around the airport and struck up a conversation with an attractive elderly lady

from Chicago. Finally she asked me where I was going. When I replied, "Moscow," I suddenly realized where I was headed and became overcome by fear. I broke out into a sweat. I thought to myself, "My God, where am I going? Will I ever get out of there alive? Why am I doing this?" I ran like lightning to the restroom and out came the steak and dessert. Suddenly I heard them call the Lufthansa flight to Frankfurt. Somehow I managed to leave my safe haven and board the jet. I was still too scared to speak. Marlyn Lebedzinski sat next to me. She felt something was wrong. She tried to comfort me: "Well, I guess this is what Professor Krupensky prepared us for." But, did he?

Any kind of motion puts me to sleep, especially an airplane. Usually by the time the passengers are being fed, "yours truly" is asleep. I'd say we were in the air no more than two hours when I heard an announcement in German to the effect that the plane was having engine troubles and we were heading back to New York. By the time I opened my eyes, I saw Marlyn and heard the same announcement in English. By then I knew it was not a dream. Indeed we were on our way back to JFK. We spent the night at an airport motel as guests of Lufthansa. Around 11am we were once again in the air headed for Frankfurt...at least we hoped. We had already missed the connecting flight to Moscow. Lufthansa sent us perhaps the one agent who did not speak flawless English. He had booked us on a flight to Berlin and on to Moscow on Interflug (the East German airline). When I saw that he and our accompanying officer, Jerry Verner, were not understanding each other, I volunteered to interpret. The agent was delighted, but Verner—the consummate new American diplomat—saw it as some young, German-speaking greenhorn overstepping his boundaries. Finally it was decided to send us to Helsinki where we would spend the night and fly in to Moscow the next day on Finnair. To add to the friction between Verner and me, the agent booked me First Class to Helsinki as a sign of gratitude. What the Hell, I felt I had done nothing wrong, so I accepted. I resented Jerry's attitude. This resulted in a lengthy conversation in German with the agent during which I kept looking at Mr. Verner and laughing. The truth is I was relating to him how I barfed in the airport when I realized I was on my way to Moscow.

The side trip to Helsinki was an unexpected delight. The city was immaculate. We got to do some last minute shopping at Stockmanns' department store and, for the last time in the next six months, see fresh fruit and veggies.

Next morning we boarded the Finnair flight to Moscow. On board they served us a full and tasty lunch. Next thing we knew we were landing in the Soviet capital.

We had arrived at last! I'll never forget getting off the plane and seeing Red Army soldiers armed with rifles at the bottom of the stairway. Even more memorable was the immediate stench we all sensed. Later an American diplomat told me it was the combination of low grade fuel, lack of dry cleaning and the aroma of Soviet soap, which was worse than not bathing at all. We were hoarded onto an Embassy bus and taken straight to the Embassy on Tchaikovsky Street. We did not see any well-known tourist sights along the route. All of Moscow seemed to be tall, ugly apartment buildings and Communist slogans everywhere. "The Party and the People are One!" "Ours is the Way of Lenin!" "We shall Fulfill and Over-fulfill our Five Year Plan!". Once again I wanted to do what I did in the New York airport! We also noticed the lines—people standing in line every-where...but for what? We could not tell from the bus. Then our bus pulled into the U.S. Embassy complex. We were whisked into a reception room and were treated to a buffet. Needless to say no one was hungry. Two weeks later we were all sent a bill for ten dollars to cover the cost of the buffet. Ambassador Foy Kohler and his wife were there to welcome us. I was fearful to approach the Ambassador, but I drummed up the courage to go up to Madame Kohler and ask, "Well, what is it like living in Moscow?" "Please, dear," she replied, "how many times can one watch Swan Lake?"

The one diplomat who treated us kindly and with respect was Nick Moravsky. He spoke the best Russian at the embassy and seemed NOT to be afraid of the Soviets. Above all, he had a sense of humor. Indeed he always looked out for our well-being. The other person who seemed human and intelligent was our embassy doctor, an Air Force physician named Jim Bazzell. We became close buddies and I stayed at his apartment a few times when one of us had to travel by air to Moscow once a week to pick up the mail (which arrived by the diplomatic courier) and to buy a limited number of items at the Commissary. Dr. Bazzell had recently returned from visiting an American cardiologist, who suffered a heart attack while attending an international symposium in Kiev. Because of the doctor's international reputation, Dr. Bazzell was sent to make sure he was get-ting the proper care. When our doctor arrived at the Kiev hospital (first of all, they did not want to let him in), he almost fainted when he found the cardiolo-gist covered with leeches. It was an old Russian method of treating a heart attack. We wondered if the good doctor was just pulling our leg. Was he saying in effect, "Keep healthy, so you do not land in a Soviet hospital"?

After spending several hours at the Embassy we were bussed to one of Moscow's railroad stations for the overnight trip to Kharkov. We arrived around midnight, but the train did not leave until 2:00 am. The sight at the station is one none of us will ever forget. There were so many homeless people sleeping on the floor (men, young and old women, babies) that we had to step over them to get to our train. Nick Moravsky assured us we had first class accommodations on the train; two to a compartment. If that was first class, may we NEVER see second! I shared the cage with Charlie Trumbull. However, I was unable to lie down due to the pungent smell of urine on my mattress. Most of us roamed the car all night. Molly Nelson found an orange she bought in Helsinki, tucked deep in her pocketbook, and shared it with me. By the time the sun had come up we were somewhere in an area which had not changed in 200 years. The train slowed down to a snail's pace and local peasant women were selling the passengers hard-boiled eggs, meat pies *(pirozhki)*, yogurt and some other goodies. But we foreigners had no rubles yet, and giving dollars to Soviet citizens was strictly forbidden. This magnificent Soviet train had no dining car either. Around 10:00 am the train pulled into the metropolis of Kharkov, our first "home" in the Workers' Paradise.

TRADITIONAL UKRAINIAN HOSPITALITY

✦

[SOVIET STYLE]

We entered the Intourist hotel and immediately noticed a huge poster in the lobby written in English: "We shall welcome you with traditional Ukrainian hospitality." As a teenager we had some Ukrainian neighbors; and, believe me, they were as hospitable as one could get. I had my doubts though about the residents of Communist Ukraine. Perhaps I was predisposed to expect a real dump for a hotel room (after the first class train) so the room did not actually seem that bad. The walls were a canary yellow, which had been freshly painted. I use the word "painted" loosely. The walls were more like yellow chalk. If one touched them by mistake, the chalk came off on our hands, our clothes, whatever came in contact with it. Charlie Trumbull and I thought perhaps the Soviets had discovered a new wall covering which contained devices to transmit our conversations. "Yours truly" put it to the test. I said to Charlie in Russian: "Such a beautiful room, a comfortable bed, lovely view...Too bad the bathroom light is burned out." About ten minutes later a maid came to ask if all was okay. "Did we need any light bulbs, for instance?" When I said no, she could hardly contain the look of frustration on her face. Later that evening I called to see if I could order room service. I was told, "Only in case of illness and a note from the hotel doctor." A few minutes later I called Marlyn to say Charlie and I would join the rest of the gang for dinner. When I picked up the phone, I heard a recording of my voice asking for room service, but NOT the reply. "James Bond is alive and well," thought I!!

We had the rest of the day to catch up on our sleep and perhaps see a bit of the industrial city, which had one previous American exhibition a few years back. In other words, the Kharkovites already had experience with Americans. Nevertheless people recognized us on the streets, in shops, etc. And indeed, people were extremely hospitable. In those days all Soviet hotels had a clerk (dezhurnaya)

35

seated at a desk directly in front of the elevator on each floor. You told her your room number, and she gave you your key. When you went out, you left the key with her. This afforded the KGB the opportunity to search the room or simply know you had left your room. Follow the foreigner! These women all fit a certain mold. They were elderly, wore their hair in a bun, had a few gold or tin teeth (the ones with the gold were obviously of a higher KGB rank), just a little bit of body odor or bad breath and were not above accepting small gifts. We had one woman in the hotel who seemed to really like me. In fact, she called me *Golubchik* ("Little Dove"). Since Ukrainians tend to pronounce the "g" like an "h," I was actually "holubchik." Sounded nice. I rewarded her later on with some sweets from the USA and a ball point pen. In days past a ball point pen was a cheap but excellent gift for any Soviet.

Charlie and I hit the streets. We decided to take a bus to the central square. Once we were on the much-overcrowded bus, the passengers—realizing we were foreigners—insisted on paying our fare (about three pennies for us) and insisted on giving us a seat. We refused. There were old ladies and invalids standing. They would not take no for an answer. In the aisle were two middle-aged women with enough underarm hair to braid. Their sweat continued to drop on my arm. Just as I was about to suggest to Charlie that we walk the rest of the way, an interesting scene occurred. The bus stopped. A young African student with a blonde girl boarded the bus. Suddenly we heard shouts of, "You black bastard, what are you doing with our Russian girl?" Was I hearing correctly? The man must have been used to this verbal abuse, because he did not react at all. Maybe he did not speak Russian. The girl seemed not to pay attention either.

Later that evening we prepared for our first meal in Kharkov. Special tables with an American flag were reserved for us in the dining room. As we entered we could hardly hear each other due to the loud music, pop music Soviet style, played by a band of fifty-year-olds. The male singer—also no spring chicken—later sang a favorite Ukrainian song "Moya Milaya Mama" (My Sweet Mama…NO connection with anything Al Jolson ever did!) in honor of the American guests. We mistakenly applauded loudly, giving him the wrong signal. He sang it every night until we left Kharkov. It annoyed John Aldriedge and me so much that one evening we rewrote the words, using every vulgar word we knew in the Russian language. It was our first experience as well with Soviet service. We waited a good forty-five minutes before a waitress made an appearance with menus. The only reason she showed up was because Mr. Aldriedge stopped another waitress and asked her sarcastically if our waitress had defected to the West. The menu was impressive. It had several pages. At least six soups were listed, several salads, meats, fish and desserts. However, as we ordered the reply was always the same: "Out of it." In other words, forget the menu, ask them what they really had available that evening. The answer was: "Borscht, Capital salad, Chicken Kiev and Beef Stroganoff." Our witty director, Fritz Berliner, ordered the Chicken Kiev and was the first to be served. The meal came so cold that the grease had solidified. Fritz turned the plate upside down for all to see. The chicken stuck to the plate. In all fairness, my Beef Stroganoff was not bad, so I ordered it almost nightly.

In Kharkov we learned a few more facts about what to and what not to order in restaurants. One hot afternoon we were dining in the park outside of our exhibit hall. We ordered bottles of what they called "lemonade," that is, "orange soda" in English. The bottles were warm, almost hot. I asked the waitress for a bowl of ice. "Ice???" she replied. She looked totally confused. Nonetheless she did bring us a huge chunk of ice in a tin bowl and left. We chopped up the ice as best we could, put it in our glasses, poured the soda and were enjoying a refreshing drink when she returned. Suddenly the waitress screamed as if she had seen a tiger. "What are you doing?" she demanded. It turned out that they made ice out of dishwater. It was only used to keep covered items cool. Live and learn!

The following morning—in our work clothes—we set out for the exhibit site to begin putting the show together. The first thing we noticed was a huge sign directly in front of the pavilion stating: "The more the aggressors commit crimes on Vietnamese territory, the more severe will be their punishment." How original! Most of the heavy work was done by Soviet laborers, but we did our share as well. Later we found out that our Soviet hosts were charging us American wages, most of which the workers never saw. More about that later. Things were running smoothly when I suddenly felt the need to use the men's room. The smell led me right to it. The WC had two sections. One was like a long trough against the wall for "liquid release." The other was a huge room, completely open, with about ten elevated foot rests (the kind one sees in a shoe shine parlor). Behind them was a gutter and a tile wall. I did not have time to think about what was really going on, so I hopped up on the rests and dropped my jeans. Just about that time I heard what seemed to be Niagara Falls coming down the wall. It scared me so badly I fell forward, almost breaking my nose. Just then a Soviet workman walked in to catch me in my embarrassed state. He said with a grin, "You Americans have to learn how to shit Armenian style. Look, I'll show you." And he did. I wanted to die.

By the second day, we were getting enthused about how well we were setting up the exhibit. Around 11:00 am we were taking a break outside the pavilion. I was sitting with Sid Smith chatting about a possible trip that evening to a movie house. An elderly woman walked by. She stopped and asked, "Are you the Americans with the exhibition?" We nodded. She examined Sid and me carefully from head to toe. We were both under 150 lbs. "Why are you so skinny? Don't they feed you in America?" We laughed, and she went away. Ten minutes later she returned with a package wrapped in a Pravda newspaper. "Here," she said kindly. "These are from my garden." We were told not to accept anything from Soviet citizens, but it all happened so quickly that we did not think twice about taking the package. We opened it in front of everybody. It was a cluster of white grapes. By this time the woman was only half a block away. We could still see her thin frame. All of a sudden two bulky men approached her and began to beat her severely. We could hear them yell that she was "selling state secrets to the American spies." Sid and I were so incensed we began to run in her direction, but Jerry Verner said not to. Unfortunately, this was neither the first nor the last example of brutality we witnessed in the USSR. It did, however, fill us with fear and disgust. We were unable to eat that night, much less go to a movie.

While we were in Kharkov, the much awaited, new Soviet film version of "War and Peace" was released. Our Soviet counterparts—the All-Union Chamber of Commerce—invited us to the Kharkov opening. It was a splashy affair by their standards. Unfortunately, the movie lasted about five hours, during which the projector broke down at least seven times…and always at the most inappropriate moments. Tolstoy would have turned in his grave.

Opening day finally arrived. All the local dignitaries attended a reception, for which we imported food and drinks from the United States,as well as local delicacies. Believe it or not, caviar was plentiful and inexpensive in those days. Although most Soviets could drink us under the table with vodka, these boys could not hold their scotch, rum bourbon or gin. Our Ambassador and many from the Cultural Section arrived from Moscow for this happy event. It was also our first encounter with Soviet officials from both Moscow and Kharkov.I became friendly with a woman from the Chamber named Valentina Stepanova. She was probably in her 40's, but looked to be in her 50's and was without doubt tightly connected with the KGB. Who there wasn't? But, in her way, she liked me and I liked her. It was through her much later that I met Natalia Makarova and other ballet figures. It was our interest in ballet that bound us. She could not believe that I knew so much about Russian ballet. We talked freely about Karsavina, Dhiagilev, Nijinski and Ulanova, Makarova (who had not yet defected), but when I mentioned Rudolf Nureyev her eyebrows arched, and she walked away.

The following day we opened to the public. Although the Soviets broke their word—as they usually did—and did not place any of the exhibit posters around the city, people heard about the opening on the Voice of America. Word then spread by word of mouth. When we arrived at the site, there were lines as far as the eye could see. Each visitor was greeted by two of the guides—we took turns—and received an exhibit button and colorful brochure. The visitors proceeded to an area where a three-minute film about hand tools in America was shown. Next they entered the main room, which had about five or six elevated stands. Each stand had a theme, such as metal, automobile, wood. The guide demonstrated several tools and explained their usage. My first stand was the Automobile section. (I, who do not know an engine from a muffler!) For instance, I demonstrated a new (to them) device to change spark plugs more quickly and other tools used to make and/or repair automobiles. After the 2 to 3 minute demonstration I would say: "Do you have any questions?" Ninety-eight percent of the questions had nothing to do with the subject of hand tools.

Here is a sample of the questions we were asked three hundred times a day:
Who are your parents?
Are you of Russian ancestry?
Are they politically connected?
How did you get selected for this exhibit?
Who killed President Kennedy?
Do you have unemployment in America?
Is there discrimination against blacks and other minorities?
How do Russians live in America?
Is Alexander Kerensky still alive?
How much is a loaf of bread?
How much is a kilowatt hour of electricity?
How much does an education cost?
Is it true your roads are pay roads?
Do you have free medical care like us?
How do you like (a) the USSR? (b) Kharkov?
What do you think of our Russian girls?
Are you married?
Why are YOU so skinny?
Why do YOU wear glasses?

What is your vision?

Why are you killing women and children in Viet Nam?

Do you believe in God? Why?

Have you read the works of Lenin?

Do you know about the Great Fatherland War? (WWII)

What is your apartment like? How many square meters?

What do you think about Francis Gary Powers? (the U-2 pilot)

What do Americans know about us?

Are Soviet newspapers available in the USA?

Do we have a similar exhibit in America?

Is there prostitution in the USA?

Do Americans receive a pension?

How do old people live there?

Do you have internal passports?

Do American men pay alimony?

What do you do in your spare time?

I could go on and on. Most of these questions were sincere. I was usually happy to answer every question as if I were asked it for the first time. The KGB sent their goons to make sure our comments did not make America look too good. They would try to crucify us about the unemployment, race or Vietnam war issues.

As a matter of fact, I was their victim the very first day. Some teenagers in the crowd asked me if I knew how to dance the new craze in America, the "Monkey?" "Of course!" "Show us." I told them that this was not a dance class, and I preferred to talk about hand tools. "Oh, please…dear friend…just show us a few steps." So, I lifted my arms in a position to dance the "Monkey" when—out of nowhere—popped a camera and snapped my picture. A few days later the photos arrived by mail at our Director's office. Indeed, I did look like a monkey! Fritz made nothing of it, nor did I. Yet, we knew they were on my tail. An "akt" is something we do not have in the Free World, but it is like a citizen's complaint, better known as "ratting on a fellow human being." It was a daily occurrence in Soviet Russia. Many people moved up the ladder by writing up "akts" against their fellow citizens. Knowing my personality and inability to keep my mouth shut when I should, I wondered how soon there would be an akt against me. It happened the third day of our presence in Kharkov. That afternoon an entire brigade of KGB imbeciles invaded our exhibit. One could always tell who they were. In the winter they often wore green felt hats. In addition, they would push their way to the front of the crowd and begin their comments with the words "young man." They had been pestering me about the war in Vietnam for nearly an hour. "Nam" in Russian means "for us" or "to us." So, I made a pun by saying, "The country is called Viet *Nam* (for us) not Viet *Vam* (for you)." Ah, that brought me to the attention of a real KGB pro. The conversation went like this:

"Young man, are you a believer?" (in God)
"Yes, I am. A Roman Catholic."
"Have you any education?"
"Sure do, a Master's degree."
"And you still believe in God?"
"More than ever. Some of the greatest minds in history, including many Russian writers, composers and educators had deep religious convictions."
"Well, that was the past. Scientific Communism has replaced those outdated theories."
"Only in Communist countries."
"Well, let me tell you, when our Kosmonauts were in outer space, they did not see any God."
"Well, let me tell you, my friend, God would not be seen with a Communist!!!"

The crowd roared. The old "babushki" (grandmothers) blessed themselves and cheered me on. The KGB swine and some Young Communist Youth Leaguers demanded an apology. I refused. Then I added:

"Hey, want to hear a cute joke about the space programs? It seems the USA and the USSR sent up two satellites with scientists aboard. They crossed above Mars, and both ships rolled down their windows and said: 'Jetzt koennen wir wieder Deutsch sprechen!'" (At last we can speak German again!) This was the straw that broke the camel's back. I had not one but two "akts" (denunciations)—one for spreading religious propaganda and one for insulting Soviet science. I had to appear before the Soviet Director of the exhibit. No apology from Bill McGuire! I screamed obscenities at him for allowing these KGB hatchet men in to annoy me. What kind of cultural exchange is this? Had he no shame? He could send me home, and I would write about it for the entire world to read…and I would give his name! He finally said to me, "Get out of my office."

TURNING WATER
INTO WINE

♦

[IT'S BEEN DONE BEFORE,
COMRADES!]

Of all the funny things that happened to me during my trips to the former Soviet Union, perhaps the one that evokes the most laughter from those friends to whom I relate the incident is my "Miracle in Kharkov." We were there in the summer. It was hot but without the humidity I was used to in Washington. Needless to say, the Intourist hotel was not air-conditioned, nor was any other building that I can remember in the USSR with the exception of Lenin's tomb. My room had a small transparent pitcher with two glasses on the night table. We were told that we could drink the water, which we did. However, I also learned that not far from the hotel was a field with about ten large spigots from which ran cold, clear water. Many of the older houses in the outlying areas had no running water. In the evenings women would go to the field with huge buckets to fill for their families' consumption. There was a festive atmosphere in the field. Women would chat about their families, events of the day (I hope the American exhibition was one of them!). It was a chance to relax and at the same time get fresh, clear water. One evening I decided to go to the field and get some for Charlie and me. Before leaving the hotel, I opened my suitcase and found a few packages of cherry, strawberry and lemon Kool Aid that I had brought from the States. I thought how nice it would be to have some cool, refreshing Kool Aid. I chose the strawberry. At first the old ladies looked at me strangely. They knew I was a foreigner, probably with the exhibit. Two of them actually spoke to me and wanted me to go to the head of the line. "No way" was my reply. "I'll stand here like the rest of you. This way I get a better understanding of how you live, how you get your water, etc." I also made it clear that I was on my own time and was not about to answer any questions. "Leave the boy alone, girls," yelled a babushka. And so they did.

It took about twenty minutes for me to reach the spigot. Just before I approached the water, I emptied the Kool Aid into the pitcher. Needless to say the water turned bright red. I thought nothing about it. However, suddenly the women around me began to scream. "Blood!" shouted a local woman. "Blood is flowing from the well. Oh, my God!" Some of the older women dropped to their knees and blessed themselves three times. Others simply panicked and ran away. One did, however, say, "What have you done to the water, you foreign spy?" I began to laugh hysterically and replied, "Citizen" (I NEVER used the communist word "comrade"), "I just turned water into wine. It has been done before. It is the first time in Kharkov, perhaps." As I walked away, not one soul came anywhere near me. I laughed so hard, I almost cried.

One morning while riding the bus to the exhibit hall, I suddenly remembered some words said to me by my dear friend, Tamara Azarova (who by now had married a man named Kit), and who had worked on the exhibit Architecture USA in 1964. She said it was necessary to meet with Soviets three times (assuming they have not been picked up by the KGB before the third meeting). The first time they tell you what the Soviet government wants them to say. The second time they say what they think you want them to say. By the third meeting, they tell you what they really think. As usual, Tamara Gerasimovna was right. That was true in many cases.

I'd like to say a few words about some of the people I met and befriended while in Kharkov. My closest friends were Volodya and Luda Prostov and their handsome three-year-old son, Oleg. One evening while sitting and reading on a park bench near the hotel, this young couple was watching their son play with some other children. Never did I trust anyone who approached me first. But in this case I began to speak with them. I believe I said something to the effect that I could not believe there were about five children playing and yet there was hardly any of the noise one associated with kids at play. "You're with the American exhibit, aren't you?" asked Volodya. "How did you guess? Is my Russian that accented?" He laughed. My new Ukrainian buddy pointed out that—even if I had not uttered a word—my clothing, especially my shoes, were like holding up a sign "I'm a foreigner." He said he had not yet seen the exhibit because the local bosses at the factory where he worked "warned" them about the possibility of losing their jobs were they to visit the American pavilion. Contact of any kind was not to be tolerated. I asked him why he was planning to go anyway? He said he hated his job, the boss, and even Kharkov. If he were fired, it might be the stimulus he needed to get his family to another city and begin life anew. Volodya also pointed out that two years ago he met a young African student from the university and they became good friends. The KGB interrogated him for two hours and said he could meet with the "nigger," but any anti-Soviet talk from this foreigner must be reported immediately to the Big House. Volodya said that his friendship with Hassan (I believe from Somalia) had caused him to think more about the West, philosophy, religion and other matters. Hassan had taught the family a lot. Volodya was afraid to invite the student to their apartment for fear that the neighbors—all of them rabid anti-African in their outlook—would harass the boy, or, even worse, harass the Prostov family. Why were they so against a student who had done nothing to them? The answer was even news to me. First of all, Volodya explained, these "students from the Third World" had more money than their Soviet students. They had better clothing, better dorms and, above all, they could return home for the summer vacation. Even the professors were convinced the Government was wasting money on these "savages." They would never be good Communists. Many students voiced open hostility to the Communist system. Above all, continued Volodya, many—not all—these students were what the Soviets called contrabandists. They returned each semester with suitcases full of consumer goods (toothpaste, perfume, jewelry, transistor radios...name it!) and sold them on the black market. That's why they had more money. Another sore point was that only the children of Party hacks could buy these items. There was resentment from many angles. I had to ask the question, "So, you do not dislike them because of the color of their skin?" "Of course we do!" snapped my new friend. "If they were on our level, they'd be white." All I could think of was how at the exhibit the Russians accused us daily of racism. These people were unbelievable racists, bigots and hypocrites.

Speaking of blacks, we had a guy on "Hand Tools" named Elliot Gilmore. Elliot was a big football-player build, light-skinned, funny, educated Afro-American, who actually made many friends among the African students studying in the USSR. I hope one day he will write a book about his experiences. At any rate, I must tell one short story about Elliot on the exhibit stand in Kharkov. One day a middle-aged woman in his crowd asked him to say a few words in his "native language." Elliot said a few words in English. The woman shook her head. "No, she insisted, in your NATIVE TONGUE. You're a black, not an American. Speak to me in your native language." Elliot began to bark loudly like a dog. She simply walked away...unsatisfied, of course.

Let's get back to the Prostov family. Since I blended into the scene more easily than Hassan, I finally got to visit them in their modest two room apartment, in which lived Volodya, Luda, Oleg and Volodya's mother, a sweet, caring woman of about fifty. This was my first visit to a Soviet apartment and was typical of what I would see later in other cities in the USSR. These were not Party people. They were ordinary workers. The apartment was small. They shared the kitchen and bath with other families. The furniture was shabby and old. They did not have a radio, but did have a TV. The first night I arrived, Mama Prostov had visited her sister on the outskirts of town and came back with fresh tomatoes, cucumbers, radishes and homemade kvas (a drink made of yeast that tastes like cardboard). There was also a bottle of Armenian cognac. All in all it was a friendly, family-oriented evening. Politics never came up. We talked mainly about the exhibit, about little Oleg and his kindergarten, about closer ties with America. The family said that, based on what they knew about Americans, NOT the US Government, there was a lot of common ground for us to live in peace. I agreed. These were not sophisticated nor educated people. In fact, they asked many of the naive questions I heard every hour at the exhibition. I would also say that the Soviet government did a good job at convincing this family that they lived better than people in other countries. The adults mentioned several times that the Soviet Constitution guaranteed them the "right to work." That seemed to be the most important thing in their lives. Finally they asked in an embarrassed tone, "What do the unemployed in America do to survive?" They were under the opinion—as were most Soviets—that the unemployed in America remained unemployed their entire lives. I felt they did not believe me when I talked about unemployment compensation, training, food stamps. They really freaked out—again probably did not believe me—that many unemployed had homes, automobiles, TVs and enough to eat. Finally I remarked that I was not here to promote the United States but simply to enjoy an evening in a family setting, that I missed being with my family in Philadelphia. "Oh," said Mama Prostov, "you're from the best homes of Philadelphia?" That was the first time I ever heard the phrase "iz luchikh domov Filadel'fii" (from the best homes of Philadelphia). Apparently it was a common Russian phrase used to denote the "creme de la creme." I was touched. By the time I left the USSR, I must have heard the phrase a thousand times. In fact, I began to use the words at the exhibit whenever I was asked from where I came. My response always brought about a chuckle from the audience. Just before I left Kharkov I purchased a short wave radio for the family as a token of my appreciation for their hospitality and friendship. A few years later they were listening to me on the Voice of America. In all honesty, at the time I had no idea I would one day be working at the VOA. But their association with Hassan and me instilled in that family a desire to learn more about the West. I was happy to be able to do that for them.

Another day I was doing my thing at the exhibit. A teenage boy stood in front of my stand for the entire hour (we worked one hour on the stand and had one hour of rest). When I returned an hour later he was still there. The boy kept staring at me, taking in every word I said but did not ask one question. When I went for my second break, he followed me into the courtyard and sheepishly asked me if I had a minute to spare. I noted that he spent two hours listening to me without asking a question. "Is there something you want to ask, but not in front of the audience?" "No", he replied. "My aunt was here the other day, and she heard you say you speak German. My mother teaches German and would like to have the opportunity to speak with you in German. She is afraid to come to the exhibit for fear of losing her job. The teachers were forewarned not to go near the American exhibition. Mother is fascinated to speak with an American in a third, neutral language," said the boy. His name was Igor. There was something so innocent and pure about the boy, I was certain he was not a KGB trap. I said I'd try to meet with them on my day off, Monday. That evening, as usual, I was reading in the park. Along came Igor with a school mate. They seemed surprised to see me there. "Mama is home now," he exclaimed. "Why not come and have a cup of tea with us?" The number one rule for us was not to go anywhere without another American. Nevertheless, I was not about to ask my colleagues to go listen to me speak German with some local schoolteacher. Off I went with the boy. The apartment was quite close to the park and our hotel. As we entered, I saw a woman in her late 30's, rather well-preserved for her years (living in that society where age creeps up fast). She seemed shocked when I said, "Guten Abend. Ich heisse Bill McGuire. Wie geht es Ihnen, Frau Kwitnitskaja?" She seemed dumbfounded. "Igor, go boil some water for tea. We have an important guest." We sat at the table and had a delightful chat about Goethe, Schiller and other German writers. She was completely unaware of the modern German writers and even took notes about the Group 47 that was popular in the 60's in West Germany. She had visited East Germany once with a group of local German teachers. To her it was a paradise. Nevertheless, she sensed great mistrust between her group and the German teachers of literature. Everybody was "correct," she remembered, but not warm. As a child she heard from her parents how the Ukrainians welcomed the German troops as liberators, but was always warned not to ever mention it in school or in front of strangers. That fact of Soviet history was "verboten". Just as I was about to leave—it was around 9:30—the door opened. It was her half-drunken husband. He took one look at me and shouted: "Is he a foreigner?" Before she could answer he gave her a swift slap in the face. Then a second. "You bitch! Don't you remember what happened to the Grishins when they had an unauthorized foreigner in their apartment?" Nina began to sob bitterly. Little Igor begged his father "not to hit Mama in front of a foreigner." The man became more enraged. He thumped her a few more times. I finally screamed: "Stop it, you 'govniuk' (piece of shit). I'll call the police and you'll really be in trouble." (It came out more vulgar in Russian.) With those words I took leave of that unfortunate family. "No more visits to German teachers," I thought to myself.

CAN YOU TAKE A LITTLE MORE BRUTALITY?

Once a week one of us had to travel to the embassy in Moscow with one of the administrative staff to pick up and deliver mail, buy some limited items from the Commissary and inform Moscow and Washington how things were going. It was my turn to go with our Finance Officer, Marv McClure. Marv and his charming southern wife, Leah, known to all of us as Mama McClure because of her maternal instincts, and I had become lifelong friends. Somehow she managed nightly to cook a series of tasty meals on two hot plates in their hotel room. I was often the guest for dinner. Anyway, Mama stayed back in Kharkov while Marv and I did our business in the capital. It was early in the afternoon. I had just returned from the Embassy luncheonette and was chatting with an officer on the street level of the Embassy. Although I was talking to him, my eyes were looking out on the passers-by on Tchaikovsky Street. To this day I can not explain it, but at least we Americans rarely saw a pregnant woman on the streets of the USSR. We knew Soviets had babies (probably more abortions!), but it was the first time I had seen a pregnant woman on the street. Which is why my eye followed her as she passed our window. A few yards away on the right was the entrance to the Embassy with two armed Soviet guards on each side. Without warning the woman ran right into the entrance into which all the vehicles came in. The guards ran after her. By the time I got to the door they were beating her and kicking her in the stomach. The woman was crying and covered with blood as they dragged her out of the compound. I could not believe that our people stood there and allowed this to happen. After all, these thugs illegally entered and committed a violent act on American territory. "What are we going to do about this travesty?" I asked one of the diplomats. His answer: "We'll complain to the Soviet Ministry."

SEX…STUPIDITY…
SECURITY

When Lenin and his original group of Communists came to power they soon discovered the benefits of "advertising" in the form of posters and billboards. Throughout the new Soviet Union one could see huge billboards announcing: "Communism means the electrification of the country" "Communism means equality for all" "Communism guarantees the right to work" "Communism means the end of prostitution." Communism means the END of prostitution????? No government in the history of mankind has used the world's oldest profession for its benefit like the Communists. One might argue that during the period of free love in the Twenties there was less need for these ladies of the night. Nevertheless, prostitution survived with a lot of help from the KGB especially.

I heard how a young, married American diplomat arrived in Moscow for his first assignment and was seduced by an attractive KGB agent many years ago. Since he was so low on the totem poll, the files remained in a vault until they could be of real use to the KGB. They had a talent for knowing who would one day be a good target. Indeed many years later the diplomat was assigned to the US Embassy in Prague. Suddenly the photos surfaced.

An even more delightful story—if true—that floated around Moscow for some years was about the visit of Indonesian President Sukharno some time ago. The KGB got some juicy photos and videos of the dignitary engaged in rather hot activity with a voluptuous KGB officer. However, according to the story, when Sukharno was shown the video—in an attempt to blackmail him—he simply smiled and thanked the Soviets for supplying him with an outstanding visual aid. He assured his Soviet hosts that the film would be multiplied and shown throughout Indonesia to teach the people just how lovemaking should be done.

Well, what about Bill McGuire? Did they or did they not try to use seduction to nail me? I once heard an expression that "just because you are paranoid does not mean that they are not trying to get you." If you did not become paranoid in the Soviet Union, it was amazing. Again, I am certain that what I am about to relate was carefully planned at KGB headquarters in Moscow. I do not and never did believe in coincidences in that country.

It began a few days after we arrived in Kharkov. I suddenly had three new neighbors in the room next to Charlie's and mine. They were three rather attractive, blonde, buxom East German girls around my age. Every morning when I was leaving and every evening when I was returning from the exhibit they were outside their room, speaking in German, looking at me with a nice, big smile. The second day one of them said, "Ask that cute guy if he has a match." Another one said to her friend, "I wonder if he speaks German?" (She wondered???) I never answered; in fact I never looked at them in the face. I think they finally had a conversation with Elliot Gilmore, whose blonde German wife did not accompany him to the USSR because the Soviets did not issue her a visa. I never found out what was said between Elliot and the German girls, but I remember him saying that he finally spoke with them. I ignored them totally.

Within a few days of the arrival of the East German gals someone asked me at the exhibit how I liked the local girls. I diplomatically said that they were pretty. The next question was, "Did I prefer blondes or brunettes? What women did I find most attractive?" This time I told the truth. I said that in my opinion Spanish, Italian and Latin American women were the most beautiful in the world. The Spanish Civil War heroine "la Pasionara" (better known as Dolores Ibarruri) had been living in Moscow for many years. I wondered if she would arrive at my door one evening! Instead of La Pasionaria, I received a phone call one evening around ten o'clock from a woman who identified herself as Olga. She proceeded to say she had seen me at the exhibit and was in love with me. Would I just meet her for a coffee? Olga described herself as "Spanish looking." Well, how could I resist? I could and did resist because any fool knew that an ordinary Soviet citizen had no way of knowing how to call into the Intourist hotel, much less the room umber. Finally, there was nowhere in the city of Kharkov where one could have a cup of coffee at 10:00 pm. Nice try, Olga! I knew there would be other attempts.

During one of my vacations I decided to visit Vilnius, the capital of Soviet-occupied Lithuania. My Godmother came from Kaunas (a closed city, so a visit there would be impossible). When I was a child she often told me how she yearned to revisit Lithuania. I used to tell her that one day I would go to Lithuania and bring her a vial of dirt from the homeland. I was about to keep my promise. My parents had many friends of Lithuanian origin. As I child I attended many weddings, funerals and just plain Sunday mass at St. George's Lithuanian Catholic church in Shenandoah, Pa. I knew the food, some folk music and a few words, so it was not that strange for me to want to visit that country. On the other hand, Intourist (the official travel agency with strong KGB connections) was not that happy about my request to visit Vilnius. Few, if any, foreigners put that town on their itinerary. Furthermore, the United States did not recognize Soviet power in the Baltics, so there was no American presence there in case I got into trouble. At first Intourist said there were few tourist facilities. The ones they had were all booked. I requested a week there, and I persisted. I went to the Intourist office daily. Finally one day I began to scream and use profanity. A day later I was told that "Vilnius could receive me for two days only." My buddy John Aldriedge and I boarded the short flight from Kiev to Vilnius one cold November afternoon. Keep in mind it was a Soviet (Intourist) custom to put all foreigners on the plane before the locals could board. Foreigners also sat together. Not this time. John and I were the only foreigners on the flight. And our seats were not together. When I boarded and found my seat there was already a young, Russian (very good-looking) couple in the first two of three seats. I had the window. Aldriedge was across the isle at the other window. The woman, whose name was Marina, looked a bit Spanish. The man also had dark hair and was movie-star quality. They were reading an outdated Herald Tribune in English!!! I had never seen the Tribune in any Soviet kiosk in my many trips there. The couple spoke English very well. "Are you American or British?" she asked. (Like she did not know!) "A Yankee imperialist, as Fidel Castro would say," I replied. They did not get the joke. Moscow State University's special English department for spies did an excellent job at teaching the language, but when it came to American humor, they failed miserably. Anyway, this lovely, sincere couple offered me their Tribune. I refused. A few minutes later the rest of the passengers boarded, and the stewardess arrived offering the daily rag sheet Pravda in Russian or Lithuanian. I asked for the Lithuanian version and proceeded to read it as if I understood. The couple looked totally confused. "Do you speak Lithuanian?" the man asked. I continued to read *Tiesa*. Finally they began to try to converse with me once again. Guess what? They claimed they had just married that morning and were going to Vilnius on their honeymoon. For me that was like American newlyweds going to Bucyrus, Missouri on their honeymoon. To add to my amazement, Sergei and Marina were staying at the same hotel as John and I in the room next to ours!!!!! So many coincidences!

That evening John and I were having dinner in the dining room—as a matter of fact, the best meal we had so far since arriving in the USSR. But this was not really the USSR, was it? My eyes wandered over to the entrance. Sergei and Marina entered and came directly over to our table and sat down. Again, no Soviet citizen would do such a thing. The table had an American flag on it. In spite of it all, we had a tasty dinner and a pleasant conversation. What bothered me was that after dinner they absolutely insisted that John and I go up to their room for a bit of champagne. By that time a pretty, blonde Lithuanian woman named Grazvyda arrived. She informed us in English that she would be our Intourist hostess while in Vilnius. Grazvyda discussed what we would be seeing on the city tour in the morning. I introduced her to the newlyweds and explained that they had invited us to their room for a drink. I continued to say that. Although I would be happy to join them, my sixth sense told me they had "more important matters to attend to." "Oh, no," exclaimed Marina. "We are happy to share this happy day with you, our new American friends." "In that case we shall ALL go up to OUR room and John and I will order champagne from room service." I insisted that Grazvyda join us. The three of them came reluctantly. When I got out my camera to snap pictures, all three were very uncomfortable. But Bill McGuire snapped away. As I recall now, one final remark convinced me that these three were on the same KGB team. Grazvyda asked me where I learned Lithuanian. I looked at her strangely. "You were reading a Lithuanian newspaper on the plane." Only the newlyweds knew that, right? In addition, I never introduced them by name. Yet, Grazvyda was calling the "wife" Marinochka, the Russian diminutive for Marina. In conclusion, I must admit that, in spite of it all, it was a very pleasant evening. We avoided politics, drank much champagne, toasted to peace and friendship (how the Soviets loved to mouth those words!!! Any time, any place). I was slightly disappointed not to hear any honeymoon noises coming from the room next door. But the rest of the two-day trip to Vilnius was delightful.

A short time later I was on the same vacation but in Moscow. It was mid-afternoon, and John was out buying Russian dictionaries, his favorite hobby. There was a knock at the door. I opened it. Again, a handsome, young, dark-haired Russian lad hugged me, saying, "Misha, it's so good to see you again. Welcome to Moscow." By that time he was already in the room and had closed the door. "I am not Misha, young man." "Oh my God, you're not. I'm so sorry. But you look just like Misha." It all happened so fast that I was confused. I also thought the KGB would wait until I got to Rostov before their next move. But then their best agents are in Moscow. At first I really believed the man made an honest mistake. Then he went on to say that, after seeing me more closely, I was not only not Misha but obviously a foreigner. He even apologized for the intrusion. "You know I can get into serious trouble for this," he said. "Fraternizing with foreigners, especially Americans, is a serious offense in our country." That statement led me to believe that he might be on the level. We began to chat for about twenty minutes, mainly about my impressions of the USSR. Then the man asked if he could use my bathroom. He was in there so long I began to worry. When I walked over to the bath, the door was open. He was standing there, completely naked, and was sexually aroused. "Wanna join me?," he said with a big smile. By this time I knew I had been taken. "Get your clothes on, you pervert, and get to hell out of here before I call the police."

Within a few seconds he was dressed and was about to exit without saying one word. I grabbed him by the elbow and said the following: "Listen, you pig, I want you to do me a favor. Go back to your KGB bosses and give them the following message from Bill McGuire, "I cannot be seduced by big-breasted East German sluts, nor by Spanish-looking sluts from Kharkov, nor by so-called honeymooners in Vilnius, especially by some Moscow pederast. Now, you want to know what my sexual preference is? Do you? (No reaction) I am a farm boy at heart. I love sheep! Yes, sheep. That's what I'm into!" I opened the door and pushed him out.

Every morning when I opened my door to go out, I was expecting to find a friendly sheep waiting for me, compliments of the KGB. It never happened. However, this is not the end of the sheep story. A few weeks later our group arrived in Yerevan, the capital of Armenia (another Soviet-occupied land). Our Armenian hosts took us on a bus trip one afternoon to see Lake Sevan, the largest man-made lake in the USSR, the pride of Soviet technological achievements. As we left the bus I immediately saw a shepherd with his flock just several yards away. I looked at John Aldriedge and yelled: "Look, John, sheep...beautiful, young sheep. I'm going to like this place." Then I began to run in the direction of the sheep. John could hardly control his laughter, but he pretended to be holding me back. "No, no, Vilgelm Ivanovich, not this time. Not today."

I do not wish to spend any more time on this sheep story, sordid as it is. On the other hand, the matter came up again in the year 1977. I demanded to see my USIA security file because of all the turmoil going on in the Voice of America. I needed to see what, if anything, these security thugs had on me. Sure enough, there was a statement, based on my debriefing in 1966, that—and I quote—"Mr. McGuire expressed a sexual preference for sheep to a Russian KGB officer."

THAT OLD TIME RELIGION

There are two incidents that occurred during my first trip to Leningrad that I must relate to my readers. John Aldriedge and I arrived in the "City that Peter Built" on a cold October morning. We checked in to the Evropeiskaya hotel, which was built in the 1820's and was a showcase before the Revolution. Matter of fact, I returned there in 1993 after it had been completely restored. It is now the Hotel Grand Europe, a five-star hotel as it was meant to be; but in 1966—although a luxury hotel by Soviet standards—it was a fleabag by Western terms. The people at the reception desk were as rude and crude as any I had ever encountered in the former USSR. And that's saying something. It was one step up from the Intourist hotel in Kharkov. The walls were not painted with chalk and there was no crooner singing "Moya Milaya Mama." I cannot remember exactly what caused my first run-in with the desk clerk, but it ended in a screaming match. The wretch looked at me and announced: "I sense that you hate everything Russian!" "Wrong, woman, I love most things 'Russian.' I hate everything 'Soviet'. And there is none more Soviet than you." This nasty attitude carried over to the disgusting female Intourist guide that we were given that afternoon. We had prepaid for a four-hour city tour with a private auto and a guide. It was one of these unfortunate cases in which she took an immediate dislike to us and we to her. In her permanent nasty tone she asked us if we wanted her to speak English or Russian during the excursion. "Speak English," I demanded. "You are here to serve us. We paid in American dollars. Treat us with the respect Americans deserve in this damn country."

Leningrad/St. Petersburg is indeed a beautiful city. Even after so many years of Communist rule, they did not manage to ruin the city, often called the "Window to the West," built so magnificently with considerable help from the Germans and Italians some centuries ago. It is a city that requires days, not hours to see. Nevertheless, our beloved Intourist guide Marina finished our city tour in two hours. When I heard her tell the driver to return to the hotel, I reminded her we had paid for four hours. I intended to have what I paid for.

"Well, what do you want to do?" she asked in her usual surly manner. "Marina, I am a devout Roman Catholic," said I. "I know that there is a Catholic church off Nevsky. Take us to see it." She was stunned but told the driver to take us to the church. When we got there, Mass had just ended, and the priest was hearing confessions. Most of the parishioners were very old women of Polish or Lithuanian extraction. They looked at John, the witch and me suspiciously. Then I blessed myself the Roman Catholic way (which is different from the Orthodox) and suddenly they smiled. They pushed me to the front of the line. Next thing I knew I was in the confessional box, and the priest was sliding the window open. He was quite surprised to see a young man staring at him. "Good afternoon, Father," I said. "I am from the USA. I bring you greetings from your Catholic brethren in America." "Nice, my boy," said the padre. "Now make your confession." I was taken aback by his command (I had never confessed in Russian, nor was I about to), so I smiled and said, "Father, I just arrived in Leningrad. I have not had time to sin; but, if I do, I'll be back." I ran out of that booth like a bat out of hell. The old ladies all smiled at me, displaying their steel teeth. Again I made the sign of the cross and motioned for John and Marina to GET OUT FAST!

Marina remarked that the experience was "different." "Back to the hotel?" "Oh, no, Marina. We still have an hour and twenty minutes that you belong to us. Now, I cannot slight my dear friend John. He is a devout Baptist." (John had never been in a church in his life!) I know you have a Baptist church here as well. John, don't you wish to worship in a Russian Baptist church for the spiritual experience?" Aldriedge knew I would not take no for an answer. Besides, he had a great sense of humor and wanted to "punish" the Intourist wretch as much as I did. Off we went to the Leningrad Baptist church. Unfortunately, there was neither a service going on nor worshipers there to welcome us. But we did see the inside of what was probably once a very pretty church. Marina reminded us that during the day people worked for the betterment of Soviet society. There was little time to go to church. They go on weekends, she assured us. She suggested John return on Sunday when he would find the building packed for the service. "Back to the hotel?" "Of course not!" "Well, we have exhausted all religions," objected Marina the Adorable. "May we return to the hotel?" I looked at my watch. "Nope. What about the local synagogue?" was my next question. We still had over an hour of our paid-for tour. "Oh, come on, how can you be Catholic, Baptist and Jewish?" "Marina, darling, we have many Jewish friends. We are anxious to tell them about Leningrad's beautiful synagogue." She said she was not sure where the synagogue was. "We'll find out," I said. "There's plenty of time."

Marina said she would make a phone call. (I bet she did! More than one.) Next thing we were headed for the one remaining synagogue in a city where Jewish culture and religion once had existed openly. From the outside we could see that the building was badly in need of repair. Marina knocked on the door. A man in his fifties opened, and I greeted him with the word "shalom." I got the impression the "rabbi" had never heard the word in his life. Nor was his head covered. Our guide and mentor told the man that we were Americans, not Jewish, but wanted to tell our Jewish friends about the Leningrad synagogue. He took us inside—also in bad need of repair—and began to explain how the Soviet constitution guaranteed freedom of religion for all, how the Jews in the USSR even had their own newspaper (Yiddische Heimat, if I am not mistaken), a Jewish theater and even their own "republic" for those who wished to lead more "spiritual" lives. "The greatest threat to Soviet Jews," said the "rabbi," was the Israeli and American Zionists who seek to destroy the achievements of the Soviet Union and to "dominate the world." I had a question. "How many young Jewish Leningraders celebrate their bar mitzvahs? How many do YOU perform a year?" The "rabbi" looked at Marina for guidance. She tried to rescue him from the unwanted question. "You must realize, you Americans, that he is too busy to keep track of exact numbers. Right now he is busy working with the Soviet Committee for Peace in Vietnam to perform bar mitzvahs." Then our distinguished peacenik lashed out into an attack of U.S. policy and the war in Viet Nam. "It is a dirty war. You are committing disgusting acts. You are killing innocent women and children. Why?" I could not resist any longer. "Look, if you are a rabbi, I am a cantor. Why are we in Vietnam? So that Vietnamese synagogues will not look like this one in fifty years. So that young Jewish Vietnamese boys can celebrate their bar mitzvahs in peace. And finally so that real rabbis are not replaced by KGB hatchet men. Get the message? We were not born yesterday." Marina seemed angry. The "rabbi" seemed confused. John and I were trying to hold back the laughter.

In a way, Marina had the last word. When we returned to the car she announced that we still had about twenty minutes. "Now it is my turn. I am taking you to see the "Museum of Religion and Atheism." And that is exactly where we headed. The "museum" was right on Nevsky, the main street, and was by far the most despicable distortion of religion throughout the ages I had ever seen. She seemed particularly animated at the exhibit depicting the Spanish Inquisition. "Is that where the boys at Lubyanka (KGB headquarters) learned their methods?" I asked. No answer. When we left the building, Marina felt she had won a victory for Communism. She would score high brownie points for her work with these

American religious fools. You could see it on her face. Then she obviously wanted a reaction from us. "Uuuh?" was the subhuman sound from her mouth. I looked at John and muttered, my granddad always said, 'What can you expect from a pig, but a grunt?"

TRACES OF THE RUSSIAN NOBILITY

✦

[A CHAT WITH ANNA IVANOVNA]

The second encounter I wish to relate from my first trip to Leningrad took place the day after we had our historical, ecumenical trips to the religious institutions of the city. John and I were walking down Nevsky Prospekt and had stopped for a red light. My eyes focused on an elderly lady, shabbily dressed, who needed to see a beautician. But her demeanor was so elegant, so graceful that I could not take my eyes off her. By the time we were standing side by side, I got up the courage to speak to the lady. "Pardon me, Madame, but I see in you something I have yet to see in this country. You are a reflection of the good, old days, a pre-revolutionary lady, so to speak." She glanced at me and with a smile replied: "I am Countess Anna Ivanovna K. But I object to being called a "pre revolutionary lady." You're a foreigner, aren't you? I have not been called 'madame' in many decades." "Yes, Madame, dear Countess, I am an American visiting this beautiful city where Lenin and his godless henchmen destroyed the life you once had." She seemed impressed. I almost begged her to have a cup of coffee with John and me. She agreed. We entered a cafe nearby, and I asked what she wanted to drink. She asked what I was going to have. "I wonder if they serve hot chocolate," I asked my new friend. Anna Ivanovna gasped for her breath. "Hot chocolate, my dear? Oh yes, we used to drink hot chocolate in Tsarist days. But those days are long gone. You better order coffee or tea. Coffee for me." I bought three "bulochki" (sweet rolls) for us. The Countess devoured hers like she had not eaten in days. I brought her a second roll.

Then I made the goof of the day. She wanted to ask us a series of questions but preceded them with the words. "Please forgive me, boys, but, as you can see, I am crazy." "That is absolutely not true!" I exclaimed. "Please do not say such nonsense. That is not the truth at all." Well, the joke was on me. She had used the adjective "bezzubaya" (toothless), but I heard "bezumnaya" (crazy). Finally she pointed to her mouth. "Bezzubaya...zubov nyet" (toothless...no teeth). "Oh, my God, forgive me. As you can hear, Russian is not my native language." "Where did you learn our language?" she replied. "As a matter of fact, my first professor was born here in St. Petersburg. His name was Mikhail Georgiyevich Krupensky and his father served in the Duma under Nicholas II." There was a long pause. "Oh, it's unbelievable. Misha, my friend from childhood! Your teacher was Misha Krupensky! I want to cry. Last time I heard about him he was living and studying in Prague. How is he?" For a moment I, too, was unable to speak. John broke in and asked if she knew his professor, the Countess Slavatinskaya? "No." Another coffee was needed to continue this historical (for me) encounter. I was mesmerized.

We sat for nearly two hours while the charming, toothless Anna Ivanovna recounted the story of her life. Her family had all left the country shortly after Lenin came to power, with one exception. That was her favorite aunt, who had taken ill and was unable to travel. When the aunt had recovered enough for the train trip, Anna Ivanovna returned from Paris to accompany her. Shortly after she arrived in St. Petersburg—or was it Petrograd by then?—Lenin halted all emigration. Our Countess was stuck. Her family home was turned into sixteen communal apartments, but she was still allowed to live in just one room. Just as she was about to be exiled to Siberia for making anti-Soviet comments, another childhood friend appeared on the scene. He had thrown in his lot with the Soviets and become a Red Army officer. From mutual friends he heard of Anna Ivanovna's grave situation. He found her, married her and took her with him on his next assignment as a guard for Josef Stalin in the Kremlin. They actually had a flat within the Kremlin. The couple had two children, who were estranged from their mother by the time I met her, because they turned out to be die-hard Communists. The husband, as luck would have it, was one of the many "enemies of the State" (Stalin's favorite expression) and was executed even though he was loyal to Stalin and the Red Army. A friend turned him in by writing one of the famous "akts" I spoke about earlier. Fortunately for Anna Ivanovna, she was allowed to return to her one room in her ancestral home. And there she lived awaiting death. That evening she actually invited John and me to her room but only after taking us to a small, charming, local Orthodox church where she worshiped. We had recounted our story from the day before with the obnoxious Marina from Intourist and our visits to the local religious institutions. This little church was beautiful, but only a handful of old women like herself were there saying the evening vespers. As we exited the church, our lovely lady remarked: "I come here every night and pray that the merciful God will take me to His Kingdom." After that we went to her lonely room, filled with family pictures, a few paintings, an icon or two. I admired a bronze horse on the table. Anna Ivanovna told how her father had many horses on the estate outside of St. Petersburg. She loved to ride as a child. Her father had a favorite horse and had commissioned a local German artisan to make a sculpture of the horse. She insisted on giving it to me. I have it to this day. As the evening was drawing to an end, our dear Countess asked us not to return. It was just too dangerous for her, or any ordinary Soviet citizen, to be entertaining foreigners. We kissed her goodbye and wished her health and happiness. John and I left with tears in our eyes.

When I returned to Washington, I invited my ex-professor Krupensky to dinner one evening at the Old Europe restaurant. To be truthful, I expected Mikhail Georgiyevich to say he never heard of her. Just to be sure, I told the story without giving a name. It was only when I spoke about the horse and her father that Dr. Krupensky shouted: "Of course, Anna Ivanovna!!!!" He burst into tears. Then he raised his beer and said: "Long live the Monarchy!"

A second backup source confirmed the existence of this "pre-Revolutionary lady." I began a short correspondence with Stalin's daughter, Svetlana Alliluyeva. I was in Moscow when she defected (more on this later) and wrote to her about the reaction of her ex-countrymen. When she visited Washington in the early Seventies, she confirmed that Anna Ivanovna really did exist. Svetlana remembered her from her childhood in the Kremlin.

By this time I am certain that the Countess has finally achieved what she was praying for. Nevertheless, I just wish she had lived to see the end of the Communist domination of her homeland.

ROSTOV ON THE DON/YEREVAN

For the residents of Rostov on the Don, it was the first time they had the opportunity to see an American exhibition, much less speak with real, live Americans. Few foreigners had visited the city, and after arriving we knew why. Unlike the major cities of Moscow, Leningrad, Kiev, even Novosibirsk, Rostov was just a quiet little city situated along the banks of the Don river. It had few historical monuments and did not play a major role in the development of the country. However, the city is known throughout the country as the home of the famous Don Cossacks. Rostov's most famous monument—and certainly one I shall never forget—was a theater built in the shape of a tractor. Yes, a tractor! The only other facility that sticks out in my mind was the circus. Actually, Rostov had a first-class circus, which we attended more than once. Cultural life was scarce. Our hotel was the typical Intourist-type structure, not well constructed. On some days we had hot water and on some days cold but rarely both at the same time. I often had to fill the tub with boiling hot water and wait for it to cool down enough to jump in and bathe my weary body. We were there in the fall, and although it was not freezing, it was cold. Many days the hotel was without heat.

One story I must relate about the Hotel Rostov is how I helped my fellow guide, Molly Nelson, with her thesis on Romanian linguistics. Molly was a pretty, petite brunette, who had spent much of her life studying languages and linguistics few ever heard of. She had also worked on an American exhibition in Poland and had been an exchange student there. It was not surprising that Molly often con-fused the two languages, but her charm and enthusiasm more than made up for a few Polish words thrown into her speeches. Molly had another attribute for which she was famous. She often wore what seemed to be rhinestone-studded panty hose on the stand. I'm sure many eyes in the audience never made the trip all the way up to her pretty face. She had a wonderful sense of humor. At any rate, one evening Molly asked me to help her with her thesis. It seems that all the early textbooks on the Rumanian language were written in German. My task was to orally translate a particular chapter. The room was so darn cold that Molly and I did our project in her bed with as many blankets as we could find. It was still too cold. So, Molly put her hair dryer under the covers with us, at medium heat, and I proceeded to translate. I often thought that if the KGB had a camera in the room, they must have thought that these two Americans had really flipped their lids.

Opening day in Rostov was not much different than the one in Kharkov in that—true to tradition—our Soviet hosts had not put the posters around the city to inform the Rostovites of our presence. Perhaps ewer people listened to the VOA as well. Actually, reception was worse in Rostov than in Kharkov. As a result, the first day we did not draw the crowds we were accustomed to. I stood alone on my stand dealing with wood products and the tools used in woodcarving, etc., for about ten minutes before I finally attracted five young (ages 18-22) men. They were dressed like most Soviet youth: baggy pants, ugly shoes, caps like the one Lenin wore. They needed a shave but were smiling without the commonplace steel teeth. One of them posed the first question, "Hey, American, which is better, Communism or masturbation?" I thought I was hearing things. I asked him to repeat the question. He did. I asked if this were some kind of joke. "Of course it's a joke, a current Russian joke. The answer is: masturbation is better than Communism. Why? Because a cock in the hand beats a cunt on the horizon." Bill McGuire was speechless. I was simply not prepared for this introduction to Rostov. "Wanna hear more jokes we young people tell?" I said I was here to talk about hand tools, not other uses of the human hand. "Okay," said the boy, "tell us an American joke and we'll leave you in peace." I tried to think of a current American joke, for which another "akt" would not be written up against me. It was difficult, because American humor does not translate easily into Russian. I went into the whole business of a play on words. Finally I remembered a joke told to me by a French journalist about why the sun never sets on the British Empire. "Because God doesn't trust Brits in the dark." The boys reminded me that it was not an "American" joke. Did I not know any American jokes? Do Americans not have a sense of humor? What is a current joke floating around Washington these days? I thought and thought. Above all, I wanted to keep it clean yet funny for a young Russian audience of five. I came up with a very corny joke about a young American man from the Ozarks who had no sexual experience before marriage. He wanted to start a family immediately. A year passed, and his wife was still not pregnant. The man went to the doctor and asked what was the matter. The doctor was shocked to learn that the man had no idea about how babies were made. He was embarrassed, too. Finally he told the man to stick the longest part of his body into the hairiest part of hers. Another month passed, but the wife still was not pregnant. Finally one afternoon the irate man burst into the doctor's office and screamed, "I am tired of sticking my nose under her arm, and she still is not pregnant." The Russian boys forced a laugh. Then they began to tell what was for me the first of the famous Radio Armenia jokes. These silly jokes could be compared to the Polish jokes going around America around the same time. One example: "A man calls in to Radio Armenia and asks, 'Is it true Tchaikovsky was a homosexual?' Radio Armenia answers, 'Yes, but we also love him for his music.'" These guys spent about fifteen minutes recounting these anecdotes. I found them silly and stupid, but I was truly happy to see how much they were enjoying telling me the jokes. Finally I suggested they share this humor with my colleague, Mr. K, on the other stand. I knew K had no sense of humor and it would annoy him. I was not particularly fond of him either. The boys left for the metal tools area, and I stood all alone for another twenty minutes. By noon word had spread by word of mouth that the Americans were open for business. The exhibit hall was full to capacity for the rest of the day. I suppose the KGB gave us a day of rest, because there were no questions about Vietnam, unemployment or racism in the USA, or any other unpleasant topics. Later in the afternoon my original buddies returned with several of their friends. A second round of current Soviet jokes took place, this time less vulgar since there were old ladies in the audience. Much to my surprise, Rostov had a considerable Armenian community. They began to come to our exhibit as well and often shared the latest Radio Armenia jokes with us. One has to admire anyone who can poke fun at himself or herself. These charming, warm and friendly Armenians gave me some idea of what working in Armenia would be like in another six weeks. By day two, however, KGB thugs had sent out their hound dogs. There were questions about the war in Vietnam, unemployment, racism, high cost of education in the USA, the murder of JFK, and finally a new topic came into our discussions. The local newspaper ran a series about the "brain drain" from Third World countries to the USA. People asked how we could allow these specialists to "abandon" their homelands that needed them more than rich America? Then I explained that in the West it was common for Americans to work in Italy, for Ugandans to work in France, for Australians to work in Sweden, and, above all, it was not necessary to get government permission to do so. It was obvious that the Rostovites did not believe me. It was just beyond their comprehension.

One morning a typical Soviet provocateur pushed his way to the head of a very friendly crowd around my stand and demanded to know why we were exhibiting tools that not only existed in the Soviet Union, but were also of a better quality. "What?" I laughed in disbelief. Before he or I could say another word, the old women began to shout at him that the USSR did not have these wonderful tools and why was he annoying this nice, young man from the USA. He insisted that all the tools on display could be found in any Soviet department store. So I said to him, "How strange. Only yesterday I wandered through your local department store just to compare prices. I could find NONE of these tools." He replied, "Listen, you young smart ass. We had a WAR in this country. Millions of Soviet men, women and children lost their lives fighting for the Fatherland. That is why we do not have these tools." At the risk of another "akt" against me, I replied, "Well, if I am not mistaken, Germany had the same war. Many Germans also perished. In fact, they LOST the war. But, guess what? They have all these tools today!!" The old ladies cheered me on. One of them hit the provocateur with her purse and told him to get lost.

As I said, there was not much to do in the evenings in Rostov. At first people were reluctant to talk to us on the streets, in restaurants and at the circus. One evening I was dining in our hotel with three of our guides, Shirley Berezesky, Linda Delbell, and my roommate, Charlie Trumbull. We were all bored. I came up with a plan to find out to what extent we were being followed. After dinner, Charlie would go out alone and walk toward the circus four blocks away. Five minutes later Shirley would leave her room and do the same. In another five minutes Linda would do the same, and finally I would leave. This way Shirley could see if and who was following Charlie, Linda would see who was following Shirley, and I could see who was following the three of them. Indeed one man with a green felt hat followed Charlie, another behind Shirley, etc. We all met in front of the circus, embraced as if we had not seen each other in ages and walked back to the hotel. It might have been a silly thing to do, but that's how bored we were.

The very next day a very young, attractive Russian man named Vitali(or so he said) came to the exhibit and spoke at great length with me. He even followed me on my break. Vitali said he and his wife Luda would like to meet with Shirley, Linda, Charlie and me (how strange that he knew all the names of the "street walkers" from the night before) to meet them and some of their friends. He agreed to meet us in front of the circus at 8:00 pm. Indeed he was there to escort us (we saw nobody following us that night) to the apartment of their friend Ilona. We were shocked to see such a beautiful (by Soviet standards) apartment; spacious, well-furnished, lovely art on the walls. They had fresh tomatoes from Bulgaria, Georgian wines, Armenian cognac and even caviar. Vitali and Luda, his beautiful, blonde wife, were "graduate students." Ilona never said what she did, but she had Western clothing (although she was never in the West, she said) and lived alone in this spacious apartment. The other "friends" there that evening were KGB-looking thugs, who rarely spoke. Nonetheless the evening was devoted to music, mostly jazz, fashion and Russian art. We all enjoyed ourselves. I think by the end of the evening they also felt fairly comfortable with us. If we were spies, we were nice, educated spies. They invited us back almost nightly. I was happy to get the good food and honestly enjoyed dancing with Madame Luda. Oh, yes, I taught them to dance the Monkey. This time no pictures were taken of me by the KGB. They were not too happy the evening I showed up with a camera to take photos of them with us "to remember our pleasant stay in Rostov on the Don." But they agreed. I might add that by the fourth visit, the "quiet ones" were no longer present. In fact, Charlie became bored with them and also stayed away. To this day I am not sure if it was my imagination, paranoia or a ploy, but it seemed to me, as the days passed, Vitali became more friendly with Shirley and Luda with me, while Ilona spent more time in the kitchen. Shirley and I discussed the situation in the park one day and decided it was time to see less of the trio. We had to come up with an excuse, but what? Shirley said I was good at masterminding schemes to annoy the KGB. It was my ball game. We also decided these provincial types were less sophisticated than the Leningrad KGB "intelligentsia." It was not necessary to go to extremes to part company with them. Besides, they treated us well. As human beings we liked them. Finally the time had arrived to confront our Rostov friends with the reason why we would not be seeing them again. When I told Shirley about my plan, she thought we could never pull it off without laughing. But, let's give it a try. We arrived at Ilona's apartment at the regular time. She had her usual buffet ready and all were in a happy, joyful mood. Finally Shirley declared that Bill had an announcement to make. As I whispered to myself, "God help me and forgive me for lying." I said, "Dearest Friends. We want you to be the first to know the good news. Shirley and I have fallen madly in love. As soon as we return to the USA, we are getting married. But for the rest of our time here in the USSR, we want to spend more time together, making love, planning our future, etc." The words were greeted with a round of applause. Cognac was poured. Kisses and hugs were exchanged. Later Shirley reminded me that she and I did not kiss. Strange. The Trio had but one favor. Would we return just one more time to celebrate the engagement? Of course. The following week we arrived at the usual hour. Happily for me, that day a package from my Mother arrived in the diplomatic mail from Moscow containing several items I requested from Philadelphia. She had sent cosmetics for the girls, after shave for Vitali, and several other things that one did not see in the USSR. After a tasty meal I presented our hosts with the goodies. They were overjoyed. Our cheeks were wet from all the kisses from the three of them. Then they announced they had some presents for us. Much to our amazement the gifts were baby clothes (made in Poland). Ilona smiled and asked: "When is the baby due?" "Baby? What baby?" replied Shirley. Luda interrupted, "Of course, there's a baby. You came here as friends and suddenly you are getting married. We understand. Now when is the happy event?"

When the exhibit closed its doors in Rostov, we were given a little over two weeks of rest and relaxation. We were free to remain in Rostov (who would want to?), travel to Moscow (where we had commissary and luncheonette privileges), or see a bit of the Soviet Union. In past exhibits the guides were even allowed to leave the country (the best idea of all!), but the Soviets stopped issuing multi-entry visas and one of our former colleagues got stuck in India. In other words, we could travel within the Iron Curtain only. The Soviets at the time were unaware of the advantages of collecting dollars for hotels, meals and travel. As a result, we paid what a Soviet citizen would pay for a hotel room (about three rubles), and the same went for food and travel. We had temporary Foreign Service assignments—the equivalent of about five-thousand and some dollars year—plus per diem. It was possible to save a nice amount of money (I saved over six thousand, as I recall) and still eat well and see the USSR. I already wrote about my first vacation after Kharkov to Leningrad, Vilnius and Moscow. Believe it or not, after Rostov my buddy John Aldriedge and I decided to return to Kharkov, mainly to see our friends there. From there we went to Tbilisi, the capital of Soviet Georgia, birthplace of Joseph Stalin. We got there the night before the yearly celebration of the October Revolution, better known in Russian as the "Great October Revolution." Moscow was full of red banners proclaiming the wonders of the USSR, the Soviet heroes (Marx, Engels, Lenin, and, of course, Comrade Brezhnev, who was still in power at the time). The celebration in Tbilisi was somewhat understated. There were flags, even a parade on November 7 (it was October according to the old calendar, November according to the new), but the air of celebration was somewhat lacking. What they had in common with Moscow and other better-known Soviet cities was the number of drunks in the streets. The hotel was decent by their standards, and the fiercely nationalistic Georgians were accustomed to seeing foreigners. They even had an American exhibition or two. Above all, I must say I enjoyed the food. I happen to like hot, spicy food. Georgian food is just that. The wines were not bad either. We did the usual four-hour tour with guide (this time a pleasant, young Georgian woman, who could not have been nicer nor more informative). When I complimented her on the first-rate city tour and related to her the story of the witch in Leningrad, she simply shrugged her shoulders and said: "You realize we are not Slavs. We had a culture when the Russians were still living in trees. Pity they did not stay there!" I got the impression she was not too fond of her brothers to the North. In fact, most of the Georgians with whom I spoke were still deeply devoted to Stalin, their native son, and felt the Russians treated him shabbily.

I asked a man in a cafe that afternoon if Georgians were unaware of the atrocities Stalin committed during his days in power. The man replied in a most serious tone: "But Stalin killed Russians and other Slavs. What's wrong with that?" I switched the conversation to the fine Tsinandali wine he served. In the hotel restaurant that evening I ate alone. For some reason Aldriedge was either buying dictionaries or with some locals. An elderly man and his two sons in their thirties (I'd say) came to my table and sat down. The old man immediately asked if I were an American. I nodded. They ordered several bottles of Georgian wine, Armenian cognac and chocolates for a starter. Next thing I knew more booze and chocolates were arriving at our table, compliments of other Georgians in the restaurant. True Georgian hospitality indeed! We hada delightful conversation, even though the old man spoke Russian poorly. The sons spoke it well. The younger son remarked that in the morning he was leaving for "abroad." I asked where he was going. "To Moscow," he replied. Then the older son asked me when we would have Communism in America? I almost shouted NEVER!!! "But," said he, "Lenin said that one day America would be a communist state." I replied, rather annoyed, "Well, Lenin was mistaken. We shall NEVER live under Communism." The old man continued, "Know what? Lenin was wrong about two things then. He also said there would be Communism in Georgia. Let's drink to Georgian-American friendship." And so we did!

GE TSET AZAAT
HAIASTANNA

✦

[LONG LIVE FREE ARMENIA!]

We arrived in Yerevan, the capital of Soviet Armenia on a rather cold but clear day in November 1966. The flight from Moscow was a nightmare. The planes' pilot was obviously an Armenian national and gave chauvinism a new name. He remained on the loud speaker for most of the six or so hour trip, telling the passengers about Armenia. At first it was interesting. He spoke about literacy, education, medical care, the massacre of innocent Armenians by the Turks in 1917, about the repatriation of Armenians from the Diaspora, the high quality of Armenian cognac, including every international cognac-tasting competition it entered; for example, first prize at the International Competition in Lodz, Poland, in Plovdiv, Bulgaria, in Dresden, Germany, and even some god-forsaken hole in North Korea. This is what the Soviets fondly refer to as "international." By the end of the second hour of his lecture, the passengers were "begging" for some of that liquid joy and hoping he would drink enough to shut his mouth. No such luck.

When our bus pulled up to the Hotel Armenia (an Intourist hotel like all the rest), the manager, a portly, pleasant Armenian woman of about fifty, came out to welcome us. That was the one and only time I ever experienced such a welcome in any of the US-USSR cultural exchange programs I participated in. And it made us feel good. The rooms were like all other rooms in the Intourist chain—hardly up to the standards of the Red Roof chain in the USA!—but there was heat and both hot and cold water. We had a good meal and went to bed. Next day we were off to the exhibit site to begin setting up our tools. What a disappointment. The pavilion was about a twenty-minute drive from the city, no eating facilities, an outhouse (yes, an outhouse), and the building was so drafty we had to wear our coats during set-up. This meant another problem. The only way the locals could reach the site was by bus. The bus ran only once an hour. On the positive side, our Soviet hosts had posted "a few" announcements around the city. By opening day many of us had colds. That was not the worst of our worries. They set up a so-called kitchen for us to have our lunch. This consisted of a few charcoal burners and vats with cold water to wash the dishes. So many of us got dysentery that we almost had to close down the show. Instead the embassy doctor, Dr. Bizzell, flew down to treat us. My roommate Charlie was in bed for most of the stay in Yerevan and lost about forty pounds. I never got that ill, because I did not eat the food at the site. I would go to the local market (bazar) the night before and buy tasty Armenian sausages, local cheese, black bread and, of course, I always had my trusty jar of Skippy peanut butter from the commissary.

Attendance was way down compared to Kharkov and Rostov. On a more cheery note, there was little or no mention of Vietnam, unemployment, racism, rotten capitalist decadence, and other distortions of American life. Instead the attendees asked things like: How do Armenians live in the USA? Are they good capitalists with a lot of money? What is Kirk Kerkorian doing these days? Do you like our Armenian food? The answer was yes, when it is prepared in a real kitchen. In short, despite the hardships of our life in the pavilion, the warmth and kindness of the Armenian people left an unforgettable impression on me.

One incident in particular stands out among my recollections of Yerevan. Early one afternoon a middle aged woman walked up to my stand and in perfect Philadelphia English asked me, "Hey, are you the guy from Philly?" Dumbfounded, I answered "Yes." "Ever hear of Bartram High (School)?" "Yes, it's at 67th and Elmwood, right? You mean John Bartram High School?" Then the woman said she had gone there, and she broke down and sobbed bitterly. "Now what do I do?" I thought to myself. "What is this all about?" When she calmed down, she related how she was born in Philadelphia of Armenian parents from Turkey. After the slaughter the parents went to the USA and settled in the Philadelphia area. In the Forties the Soviet government was encouraging Armenians abroad to return to the homeland and help build it up. Many, many did. They came from Turkey, Egypt, Lebanon, the USA, France and other Western countries. Once back in Armenia there was no getting out. In many cases they were American citizens and held American passports. Needless to say, none of them ever applied for Soviet citizenship. This woman told me that she and her fellow Americans refused to learn Russian and thus could not enter the institutions of higher learning. Among each other they spoke only English and listened to the Voice of

America broadcasts in English. The American Embassy in Moscow was more than willing to issue them entry visas, but they were unable to get exit visas from their Soviet step-parents. And so they lived miserably and with little hope. She wanted to introduce me to other of my countrymen, but I was afraid it would be too risky for them, as well as for me. There was nothing I could do for her. She had asked if I could take a letter out to her aunt and uncle who were still living in Philadelphia. I remembered that both USIA Security and the US Embassy told us that NOT UNDER ANY CIRCUMSTANCES could we accept ANYTHING from a Soviet citizen to be taken out of the country. I did, however, ask the names of her relatives in Philly. When I returned home, I called the aunt. We spoke for over an hour by phone. The aunt and uncle had given up any hope of ever seeing their relatives again.

The Hand Tools staff and guides had the honor of spending Thanksgiving 1966 in Yerevan. Our Embassy sent down several turkeys for our dinner, complete with frozen pumpkin pies and other Thanksgiving foods. However, the kitchen staff of our hotel told us we could not use their kitchen for "sanitary reasons." It was the first time I saw our Director Fritz Berliner completely lose his cool. I remember his words well since I had to translate them into Russian. "Sanitary reasons? You give us a goddam pigsty for a pavilion, you feed us greasy crap at lunch, wash our dishes and silverware in dirty, cold water, and you talk to me about sanitary conditions!!!!! Screw you! I'll give you one hour to change your minds." It worked. Fritz was finally learning how to deal with the Soviets. They always misinterpreted our politeness as weakness. The only language they understood was force, determination and profanity. We finally got to use their "immaculate" kitchen facility. Happy Thanksgiving 1966, Yankees!

In each city I did at least one silly, ridiculous thing to keep from going crazy. I already wrote about the trip to Lake Sevan and the "lovely" sheep there. By the way, the local hosts never sent me one! But it was getting close to Christmas and it looked like we would be spending our holiday in Yerevan. So the Sunday before Christmas I organized some of our guides to do some caroling. We removed the sheets from our beds (which infuriated the dezhurnayas!) and paraded through the hotel using the sheets as cassocks with votive candles in hand and sang traditional Christmas carols. Some of the hotel staff were livid. Others, who had been in the West, knew what it was all about. For me and the guides who joined me, it was simply a way of releasing a lot of pent-up tension. By the way, thanks to the efforts of Fritz Berliner in Yerevan and Nick Moravsky in Moscow, we at least got to spend the holiday in Moscow. Merry Christmas, 1966!

A BRIEF INTERLUDE

✦

[IS THERE PARADISE AFTER MOSCOW?]

Moscow is not the ideal location to spend Christmas, at least in those days; nevertheless, my colleagues and I made the most of it. On Christmas eve we were invited to a tree-trimming party at the Ambassador's residence, Spasso House, an Italian-like villa where from time to time our diplomats and other visiting American dignitaries, cultural and financial figures had an opportunity to have one-on-one chats with leading Soviet authorities. The other time one could count on seeing the Soviet bigwigs was July 4. Even Nikita Khrushchev and Leonid Brezhnev showed up at these occasions. The mood on Christmas eve was festive, and few of us thought about how far away from home we were. For me it was the first Christmas in my life I did not celebrate with my entire family. On December 25 I had two experiences I shall never forget. I had been in the USSR for nearly five months and had not been inside Lenin's mausoleum, not that I ever made the effort. That day as some of my colleagues and I were down in Red Square we noticed—for the first time—there was only a short line waiting to get in to see the "Father of the Great Russian Revolution." My first thought was that God would strike me down dead for entering such an unholy sanctuary on His birthday. But, what the hell! It was now or never. We got in line and after about five minutes there we were, gazing at the Man Himself. Lines were everywhere in the former Soviet Union, and in most cases people were talking or arguing loudly as they waited in line for hours for everything. NOT in the mausoleum line! Inside there was such silence it was eerie. I looked at Vladimir Illich and could not believe it was once a human being. It had to be a wax dummy. To me it just did not seem real. When we exited, I struck up a conversation with an elderly man. He was obviously from the country by his dress. He, too, was missing a few teeth, reeked of alcohol and was extremely friendly, switching to the familiar form of "you" at once. "Well, what do you think?, he asked. "If you really want to know

73

the truth, my friend, I don't think it is Lenin," I replied. "It looks like a wax dummy to me. I could be wrong. And please do not report me for saying so." "What factory are you from?" asked my new buddy. "Factory? I am not from any factory." "Okay then, what labor union sent you here today?" "No labor union either. I am a tourist from the United States." "The USA? Sure. And I am from Mars! Now, tell me, Comrade, why are you here? By whose orders?" I had known for a long time that the local party officials and the union people took turns sending their workers to the mausoleum so that it was never without a line. Finally, he said that he knew I was not an American because I spoke Russian. But his most surprising statement was, "That is not Lenin. Lenin, as we all know, died of syphilis, and you cannot embalm syphilitics." "I'll take your word, Grandpa," I said. With that I took leave of the man.

Later that day I did what I encourage every visitor to Moscow to do. A few of us went out to the Moscow countryside and went on a "troika" ride. It is a sleigh pulled by three horses—"troika" means "three" in Russian—and it was one of the most delightful activities I ever had in the former USSR. The Russians bundle you up with heavy blankets and away you go "dashing through the snow in a three horse open sleigh." It is delightful and invigorating.

Some of my colleagues got out of Moscow as soon as possible, as soon as a flight was available. I had chosen to exit via India and the Far East. Because of that I had to wait a few more days for the Air India flight to New Delhi. It gave me a wonderful chance to see the ballet, the circus, the museums, the restaurants (especially the Russian Tea Room in the Metropole Hotel where the food was mediocre, but the balalaika orchestra was impressive, playing old Russian folk tunes with great gusto), and even to meet some more Russians who risked inviting me to their homes. Moscow was full of foreigners for the so-called Winter Festival. I was staying at the Ukraina hotel, just a few blocks from the American embassy. The hotel was used mainly by foreigners, but also by visitors from the other Socialist states and by high-ranking Communist dignitaries.

The Ukraina was one of what some called "Stalinist birthday cakes" in Moscow, because of its tiered shape (minus the candles, of course). One evening in the lobby within an hour's time I met my first Cubans in the USSR, as well as a leader of the Peruvian Communist Party, some Italian Communists and a Vietnamese woman. When I informed her that I was an American, if looks could kill, I'd be dead. To appease her I told her that the Hard Currency Food Store in Moscow, where I and other Americans bought much of our food, had the most delicious pineapples from Vietnam. She was unaware that such a store existed, as were many Soviet citizens. At any rate, I told her that we enjoyed those nice fruits that her Soviet brothers and sisters would probably never taste. When I entered the elevator there were two men speaking Spanish with a Cuban accent. From their conversation I realized that one of them was a diplomat at the Cuban embassy, and his friend had just arrived on the plane from Havana. They assumed I was another Socialist brother who could not possibly speak Spanish, so the newly-arrived asked his friend what it was like to live in Moscow. First the diplomat said it was he coldest place on Earth—he obviously had not visited Siberia—and that the Russians were "barbarians." According to him, they live like pigs, eat like pigs and therefore act like pigs. "In fact, they ARE pigs," said the diplomat. In the remaining moments of our ride together he also noted that Russians thought Cubans were lazy. "You'll see," said Comrade Diplomat. "It will not take you long to understand the realities of Russian society." As I was getting off the elevator, I said to them in Spanish: "I wish you would not talk that way about the hand that is feeding you and your countrymen, Comrade. I'll report you to the Ministry in the morning." The man looked like he was about to have a coronary. I smiled and got off, laughing all the way to my room.

The day I was to leave for India I suddenly discovered that my Soviet exit visa was missing from my passport. My first thought was that a KGB agent lifted it from my passport while I was having breakfast. Or, maybe it just dropped out of the passport without my noticing it. I had to drop by the Embassy anyway to have lunch and say good-bye to my friends there. When I told one of our officers, he began to panic. He ran to report it to security. Next thing three men were questioning me about why the KGB would do this to me. It was obviously a plot to keep me from leaving the USSR. They probably had something on me and would hit me with it at the airport. It was decided that an Embassy officer would have to accompany me to Sheremetyevo airport for my 11pm flight. It turned out to be none other than Bill Dixon of the Cultural Section, who had just arrived in Moscow. We left my hotel around 8pm in an Embassy car driven by a Soviet employee. He and I joked all the way to the airport. Moscow was covered with a thick blanket f snow, and it was snowing very hard as we drove. I asked the driver, Seryozha, are you sure we're still on the road?" "Maybe yes, maybe no" was his reply. "Seryozha, you want to go to India with me? It's nice and warm there!" "No, there are no Russian women there." "Seryozha, variety is the spice of life." "Mr. Bill, you can have those dark-assed, ruby-four-headed sluts. I'll stick to our Russian women." (Did I detect just a bit of racism in his remark?) After all,

India and the USSR were great pals in those days, as I soon found out after arriving there. I noticed that Mr. Dixon was not amused. In fact, he became more and more pale as we reached the airport. We arrived. Dixon suggested we face the music together. If I had any problems, we would head for the car and return to the Embassy. I told him to remain in place until I at least spoke with the passport official. I would not be out of his sight. So I checked into the Air India counter and headed for Passport Control. A very pleasant, plump officer (who had more than coffee with his dinner) began by asking where I was heading. I gave him the biggest line of BS I had cooked up in five months, pretending that all was in order. He asked why I was going to India. I replied that I did not really want to but that I was suffering from the terrible Moscow winter. The doctor suggested a few days in a warm climate. He looked at my American passport. Before opening it, he said: "Why do you speak Russian so well?" Then I really laid it on. I said I was so impressed with the achievements of Soviet science, (example, Sputnik), the magnificence of Soviet literature, (example, Mikhail Sholokhov), the splendor of Soviet ballet (example, Maya Plesetskaya), not to mention free education and medical care, that I chose to major in Russian at the university. I loved Moscow, the Moscow countryside, the food, the women, ah, yes, the vodka! Best in the world! By that time he had opened my passport and asked where my exit visa was. What exit visa? Isn't it inside? My goodness, it must have fallen out. Could he not issue me another one on the spot? I'll bring him back a bottle of rum when I return. Without further ado, he passed me through the gate and I was in the International Departures lounge. I waved goodbye to a very relieved Bill Dixon.

The flight came from London and was late. So the other passengers and I—mostly Indians, a few Japanese and a few Russians—waited patiently for over two hours. Finally the plane landed. Boarding the Air India airplane was like entering another world. The aroma of fine spices permeated the cabin, the stewardesses were draped in beautiful saris, and there was music coming out of the speakers. I almost cried it was so beautiful.

Fellow Americans and others who had spent a long time in the USSR had told me that wherever you land after you leave Moscow, you think you're in paradise. It was not quite that way with me. First of all, New Delhi was closed due to fog and we had to land in Bombay. We were assured that Air India would put us up at the Hotel Taj Majal, feed us and get us to New Delhi as soon as possible. It was well below zero when I left Moscow and over one hundred degrees when I got off the plane in my Russian fur hat and my heavy, black overcoat, not to mention long, thermal underwear. People in the airport looked at me as if I were a real idiot. I certainly felt like one. The ride into the city was annoying, to say the least. Undernourished, dirty children were playing in the mud. There were strange odors, even worse than what I smelled in the USSR. I shared a cab with a young British woman (we'd call her a hippie in the USA) who had been there several times to meditate. "Can anything be worse?" I asked her. She replied, "Oh, Ducky, you haven't seen anything yet! Go visit Calcutta!"

After two days of being stranded in Bombay, and with Delhi still fogged in, I decided to change my itinerary. I marched down to the Air India office and asked where the next plane was going. Bangkok. "Get me on it, please!" And so I wound up in Bangkok. After checking into a lovely hotel, taking a nap and a shower, I went down to the elegant dining room to eat. I was actually starved. However, I lost my appetite when I sat down and the band began to play "Midnight in Moscow." "Can I ever get away from that goddam place," I wondered? I thoroughly enjoyed Bangkok and the wonderful hospitality of the Thai people. The food was also superb. Still, I thought about the many dear friends I left behind in the USSR and how they would never have the opportunity to walk along the floating markets, smell the exotic fragrances, taste the fresh fruits and vegetables. Those poor, unfortunate people. How I suddenly missed them. As a matter of fact, every time I left the Soviet Union I became very saddened to leave so many good friends behind in that miserable system.

From Bangkok I flew on to Hong Kong where I spent New Years 1967 watching in the streets like everybody else there the elaborate fireworks at midnight. There I also ordered several hand-made new suits. I entered the USSR with three huge suitcases of clothes and left with just one. I gave most of my clothing to young Soviets I had met as a token of my friendship. By the time I left Hong Kong I had a new wardrobe, several electrical devices and a desire never to eat Chinese food again. My next stop was Tokyo. That city I also enjoyed immensely. It was even more expensive than I imagined. But I had to see the country that bombed my father's sub during the war, leaving him in pain for the rest of his life.

From Tokyo I flew on to Honolulu. AMERICA AT LAST!!! I am not one for outward expressions of patriotism and emotion, but I fell to my knees and kissed the ground of our American soil. It was good to be home. I stayed at the beautiful Royal Hawaiian and drenched myself in luxury for one week. Believe me, by that time the Soviet Union was the farthest place from my mind. I decided that maybe in five years I could go back on a visit, but never on an American exhibition and never for more than a week. And finally I flew home to Philadelphia where my entire family—the entire brigade!—was at the airport to welcome me home. In the car on our way home, my mother said semi-jokingly, "Well, honey, in twenty-five words or less, tell me about the Soviet Union." "There's nothing to tell, mother. It's all in the past."

MOTHER MOSCOW
CALLS AGAIN

By late January 1967 I was about to accept a job with the Government, to rent an apartment within walking distance of my office, and to enroll in the PhD. program at Georgetown University. Then one morning the phone rang. It was Mary Hourigan from USIA's Exhibits Division. She said they needed me badly to replace one of the guides on the current exhibit about to open in Moscow. Several of my colleagues from Hand Tools were offered to stay on for the newest presentation called Industrial Design and scheduled for the Big Three (Moscow, Leningrad and Kiev). It seems that one of the guides was in an automobile accident and was sent home. I told Mary thanks, but no thanks. I had enough of the Soviet Union to last for several years, if not a lifetime. On that same day, though, I had to go down to USIA to pick up my severance pay from the last exhibit. This would—I thought—end my association with the United States Information Agency, commonly referred to in the Soviet press as the Misinformation Agency.

While I was at USIA, I ran into Alexander Barmine, whom I had met during our training for Hand Tools. He was a man I liked and respected. Barmine was born in the USSR and rose to the rank of general in the Red Army. While he was stationed as a Military Attache at the Soviet Embassy in Athens in the early 1940s, Barmine decided to defect to the USA. He told a funny story about volunteering for the US Army to fight Hitler and the Nazis. His army application form had the following questions: "Did you ever serve in the armed forces of another country?" Barmine wrote "yes." "Which country?" "The USSR." "Highest rank achieved?" "General." His American sergeant thought Barmine was being facetious and almost threw the papers away. In his new homeland Alexander Barmine also rose quickly due to his intelligence, his persistence—and good looks. He married several times, including one of the Roosevelt women. For years Barmine was the Chief of the Russian Service of the Voice of America, where his staff either loved or hated him. There was no in-between. He was a no-nonsense man. Well, I happened to be one of his greatest admirers. So was Richard Nixon. Gen.

Barmine was connected with anything and everything USIA did with the Soviet Union. When he saw me in the corridor that day, he asked me to step into his office. "Look, I am not going to mince words nor waste time. You must return to the Soviet Union. America needs you. USIA needs you. Alex Barmine wants you." It was the last part that impressed me most. Then Mr. Barmine proceeded to tell me that the director and staff evaluated the guides as to effectiveness, ability to speak Russian, ability to remain calm under stress, etc. He said I had been rated number one. It was a very nice compliment, especially coming from Barmine. "Besides, the money is good, you'll get to spend time in more important cities than on your first trip. And finally, I shall personally recommend you for employment in USIA when you return." I truly felt an obligation to help out, but added that Mr. Barmine could forget about future employment with USIA. I did NOT ever want to work for the Government.

Within a week I was on a plane for Moscow. By the time I arrived the new (and old) guides were setting up the exhibition, whose name "Industrial Design" gave me an entirely different understanding than what the show was actually all about. To me it would be more tools, heavy equipment, uninteresting items for us and just as difficult to explain. In essence, the show was far better than what I saw on "Hand Tools." The exhibition traced the development of various products, among other things. One good example was a crescent-shaped series of refrigerators, from the earliest to the newest, featuring ice-making machines, huge freezers, etc. I always had to laugh when our Soviet visitors would stop at the 1930 model of a GE refrigerator and exclaim, "Oh, we have this too." Then I would ask them to walk a little farther and see what Americans were using in 1967. It blew their minds. We also had a 1967 Buick Riviera convertible on display. Another mind blower. Unfortunately we had to leave the hood down because people were stealing the spark plugs and anything else they could remove. One day I saw a very old woman take a handful of padding from beneath the hood. "Why in the world would you want a bunch of fiber?" I asked. "Ah, young man, a souvenir of the exhibit," said she. Several of the items were in plastic-covered display cases. It was impossible to steal them. Some of the items on display were ridiculous. For instance, there were women's dresses made of paper. Yes, paper! I was embarrassed every time I had to work in that section of the exhibit. I never had a good answer as to why Americans produced paper dresses. However, my colleague, Joan "Honeysuckle" Radin, had the perfect retort: "This way we do not have to use napkins." I really enjoyed demonstrating the huge forklift. Most of the time I was on the level with the visitors, who bombarded me with questions about the machine. When there were so many around me I could no longer breathe, I'd turn on the forklift and elevate myself high above the crowd. They would laugh and applaud. The best question I ever got concerning my forklift was from an older man, who asked, "Isn't that bad for your hemorrhoids?"

Muscovites were certainly more sophisticated than their Socialist brothers and sisters in the South, but they were also more rude and demanding. I'll never forget one day I was passing the stand of a girl who was trying her best to keep calm after a series of questions dealing with Viet Nam. Finally, I shouted to the crowd: "Can't anybody ask this poor girl, who cannot nor will ever serve in Viet Nam, a question on another topic?" Finally, a middle-age woman said: "Of course, I have a good question. Young lady, why are you so homely? I thought American women were supposed to be pretty? You have the best cosmetics in America." Russian women, especially the older ones, were always happy to remind you there was a string hanging from your skirt, a stain on your tie or dandruff on your shoulders. Perhaps it was a cultural thing, but we found it very annoying.

At this point I want to add that these exhibits are often the place where lasting friendships are cemented. There is a "fraternity" among those of us who served on these exchanges. After we returned to the USA, we regularly met to reminisce about our experiences. Only those of us who have gone through the ordeal can understand or appreciate what it was like to be an American working in the USSR at the height of the Cold War. I am friends to this day with several of my colleagues. I was best man at John Aldriedge's wedding (to another guide). Another of my dearest friends is a woman who likewise grew up in Philadelphia. We went to the same coffee houses (popular in the '50s), ate at the same restaurants, went to movies at the same theaters. Yet we met in Moscow. I had seen Carol Dannenhauer (later Moravsky) during set-up of the exhibit, but we only exchanged smiles. Then one afternoon on the bus I heard her say to another guide, "Yes, when I'm not as fickle as a pickle, I'm as fertile as a turtle." How could one not love anyone making such a statement? Indeed, Carol later married our diplomat friend from the Embassy, Nick Moravsky. There are many more such relationships.

Every evening I had between two and four invitations to the homes of young Soviets. I had developed a sense of who was on the level and who was not. Once again, we met to listen to and discuss American and Russian music, problems of young people all over the world, our hopes and aspirations for closer contact between our two countries. Politics was avoided. Most of my newly-found friends were fascinated by the stories I could tell about my recent trip to India, Thailand, Hong Kong, Japan and Hawaii. They could not believe that a twenty-six year old guy could take such a trip without government permission. Above all, they could not believe that I saved the money for the trip while working in the Soviet Union.

While in Moscow I also attended my first wedding at the so-called Wedding Palace, where marriage ceremonies were performed like automobiles rolling off the conveyor belt. I thought the ceremony had little meaning compared to the church weddings I had attended in Mexico and the USA. Nevertheless, for these young couples it was probably the happiest day of their lives. Getting married did NOT mean, however, a honeymoon, a trip abroad, an apartment, new furniture or any of the things we Americans take for granted concerning marriage. In most cases the young couple lived with his or her parents, grandparents, maybe an uncle and aunt or two, maybe others. The housing situation was dreadful. The government put up ugly, shoe box-like high-rises at such a pace that by the time the twentieth floor was completed, the first few floors were in need of repair. The walls were so thin it was literally possible to hear the neighbor sneeze or pass gas. One evening I visited some young friends who, thanks to their parents' standing in the Party, had a new, one bedroom apartment and a stereo from Japan. I brought several cassettes of American pop, rock and Jazz. After a nice meal of salami, tomatoes and Georgian wine, we began to dance. When I was leaving around midnight, the neighbors opened their door and thanked us for providing them with such lovely dance music all evening.

In Moscow I made friends with a couple in their early thirties who had been married for five years and finally received a new apartment. They had been trying to start a family, but the wife admitted she had received so many abortions in the past she simply could not conceive. She told me that is a common story in the USSR. When I suggested adoption, she said it was not really an option. Adoption was not popular, because orphans were usually in poor health or mentally retarded.

During this stay in Moscow I realized a dream of several years. I took the "elektrichka" (local commuter train) out to the village of Peredelkino where the great writer Boris Pasternak lived and was buried. I took pictures of his home, his grave and visited the beautiful Orthodox church in the village. It was what the Soviets called a "working church." In other words, there were services and a priest. Peredelkino was a retreat for artists, writers, musicians and Party bigwigs. Most likely the church was allowed to function to appease the mothers and grandmothers of these intellectuals who grew up before Communism and who still practiced their religion. In fact, I chatted with one old "babushka" with her grandson in the cemetery. She told me that the majority of young Russians were taken to be baptized by the grandmothers while the parents were at work. Many of these kids grew up in the Party, never knowing they had been baptized. The woman also warned me to be careful of what I said at Pasternak's grave. She assured me there was a microphone under the bench at the grave site. But, of course, this was the USSR!!!!

While I was working on "Industrial Design USA," we had a distinguished visitor to Moscow in the person of Richard M. Nixon. Most people will remember that in 1959—during the very first American exhibition in the USSR—Nixon and Nikita Khrushchev clashed in the famous "kitchen debate." He was Vice President at the time under Dwight Eisenhower. In 1967 he had not yet been elected President. This was—in the words of the US Embassy—a "fact-finding tour." Nixon met with several Soviet leaders and, in the true Nixonian spirit for which he was known, did not mince his words. When the Soviets brought up the "dirty war in Viet Nam," Nixon reminded them that it was THEIR dirty war, that the North invaded South Viet Nam, armed to the teeth with Soviet and Chinese weapons. Nixon likewise reminded the Soviets of their "dirty" crushing of independence movements in East Germany, Hungary (the invasion of Czechoslovakia came a year later) and the forceful occupation of the Baltics. In short, the Kremlin did not wish to hear what Richard M. Nixon had to say. He used more than one expletive in his remarks as well.

One day our future President decided to visit the American exhibit in Sokolniki Park. He seemed generally interested in what he saw. On the other hand, "Industrial Design" lacked the volume and glitter of the first exhibit in 1959. We were all wondering if there would be a second debate. After all, we were displaying a home trailer, complete with a kitchen. But there was no high-ranking Soviet official to argue with him. When we left the exhibit hall, we walked around Sokolniki Park a bit. In addition to the mile-long lines for the exhibit, there were several old ladies with their grandchildren playing merrily while the women chatted. Suddenly one of the "babushki" ran up to Nixon with our exhibit brochure in her hand and asked for his autograph. It stunned both Nixon and his bodyguards, but I assured them it was okay. I said to him: "All she wants is your autograph, Mr. Nixon." "Ask her name," said Richard M. It was Galina. He wrote: "To Galina with best wishes. Dick Nixon, 1967" The old lady displayed all her metal teeth and said "spasibo, spasibo" (thank you, thank you). Then she turned to me and asked: "So, who is he?" I smiled and replied: "He used to work for our-Government."

THE SAGA OF SVETLANA

It was exactly 3:15 pm on a cold, March day in Moscow (1967) that I learned about the defection of Stalin's daughter. The Russian Service of the Voice of America had broadcast on the 3:00 pm news that Svetlana Alliluyeva had requested asylum at the American Embassy in New Delhi, India. It was my hour to greet the visitors at the door and present each of them with a brochure and a colorful button of the exhibit. Keep in mind, the lines to enter the exhibit in Sokolniki Park were endless. People stood in the cold for hours to get in. Obviously the people at the end of the line passed the word on to the ones in front about the defection. Suddenly all the visitors were asking me what was going on with Alliluyeva. I had no idea about whom they were asking. Who in America even knew Uncle Joe had a daughter? How could I know Alliluyeva was Stalina, but had taken her Mother's maiden name (for obvious reasons!)? For forty-five minutes everyone asked the same question. I continued to say I did not know. From their faces I could see nobody believed me. Finally my hour was up and I headed for the guides' lounge for a coffee and to relax. I was immediately surrounded by irate visitors demanding to know about Alliluyeva. I began to lose my temper. "Okay," I said "If you tell me who is Alliluyeva, I'll tell you what I know about her. But, that is nothing. I never heard the name. Who is she?" An elderly, metal-toothed woman whispered in my ear: Stalin's daughter. In turn, I must have shouted, "STALIN'S DAUGHTER!!!!!!" because the next moment everyone in the hall seemed to be surrounding me. I asked, "Well, what about her?" The crowd's response was: "Don't you listen to the Voice of America?" "No, it's jammed" was my reply. The crowd told me that on the 3:00 pm newscast, the VOA announced that Svetlana, Stalin's only daughter, requested asylum in the United States of America. "Well, what do you think of that, young man?" they asked. "I think," said Bill McGuire, "that ALL of us have the right to live where we want to live and to change where we live at any time. This is a fundamental human right." The outlawed words "human rights" brought all the KGB listeners in the hall to my area. One of them began to lecture the crowd. "Listen to me, Comrades, the Voice of America is lying as usual. And if Alliluyeva committed this treacherous act, she should be shot! She is a cheap whore! She sold her homeland!" I was so incensed that I shouted back, "She sold her homeland? Who would buy this shitty homeland?" Well, guess what? Bill McGuire was rewarded his first "akt" of his second trip to the USSR. In fact, according to the accusation, several irate Soviet citizens wrote up "akts" against me for my "distasteful and vicious attacks on theSoviet Union." The scene which took place in Kharkov after my first"akt" several months before, in which I said God would not be seen in the company of Communists, was repeated. The Soviet director of the exhibit presented me with the "akt" to sign. Of course, I did not sign it. He yelled at me. I yelled back. He said he could have me PNGd if I did not sign it. I said he'd be doing me a favor. Then he asked why I defended the "traitor." Once again I relied on BS and said I simply could not stand by in silence while "enemies of the Soviet state" cursed the daughter of the man, who—single-handedly—won the war against the Fascists (Soviets called Nazis Fascists for some reason) for the Motherland. "Comrade Stalin is turning in his grave," I remarked. "Isn't it enough for you to vilify him? Must you call his only daughter 'a cheap whore?'"

When I returned to the USA, Svetlana had already published her book entitled "Twenty Letters to a Friend" in which she explained why she chose freedom but otherwise gave very little insight into the life of Stalin's only daughter. She was living in Princeton, New Jersey. I thought she just might enjoy hearing about the reactions of the Muscovites at the American exhibit, so I wrote her a letter. This began a short, but interesting correspondence with the author. In fact, she sent me auto-graphed copies of both her books. (The second book, called "Only One Year," described all the exciting things that happened to her in the first year in America.) By that time I was working in the Russian Service of the Voice of America. I shared my news about Svetlana with my colleagues at work. One day my colleague Mara Holmes presented me with a large photograph of Alliluyeva that she cut out of a Life magazine. Mara and some of my other coworkers were convinced that I was having a romantic involvement with her. (Word was that she liked "younger" men.) So, one morning I hung the photo above my desk and signed it: "To Bill McGuire, with all my love, Svetochka." Fortunately for me, I was vacationing in Argentina when the defector came to visit the VOA for the first time. When Svetlana saw the picture above my desk, she flew into an uncontrollable rage, screaming, "I have never called myself, nor been called, Svetochka (diminutive for Svetlana) in my life!!" She crossed out the name Svetochka and wrote instead" "Svetlana Alliluyeva." Couldn't take a joke, could she?

THE MOTHER OF ALL RUSSIAN CITIES

✦

[UKRAINIAN HOSPITALITY AT ITS BEST]

Moscow was still cold and covered with snow as we boarded the overnight train to Kiev. We had gone to the Soviet Dollar Gastronome and stocked up on salami, cheeses, the infamous pineapples from North Vietnam and a few goodies from our Embassy commissary. The train ride was not as gruesome as my first ride on a Soviet train. The compartment was clean, the bed did not reek of urine, and the female attendant served us a tasty cup of tea in the morning. Above all, when we detrained in Ukraine's beautiful capital, spring had already arrived. There were flowers everywhere. The sun was shining brightly. I knew I was going to like it here. In fact, to this day Kiev, often referred to in history books as "The Mother of All Russian Cities,"(although it is definitely Ukrainian), is my favorite city in the former USSR.

Our hotel, Hotel Moscow, was situated on a hill overlooking the main street, the Kreshchatik. Between the two sets of steps leading up to the entrance was a lovely garden of red tulips. Our rooms were typical Soviet hotel rooms, but they had big windows through which the sun brightened our mornings. The restaurant served a typical Ukrainian pot roast called Zharkoye, which I ate almost nightly.

The city is built along the banks of the powerful Dniper river. In the evenings young and old gathered there around campfires, roasting potatoes and singing enchanting Ukrainian folk songs. Some of the peasant girls from the countryside often serenaded loudly enough for all to hear. It certainly made me realize that the Ukrainians had their own language, culture and traditions, which managed to survive centuries of attempts at russification.

Unfortunately, I experienced more surveillance and provocations than in any previous city in which I had worked. The KGB was active 24 hours a day. Also, more unfortunate things happened to people who befriended me there than in any other city. Early in our stay I met two brothers, Sasha and Igor, who were studying English at Shevchenko University. Sasha's English was quite good. His brother's needed much work. Of course, Igor had only been studying for two years, while Sasha had attended one of the special English schools located throughout the Soviet Union. All subjects from first grade on were taught in English. They also had such schools in French and German, as we were told daily. I visited one of these classes later on, and I'll cover that disaster in a later chapter. The brothers took me to my first potato roast along the banks of the Dniper one evening. We made a fire, roasted our "kartoshki" and talked about English grammar, American slang and the difference between the English spoken in America and England. When Igor asked about the difference, I jokingly stated that the British invented the language and we Yankees perfected it. Both boys laughed uncontrollably. I used the same line a few times at the exhibit, but my humor was met with disdain there. In short, that first evening under the stars, the campfire, the pleasant conversation, the laughter, the gentle flow of the Dniper will forever remain among my most cherished memories of Kiev. I did notice, however, that three shady-looking men made a fire right next to ours and listened to every word we said. There was no mention of politics, not one word that could be considered either objectionable or anti-Soviet. Around eleven we left and the boys walked me back to the steps of my hotel. We agreed to meet the following evening at 8:30 on the Kreshchatik. The boys never showed up. About a week later I was walking down that beautiful boulevard and stopped for a red light. A young man with black hair approached me and in a hurried, fearful tone, identified himself as another Igor. He said he was a friend of the Zagorodny boys and said I was not to try to contact them again. They had been picked up by the KGB, roughed up and told they would be thrown out of school if they had any more contact with the American spy. I did not even have time to answer him before he disappeared like lightning. I assumed he was telling the truth, but it also occurred to me that he might be a KGB agent trying to dissuade me from pursuing the friendship. A few nights later, during my nightly walk down the Kreshchatik, I saw young Igor. He definitely had a black eye; and when he saw me, he ran like a bat out of hell. So, the boys had indeed been picked up. I felt awful.

One day an advanced English class from the university visited our exhibit with their teacher. They asked for a tour of the show in English. I was selected to take the students around. By this time I had been rotated to all the display areas, and I had a spiel for each of them. The problem was that it was in Russian. Suddenly I had to explain it in English. In a few cases I could not for the life of me think of the English word for certain items, so I used the Russian word. The teacher's eyebrows went up in utter disbelief. "Is there really a word 'provod' in English?'" she asked. I innocently remarked that, as far as I knew, it was a Russian invention (such a lie!!!); and, therefore, we used the Russian word. The class seemed pleased.

One of the young men in the group was named Sasha Zarudny, a handsome, self-confident lad whose shirt was obviously not Soviet-made. He asked more questions than anyone. At no point did the teacher seem to mind what he said; however, she frowned at the other students when they asked, for instance, whether it was true that many American college students had their own cars. When we closed the exhibit that evening, Sasha was standing by our bus and asked if he could invite me for a drink after my dinner. I told him that, one, I was not allowed to go out alone, that another American would have to accompany me, and, two, that by inviting me he was opening himself up for a black eye from the local KGB thugs. I quickly related to him what happened to the other Sasha and Igor. Sasha the Second assured me he was the son of a famous writer, a loyal Komsomol and was trusted to meet with me. This remark really upset me. For his part, Sasha was irritated by the words "KGB thugs." For reasons unclear to me I accepted his invitation. Later that evening, (I think it was) Charlie Trumbull and I met Sasha for a glass of wine at an outdoor café overlooking the Dniper. He turned out to be very charming, sophisticated and animated. As usual, we did not discuss politics. Several things he said led me to believe this kid was very much aware of the realities of Soviet society and planned to use the system, as so many did, to his own advantage. He made a few references to the obligatory courses in Marxism-Leninism at school, how boring they were and how students mocked them after class. I asked Sasha why he selected English for his foreign language. He replied that English was the preference of the parents with political influence. He had little difficulty being accepted in the English language school because of his parents. In two years he would graduate from the university and hoped to enter the foreign service. I remember him saying, "Although my father has a lot of political pull, my chances are not good for an early assignment in he USA, but things look good for one in India."

The following day I went to a book store to see if I could really find anything written by his father. Sure enough, there were five or six books. I bought one called "Your Mother's Island," which to this day I have not read. I believe it was written in Ukrainian. Maybe that's why.

I met with Sasha several times during my stay in Kiev. One evening he even invited me to the house. He warned me that in spite of his connections his father would be very upset that I was in their home. However, his parents were out of town. It was just Grandma and his younger brother at home. The brother was a born comic. Grandma was your typical "babushka" (grandmother type) who remembered better days but had accepted the life she could not change. She was a believer, an Orthodox Christian. One sensed the great love between the two generations, which made me feel very much at home. On the outside, Sasha Zarudny was your typical macho man, virile and tough. But that evening in the company of his grandmother, he was like a playful, vulnerable little boy. It was a delightful evening until the grandmother said to him, "Sashenka, I just hope we do not all end up in the clink for having this nice, young American in our home." His reply amused me. "Grandma, Stalin is dead."

Let's talk a bit more about "Industrial Design" in the city of Kiev. The audiences were more open, more friendly, more inquisitive than in Moscow. The "spooks" were more vicious. I had the absolute delight to be stationed in our house trailer with open windows on both sides. I worked with a pretty, young girl from New York named Julie F. (She does not want me to use her real name.) In all the days we worked together I never saw Julie in the same dress twice. Believe me, she could have been a model. Not only was Julie attractive, stylish and sweet, she spoke beautiful Russian (and French) and had a wonderful sense of humor…and could DANCE!!!! Oh yes, she also played the piano. Julie and I hit it off immediately because we had so much in common. We were both lovers of ballet, liked to dance to rock and roll music, adored Paris and French culture; but, above all, we did not take this USSR seriously. We were able to laugh at the entire farce called Communism. Julie and I had several mutual friends in Kiev and accompanied each other to the apartments of our mutual friends. Many a night we hit two or three homes. That's how popular we were. It was not a romantic association, since she was dating my buddy, Charlie Trumbull. The reason we were so popular is that people thought we were married. We worked out this little skit for the house trailer, which was a tacky takeoff of a 1950s' family sitcom on TV. We began our presentation by opening up the windows so the visitors could see in. Then we headed for the kitchen, where Julie—the dutiful, little, obedient wife—would make my morning coffee, and we would sit at the kitchen table making googoo eyes at each other. The crowds loved this schmaltz! Couldn't get enough of it. It was hard for us to keep from laughing out loud. This is how many visitors pictured a typical, young American couple (living in a trailer???), and it made them feel good. Maybe for that reason, we got fewer embarrassing questions about America than some of our colleagues in other display areas.

One morning on my day off I went down to the restaurant with my trusty jar of Skippy peanut butter. My breakfast usually consisted of coffee, that delicious Ukrainian black bread covered with the Skippy, and a glass of tomato juice. Suddenly I heard what could only be described as a typical Philadelphia accent at the next table. It was an elderly couple who was leaving that day for home after spending ten days in the USSR as tourists. When I asked them where they lived in Philly, they seemed amused. They lived about five blocks from my family in Mayfair. Such a coincidence. What a small world! Then I asked them if they would call my mother and tell her not to forget to send me cherry chocolates for my upcoming birthday. They agreed. Two days—rather nights—later at 2am the phone rang in my room. It was my mother in tears. She said she had received a call from a lovely lady that morning who had met me in Kiev. The woman told her: "For God's sake, send some food to your son. He weighs under a hundred pounds—I was 145—looks emaciated and lives on Skippy peanut butter. Send him some cherry chocolates, too, to fatten him up."

I had my embarrassing moments as well in Kiev. As I mentioned earlier, as the visitors entered the exhibition hall, they were greeted by smiling, young Americans, presenting each of them with a colorful brochure describing the exhibit, as well as a lapel button with the emblem of the show. These little gifts were like gold to the people. Some stood in line a second or third time just to receive an extra booklet or button. In Kiev and in other cities where American exhibits had been in earlier years, visitors often appeared wearing the buttons from those shows and with brochure in hand as well. Every hour the guides were rotated. Most of us wanted to "work the door" because the guests passed by quickly with no time to ask questions. Many of them wanted to shake our hand and welcome us. Veterans often showed up wearing their WWII medals and remarked that they had met American troops at the Elbe. "We were friends then, we must be friends now" was heard very often. The outpouring of affection and respect for the USA was clear. We representatives of America were treated (by the people) like movie stars. It was quite a boost for anyone who suffered from lack of ego. This was not the case with Bill McGuire. Nevertheless, I enjoyed shaking their hands and accepting their words of friendship for the American people. We had so many visitors in Kiev that we were running out of buttons and brochures. New ones were on their way from the USA but had not yet arrived. So Director Fritz Berliner asked us not to give any to children under twelve. I have never seen such looks of disappointment in my life. One afternoon after lunch I was working the door with my dear friend Carol Dannenhauer of Philadelphia, Pa. I became so tired of answering the questions, "Why are so many of you wearing eyeglasses? What are you, a nation of poor vision?" that I would often remove my glasses during door duty. In short, I barely could distinguish a man from a woman. A little boy extended his hand for a brochure. I replied, "I am sorry, we are running out of books. We are not giving them to children today." He said, "I am not a child." I said, "Of course you're a child. Now please move on." Again from the boy: "I am not a child." "Look, little boy, you ARE a child. Now move on." By that time Carol was laughing hysterically and nudging me in the side, saying "Give him the brochure, Bill. He's not a child." "What, are YOU blind too, Carol?" By this time, someone from the Soviet administration ran over and demanded that I give him a brochure. Not only was he a midget but also the son of a high-ranking official. The Russian man lifted the midget up to show me that he was not a child. We were slightly elevated on a wooden platform. When I realized what I'd done, I began to laugh uncontrollably. In fact, I laughed so hard I tipped backwards and fell off the platform. That just added to the confusion. When I recovered my composure, I apologized to the midget. Carol shook her head and said: "From now on wear your glasses, Billy from Philly!"

Perhaps the one event in Kiev I shall never forget happened May 1, 1967. It was May Day in the USSR. We were all invited to sit in the grandstand with the Party officials to review the May Day parade on the Kreshchatik. It was a beautiful, sunny day. The parade lasted for hours with the Soviets displaying all their weapons they'd developed, just in case we rotten Capitalists ever attacked them. As usual, the dignitaries reminded the citizenry of the great sacrifices the Soviet peoples made during the Great War for the Fatherland. All I could think about was, "Wasn't I currently in the land that welcomed the Nazi troops with garlands as liberators?" Of course, that episode in Soviet history was never recorded in their history books.

May 1 was an even more important day for Bill McGuire. It was my twenty-seventh birthday. As the Red Army marched by, I waved as if they were marching in my honor. The Soviet hosts seemed pleased that I was enjoying the parade so much. If they only knew! After the show ended, Valentin Brazhnikov, from the

Soviet administration of our exhibit, came up to Fritz Berliner (our director) and me and invited all of us to a reception on the second floor of the Hotel Moscow. Then he said to me, "Happy birthday, Bill. My colleagues and I have organized a little party for you in honor of the occasion." I almost fainted. I always thought Brazhnikov disliked me. He often stood in front of my stand, especially in Moscow, and stared angrily at me. Once he even remarked that I talked about being a believer too much. Suddenly, Comrade Brazhnikov was organizing a party in my honor. It turned out to be a wonderful party indeed. The Soviets brought the biggest, most exquisite birthday cake I had ever seen. It was the size of a card table and was decorated with chocolate roses, baskets and animals. Mr. Brazhnikov asked me, "You do like chocolate, as you said so often at the exhibit." My friend Julie played the piano. We sang the Soviet and American national anthems, a few popular Russian and American songs, and then everybody danced to some of the cassettes I brought from my room. There was complete harmony and genuine friendship among all of us. Deep down our Soviet hosts were probably very decent people. We saw a part of their personality we had not seen before. They saw a group of Americans that loved to have a good time, to party, to relax. I believe some of this rubbed off on them. It was cultural exchange at its best; what cultural exchange was meant to be. I was happy to be there.

THE SOVIETS CALLED IT "SPONTANEITY"

✦

[LENINGRAD FOR BUSINESS, NOT PLEASURE]

We had a brief rest period after Kiev and then headed for Leningrad, the last of three cities for Industrial Design USA. In a way I felt like I was going home, since I had been there during my first break after Kharkov. Yet there was so much more to be seen in this lovely city. Our very first day in Leningrad I met a charming couple in their forties at the Gostiny Dvor department store. They invited me to their apartment for coffee. I warned them of the possible repercussions, but the wife taught English and had never met an American before. She could not imagine that anything bad could happen to her just for practicing her English. After all, I was there on a cultural exchange program. I came in peace. (It did not mean I was received in peace!) I never found out what happened to this pair for having me in their home. Maybe nothing. At least I hope nothing bad happened. They never showed up at the exhibit and I never saw them again. The English teacher had a wonderful sense of humor (which is one way a person could survive in that country). She recounted a fictitious encounter between a Russian woman and an American woman, which she thought I would enjoy. The American asked: "Where were you born?" Answer: "In St. Petersburg." "Where did you attend elementary school?" Answer: "In Petrograd." "College?" Answer: "In Leningrad." The American noted that the lady had lived in three different cities. "No," said her Russian friend. "In the same house, the same city all my life." It must have been very painful for the proud residents of Peter's City to have its name changed so often, especially in honor of the founder of the Communist state, who degraded the country and its people for decades.

I met a younger couple—not yet married—at the Kirov theater one evening, and we became close friends. They were more aware of the realities of Soviet society. Every meeting with them was like a scene from a James Bond movie. I would take the metro a few stations, then a cab, then walk to a park where they were waiting for me. A friend would follow to be sure the KGB was not following us. Unthinkable for a Westerner, right? On the other hand, by that time I felt that the Security Sovs were convinced I was not doing anything wrong. I really do not think I was followed as closely as before. One evening the couple announced to me that they wanted me to see a film the following evening. After hearing one line in the film, they said, Bill McGuire would understand COMPLETELY the essence of Soviet life. They told me where to go to buy a ticket. They would already be there, holding a seat for me. I was not to greet them like a friend but simply sit down and enjoy the movie. Stanislav would warn me when to listen to the "magic sentence." I cannot remember the name of the film. It was sort of a modern Soviet version of the biblical "Patience of Job." The hero's wife dies, his children abandon him, his house burns down, he loses his job. At one point he stands on the bank of a river weeping and recites the "magic words" of the film (about which my friends almost jumped out of their seats). "Here it comes. Listen carefully. This sums up our lives." The man exclaimed, "Khorosho, chto nam tak plokho!" (It's good that we have it so bad!)

Although I have visited St. Petersburg several times and admire the city for its history, architecture and general beauty—not to mention having met some of the most wonderful and sincere people in my life in that city—I shall always have a bad taste in my mouth for Peter's City because of what happened to my colleagues and me on opening day of "Industrial Design." It began on a very positive note. The food and drinks were at the pavilion, the most important people in Leningrad had been invited, the Ambassador and other American dignitaries had arrived in town, and we were ready to open our doors and our hearts to the people of Leningrad. Our bus took us to the site about an hour before the opening to make sure everything was in order. I took one look at the tables, filled with all kinds of delicacies, and could hardly wait for the reception to begin. The official opening was to take place at noon. All of us were gathered at the door to welcome the first arrivals. 12:15, 12:30, 12:45. Not a single soul. What was going on? We checked the invitations. They clearly stated a noon opening. There was a great sense of frustration. Our pavilion was located on the southeast corner of a huge square. Suddenly we noticed that on the northwest corner there were barricades, behind which there were crowds of people, many holding banners and signs which we could not read from the distance. At exactly 1:00 the iron fences were removed, and the crowd began to march in the direction of our building. Within a minute we could read the first sign, "Shame on the murderers of our Soviet sailor." A second sign read, "Down with U.S. Imperialism." A third read, "Hands off the Peoples' Democratic Republic of Vietnam," and still another banner stated, "Death to the murderers of our Soviet sailors." Sailors? The first sign said "sailor." Now there were "sailors." What gives? We soon found out that the previous night American jets bombed the Vietnamese port of Haiphong killing two Soviet sailors from a ship docked in the harbor. Obviously sign number one had been written before word reached Leningrad that a second sailor had died. The unit in Viet Nam was home-based in Leningrad. According to the Soviet version, the people of Leningrad and the families of the fleet organized a "spontaneous" demonstration to vent their anger. To me it seemed there were two hundred demonstrators, but in essence there were probably fewer. Needless to say, not one Soviet official showed up at the opening. We decided to just leave the pavilion (and all that glorious food and drink!!) and return to the hotel. We called to have the bus pick us up. The crowd continued to chant anti-American slogans and typical Communist Party slogans in front of our hall. What amazed most of us was they really did not seem to be very serious nor angry. However, there were men and women trying to incite anger by yelling things like, "Comrades, are we going to allow these murderers to get away with this act of barbarism?" Most likely these were workers from a particular plant or factory, instructed to show up to demonstrate against us. There never was a spontaneous demonstration in the history of the Soviet Union, until maybe toward the end of Communism. Soviet citizens knew only too well the dangers of any unofficial meeting or demonstration.

Our bus was parked about one city block from the pavilion. Therefore, we had to pass through the crowd to board the bus. This was the most disgusting and unforgivable part of the saga. As we walked through the masses, some spat on us, others jeered, and still others shook their fists at us. Like martyrs we marched expressionless toward the bus. But it did not end there. By the time all of us were on the bus, the crowd began to push the bus as if trying to overturn it. Our girls were screaming and crying. I seemed to feel some warm drops of something running down my leg. There was pandemonium on the bus. Our people were screaming, "Start the bus. Move on." The driver looked like he was waiting for a sign from someone to move. The crowd finally stopped and dispersed. At that point our driver turned on the ignition and took us to the hotel.

Unfortunately, there were no Western journalists there to cover the event. To our shock and chagrin, the embassy—most of them spineless, Soviet-fearing bureaucrats—did nothing to publicize that disgusting page in Soviet-American cultural history. But ask any guide from "Industrial Design USA" or our administrators, and they will tell you that the episode left a very bitter taste in us for Peter's City. There is a positive footnote to the demonstration. Most likely the KGB decided to go easy on us for the rest of our stay in Leningrad. There were fewer questions about Viet Nam, about unemployment and racism in the USA. People were still anxious to find out about the fate of Svetlana Alliluyeva and also about Rudolf Nureyev and other defectors. I brought up the anti-American demonstration as often as possible. When someone would ask about a defector, I would begin my answer by saying that after our welcome in Leningrad, I could understand why anyone would want to defect. It was very difficult for my colleagues and myself to be outgoing and tolerant with the visitors after the trauma on opening day. When people would ask which historical or cultural sights appealed to us, I'd respond, "The Leningrad airport—my ticket to freedom and happiness."

I was in Leningrad during a very important historical and sociological event in world history, namely the Six Day War. Much has been said over many years about Jews in the Soviet Union, anti-Semitism, etc. It could be that, in my personal experience—since I am not Jewish—the subject rarely came up. Readers will remember my trip to the Leningrad synagogue during my first visit to the city. In one or two conversations, mainly in Rostov and Kiev, non-Jews told me that Communism was a "Jewish political system" based on the fact that Marx, Engels and most of the first Commissars were Jews. But I did not sense deeply-rooted anti-Semitism in Russia. Rather, I sensed that Estonians hated Russians more than any Russian hated Jews. That having been said, no one had ever said to me, "I'm Jewish." This all changed during the Six Day War. Suddenly Jews were not only more visible but also proud of their ancestry. Everyone was asking us about the latest news from the Mideast. When Israel devastated her Arab neighbors—using American weapons, as everybody knew—the Jews of Leningrad celebrated like never before. This was the impetus they needed to begin the long struggle for emigration to Israel. I must also admit that I did hear more anti-Semitic remarks both at the exhibition and in public places after the war. There seemed to be a lot of frustration about America's support and involvement in the Mideast. At the exhibit people, mostly men, would say, "Why is the USA supporting the warmongering, aggressive Israeli government?" They did not seem to understand my answer that the Soviet Union was supporting and arming the

Arabs, the North Vietnamese and anyone else that was committing aggression. When visitors brought up World War II (known there as the Great War for the Fatherland), I always made the parallel to the "guns instead of butter" politics of Hitler with the present-day USSR, where there seemed to be guns for all foreign aggressors but little butter at home. I am not sure they understood the comparison. So many ordinary Soviet citizens were so pitifully brainwashed by their heartless government, and it showed.

I began to accept fewer invitations to private homes in Leningrad. Instead I tried to take advantage of the many cultural activities the city offered. I especially liked the gypsy theater, the Leningrad symphony, the museums and the chocolate cake at the Astoria hotel's restaurant. We were there during the White Nights, which was also a sight to behold. And although I enjoyed walking along the banks of the Neva at 1:00 am, when it seemed like 1:00 pm, I was appalled by the number of drunks—especially drunken women—in the city.

Perhaps the most pleasant thing that happened to me in Leningrad was the evening our Soviet colleague, Valentina Konstantinovna Stepanova, affectionately referred to by the guides as the "Dragon Lady," asked me to accompany her to a performance at the Kirov ballet. I gladly accepted. After the show she shocked me by taking me backstage to meet none other than Natalia Makarova. I was speechless to meet this world-renowned ballerina. Makarova was such a giant on stage and such a quiet, little kitten off-stage. She was obviously a shy, introverted person. The meeting did not last long, but I met other dancers as well. They were obviously tired after the performance, so I did not want to detain them. Why Stepanova chose me for this honor, I'll never know. After she defected a few years later, I met Makarova at the Watergate in Wshington. To my grief she did not remember meeting me in Leningrad. O, well.

I remember how happy all of us were the day we not only left Leningrad but also the USSR. Some of us remained an extra day or two just to leave by SAS rather than on Aeroflot. We took the direct flight to Stockholm. When the pilot announced we were out of Soviet airspace, we burst into applause. Champagne was ordered, and we drank our way feverishly to freedom. This happened just about every time I left the USSR. Semi-crocked, we arrived in the Swedish capital. I remember seeing a fruit stand in the airport and went berserk. My friends and I bought up just about everything the woman had on her stand. She must have thought we were crazy. We were starving for fresh fruits. In fact, we ate so much we had to spend a few hours in the bathroom that second day. The first evening the four of us traveling together went out for our first meal. We went to the best restaurant in the city and ordered the finest French wines (that cost a small fortune). A few days later we said our good-byes and looked forward to a reunion in Washington in a month. From there I returned to visit friends in Germany and finally to my beloved Spain. After two weeks in sunny, delightful Spain, I had recovered so well from the USSR it seemed like ancient history to me. Another strange phenomenon about having a great vacation after the USSR, one puts out all the horror and remembers only the positive moments from that country. Once again, I thought about the dear friends I left behind, friends that I thought (at the time) would never bask on the beautiful beaches of the Costa del Sol, eat paella, drink sangria and dance all night at the Spanish discotheques.

I arrived home feeling completely rejuvenated and ready to look for a real job.

USIA "Hand Tools" exhibition, Kharkov, USSR, 1966. The sign says "woodworking."

Opening day of a USIA exhibition in Rostov-on-Don. U.S. Ambassador,
Embassy dignitaries and Soviet guests. Yours truly explaining.

US exhibit guides (Charlie Trumbull, John Aldriedge, Emily Maltby, Alex Koltsev-Mosalsky (hidden), Bill Cuthbertson and a stunned Bill McGuire having lunch at a Soviet greasy spoon.

Yerevan, Soviet Armenia. Yours truly greeting visitors. Each guest a free lapel pin and a colorful brochure from the exhibit. These became collectors' items. Exhibit Director Fritz Berliner in the background.

Author paying respects to Boris Pasternak, Soviet poet and author of the banned book *Dr Zhivago*, at his grave in Peredelkino (a Moscow suburb), 1967.

Author and fellow guide Carl
Modig visiting Peter's Palace
outside Leningrad.

The first Soviet family I met
in the USSR (Volodya, Luda
and baby Oleg). Kharkov,
Soviet Ukraine, 1966.
Note the smiling faces.

Singer-composer Stevie Wonder
and author during a cultural
exchange program for the former
U.S. Information Agency (USIA).

Bill and actress Meryl Streep, a delightful, intelligent and talented woman with a personality to match.

Author at the Arab-Israeli Peace Accord ceremony with the Russian delegation. The White House. September, 1993.

TELLING AMERICA'S STORY TO THE WORLD

✦

[THE VOICE OF AMERICA 1967–1970]

This is the most difficult and painful part of the book for me to write. I worked at the Voice of America in the Russian Service for eighteen years. They were the best and the worst years of my life. I believe I worked there during the "Golden Years" of VOA's history when attempts were made to "Americanize" the station, at least the Russian Service. In 1976 there was a reversal of this policy, and our Service became "Sovietized" to the horror of all of us who worked so hard to make our programs interesting, truthful and friendly with a distinctly AMERI-CAN slant and flavor. But, first, I want to give a very condensed history of "America's Voice to the World."

The VOA began to broadcast in the early forties to counteract Nazi propaganda. Later they added new languages. As the Cold War developed, Russian became an important language, as did some of the other languages spoken in the USSR (Ukrainian, Georgian, Armenian, Uzbek and Azeri). When the U.S. Information Agency was established under the Eisenhower administration in the Fifties, VOA—which had been broadcasting from New York—was moved to Washington and became part of USIA. VOA kept an office in NYC and later opened branches in Miami, Chicago and on the West Coast. Unfortunately for our country, language study was never a priority in those days. The VOA had to rely on immigrant groups to staff the offices. The USA had and still has a wealth of ethnicity from which to draw writers, announcers and producers for the programs. Perhaps because it was a "government" agency, the Office of Personnel took the easy way out—hire immigrants, that is, native speakers. In most cases regarding refugees from Communism countries, the applicants' background could not be checked thoroughly for a security clearance. As a result, more than one foreign agent easily infiltrated the Voice of America. What was even more appalling, the VOA was like a mini-United Nations. Every ethnic group who hated each other at the UN also hated each other at the Voice. A good example is a woman who worked in another language service. I did not know her name, but we always arrived at the same hour in the morning and on the same bus. I said, "Good morning!" several times without ever getting so much as a smile. So, I stopped. Three years later I was introduced to her at a private party in George-town. For the first time she heard my last name. Her response was that McGuire was not a Russian name. Was my mother a Russian? No. She suddenly became very friendly toward me. I was so shocked and disgusted by her attitude that I asked her to please continue to ignore me. I did not need bigots as friends.

Another major problem we faced in the Russian Service was that many of the staff were highly educated, spoke several languages, lived in many countries and were professional journalists; however, others had a high school education only (we hope!). Others had a DP (displaced person) mentality picked up in refugee camps in Germany. For some, not all, family feuds dating back to the last century arrived in America with them. In other words, "If my grandfather hated your grandfather in Russia, I hate YOU in America."

In spite of these problems, most of the Russian staffers were very dedicated to their work. When Gen. Alexander Barmine was the chief, he ruled with an iron hand. His employees either hated him or worshiped him, but there was order and peace. The work got done.

For obvious reasons, the programs became very political and anti-Soviet in nature. Culture was almost ignored. There were no native-born Americans of non-Russian background behind the microphone. Iheard from several sources that when Nikita Khrushchev visited Washington in the late '50s, somebody asked him why his government was jamming VOA broadcasts. Rumor has it that the former Prime Ministersaid the programs were too offensive and that VOA announcers spoke antiquated Russian. (NOT the truth!) Then, supposedly Mr. Khrushchev asked why there were no "American voices" on the air? As I said, I can not attest to the truth of these rumors. However, after the visit, Mr. Barmine was promoted to a post at USIA, and Mr. Terrence Catherman, a USIA Foreign Service Officer was brought in to be chief. Under his tutelage the first Americans of non-Russian extraction arrived for training to become broadcasters. Before the arrival of the Yanks, people did one job only; i.e., they wrote, announced, edited or produced. It was decided to train the new arrivals to do everything. In short, we were trained first in production, then in writing, announcing, etc. It worked.

The Americans were talented, educated, dedicated and had enough of an American accent that the listeners knew these people did not grow up in Moscow. The entire tone of the broadcasts changed to have a more friendly and informative nature. More cultural programming was introduced. Above all, there was little or no resentment on the part of the older staffers. In fact, there was great cooperation and respect among the two groups. Our office parties were the envy of the Voice. (Matter of fact, my homemade cakes were very well received.)

So, how did Bill McGuire wind up in the Russian Service in August 1967? It had become common practice for VOA Russian Service to interview some of the returning guides from our exhibits in the USSR. Some were even offered jobs. I was brought down one day for such an interview. By this time the Service Chief was McKinney Russell, an extraordinary linguist, a great believer in the VOA; and, as a talented USIA Foreign Service Officer, more than capable of fulfilling and enhancing VOA's mission. The panel also consisted of Victor Franzusoff of the Political Section and one of the original broadcasters, and Vladimir Mansvetov, Chief of Features (the Cultural Section). Mansvetov was an extremely talented writer, highly educated, highly motivated and, above all, the "Great Defender" of careers for young Americans in the Russian Service. After my professor of Russian, Mikhail Krupensky, I guess I admire and love Vladimir Fedorovich (as we called him) most. He was soft-spoken, gentle, funny, delightful and dedicated. During the interview Victor Franzusoff asked me about all the people I had met in the USSR that constantly listened to the VOA. My reply was that I never met anybody that listened all the time. First, I explained, the VOA was jammed; and, secondly, there were not enough programs for young people. I pointed out that over fifty percent of the population was under thirty years of age. "Young people in the USSR want to hear about Elvis Presley, the Beach Boys and Connie Francis," I told Mr. Franzusoff. He seemed shocked, if not irritated, by my statement. So he said, "You are the first person to ever say that to me, and I do not believe it." "Well, Viktor Adolfovich, perhaps I am the first person to tell you the truth. Take it or leave it." I am convinced he never forgot my impudence. Then Mr. Mansvetov asked me, "Could YOU write programs that would appeal to Soviet youth?" I was taken aback by this question. In fact, I thought he was joking. So I began to say that my Russian was far from perfect, I had no background in journalism, and I did not like my own voice. "It is not a voice for radio," said I. "Good," exclaimed Vladimir Fodorovich. "You're exactly what we are looking for. We'll train you. Can you begin on Monday?"

I took the entire matter as a joke. Besides, I did not want to work for the Government. My two dear friends Tamara Kit and Marie Ciliberti were already on staff. That day I had lunch with them. They convinced me that jobs were hard to find in the Russian area. One taught Russian, or one worked for Uncle Sam. The thought of teaching was even more repugnant to me than working for the Government. With all in agreement, I decided to give it a try. I'd work in the day, get a Ph.D. at night and finally look for a real job in two years. Well, I stayed for eighteen!

Several things happened the first week in the Russian Service that convinced me that this was NOT a normal work environment. I am about to relate them. First of all, as one entered or exited the door to the Service there sat an elderly lady named Maria Georgievna, who resembled a madam at a Budapest brothel of retarded whores, circa 1900. Her face predated the Tammy Faye Bakker look but was even more painted. Revlon must have made a fortune on her! She was supposed to be a typist, and, indeed, she sat behind a typewriter, which I never saw her use. All day she chewed on pumpkin seeds and spit the shells on the floor beneath her typewriter. As a matter of fact, I never heard her speak either. The woman put an evil eye on all strangers. After a few days, however, she paid no attention to me.

My second day on the job, another of our ladies came flying out of the Chief's' office screaming and crying, "Imagine, he ate my *pirozhki* (meat pies) and does not want to give me a promotion!" I sat between two women in their forties, who at one time were the closest of buddies but were now bitter enemies. According to Woman X, one evening Woman Z arrived at her home with a gentleman friend. Woman X went to the kitchen to make coffee. According to her, when she entered the living room, Woman Z was naked and making love on er new, $3,000 sofa. "How could I explain those spots to my husband?" asked Woman X. "He would think it was I who was fornicating on the couch." Result: they did not speak. At times they communicated through me, if it was work-related. I was the buffer zone. At other times, Woman Z would remark to me that Woman X was wearing a dress two sizes too small for her "aging, fat body." This was said loudly enough for all to hear.

Another morning as I entered the Russian Service, one of our editors, Anatoli Petrov, was arguing about grammar with one of the writers, that is, about the instrumental plural of the word "blyad" (slut) in Russian. When he saw me he suggested that, as a foreigner who had to learn Russian grammar well, I would be a good and neutral judge. Was it "blyadmi" or "blyadyami"? Having just returned from the USSR where I heard the word declined daily, I answered proudly that the correct case ending was "blyadmi." It was an irregular noun. The woman became incensed and refused to accept my pronouncement, saying: "What the Hell does some young American punk know about Russian grammar?" At this point, Mr. Petrov turned to me and remarked, "Can you imagine, Bill. Here is a Russian woman who spent the war years shacked up with a Nazi officer in the Black Forest, bore him a bastard son, and she does not know how to decline the word slut?" I simply headed for my desk.

I was surrounded mainly by the desks of elderly ladies at first. One was a sort of a hypochondriac. The third morning at VOA I was sitting at my desk reading the newspaper. Most of the other women were at their desks as well. The hypochondriac arrived, uncovered her typewriter and began to type. Suddenly she began to cough loudly and fiercely as if she were choking. Then she stood up and said, "Girls, the air in this place is contaminated. We are all going to suffocate. I can't breathe, can you?" Sure enough, within seconds all the women in my section were coughing. It was a chain reaction. There was nothing wrong with the air. The place was air-conditioned, and the rest of us felt just fine.

The same day I was walking toward Mr. Mansvetov's office when I spied a woman I had been introduced to the day before. I greeted her with, "Good morning. How are you?" She yelled, "HOW AM I? HOW AM I? Listen you, don't you EVER ask that question of me again, UNLESS you really want the answer. Because I'll TELL you how I am, and it will take an hour!" I never asked again.

This explosion over a simple "how are you" upset me. As I was returning to my desk, Katya Elene came up to me to share some words of wisdom. "Listen, Young Man." (I guess she had not bothered to learn my name). "I want to set the record straight. People here will tell you this Service is a whorehouse. It is NOT. There is some semblance of order in a whorehouse. There is NONE here." I took her word for it. Yet, I always wondered how she knew about how well a brothel was run.

My first few weeks I was assigned to what they called "Traffic Manager" (an elegant way of saying office boy) delivering mail, tapes, feeds from our correspondents around the country and the world, doing just about everything except making coffee for the bosses. I also began to train as a program producer. Within a month I was ready to do my first "live"air show. It was the "Night Owl" show, the last program of the day, and it was midnight in Moscow. We had learned that in many places the jammers stopped their work at midnight, so that final hour was when a lot of our information got through. The program began with a newscast, a short musical piece, followed by several two to three-minute reports on events of the day. The second part of the program was whatever the emcee wanted it to be. Some wrote about science, art, music, covered seminars, etc. My first emcee happened to be Tatiana Grivsky Berls, whom I knew from Georgetown University, a Russian-American, born in Belgium, with a very pleasant voice. Tanya assured me that everything would go well and not to worry. The newscast went smoothly. This was followed by a popular song of the day (There's a Kind of Hush All Over the World"). This musical number seemed to calm my jitters and the rest of the program went like a piece of cake. After the show, Mr. Mansvetov complimented me on how I handled it. He took great interest in how the programs sounded, unlike some of his replacements after his death.

By this time, my old buddy from the exhibit, Carol Dannenhauer, came on board. We were given the task of translating Willis Conover's International Jazz program into Russian. Willis remained the VOA's top attraction for many years. He was especially popular in the Soviet Union. The top brass decided that it would be nice for the listeners that did not understand English to at least know what Conover was saying. To be quite honest, I'll never understand why Conover was so popular, except that he played the music people wanted to hear. Our job of translating was far from difficult due to the simplicity of his remarks. Basically all he ever said was, for example, "And now we'll hear a song by Ella Fitzgerald with the Duke Ellington orchestra. John Smith on piano, Bud Jones on sax, Carl Johnson on trombone," and then the song. After the song, Conover would usually say, "That was Ella Fitzgerald on the Voice of America." For this the man received an outrageous salary, his own studio and engineer! In addition, he was difficult to work with. I feel I am denigrating an American icon to many of the VOA listeners, but what I say is the truth.

I began to work more and more with the voice coach, Henrikas Ironimich Kacinskas. Before the war he was a well-known Lithuanian actor who had studied in Moscow and spoke Russian as fluently as his native tongue. Everyone loved Mr. Kacinskas dearly. He was very mild-mannered, kind, thoughtful, witty and helpful. He once said to me that, if he just read what I wrote, it made no sense. But when I read it—and I read like I spoke—it made a lot of sense. Evidently it was this "American style of speaking" that they were looking for.

And so one Wednesday morning in February 1968, Vladimir Mansvetov announced to me that I would be emceeing the "Night Owl" that day. I panicked. Was I ready? He said it was now or never. Start preparing. I began looking all over for material. First I had to check with the Political Section to see how many minutes of their material I was obligated to put on. I began to translate articles from the newspaper, from magazines. It all wound up in the trash can. Then I decided that—since this was my very first program—I would talk about myself, about who I was, where I came from, where I'd been (the USSR!) so that the listeners would have a better idea who this newest VOA announcer was. I checked with Mr. Mansvetov, who replied with a smile: "I knew, if I left you alone, you'd come to that conclusion on your own! Molodets (Good Boy), Bill!" What a genius this man was! What a credit to the VOA! I wrote feverishly. If I seem to be showering Vladimir Mansvetov with a lot of praise, it is because he deserved it. When my script was ready, he made very few changes (the sign of a good editor). Mr. Mansvetov had a talent for taking a paragraph that made no sense, changing a few words, and making it sound wonderful.

At 4:45 I entered Studio 4 and prepared for my debut. To be honest, all the fear was gone. I felt I would either sink or swim. Life would go on, no matter what. In addition, I made a pact with myself that day, that for as long as I was at the VOA, I would always finish my programs in time to sit and relax with a cup of coffee fifteen minutes before air time. I never broke that promise to myself in eighteen years. Five o'clock. The red light went on. We were on the air. "Good evening. You are listening to the Voice of America from Washington. This is Bill McGuire at the mike. It is 5:00 pm here in Washington, midnight in Moscow. After our newscast, you'll find out more about this new voice on the VOA airwaves. But, first, the news." The news lasted about twelve minutes. As usual, we had a short musical piece between the news and the program. That day I played an old Russian folk song, which had been recorded recently by Mary Hopkins in English, "Those were the Days." It was number one on the charts. The song ended. I continued. "I'm sure you all recognize that famous, old Russian song, which is now number one in the United States and performed by Mary Hopkins. [Here comes the blurp!] I wanted to say Mary Hopkins is a nineteen year old singer from England. In Russian, nineteen-year-old is rather lengthy—*devyatnadtsatiletnyaya* (a real tongue-twister). I first said "devyatnad...." then "devyatnadtsati...." I could not get it out. At which point I began to laugh out loud and said, "Please forgive me. I AM an American, and this is my first program. Mary is nineteen." The producer played a little more of the song while I tried to stop laughing. The rest of the program went very smoothly, and I was as calm as could be. After the show I went to Mansvetov's office for my sentence. I was sure he would say one of three things: (1) you're fired; (2) you'll never go on the air again; or (3) you need many more months with Mr. Kacinskas. Can you imagine my surprise when I entered VM's office, and he stood up and applauded me? "This was the cutest error I ever heard on the VOA. It is so human, Bill. I was right about you all along. You were meant to be here." I guess he was right. During several meetings in future trips to the USSR, as well as meeting our listeners who got to visit the USA after the collapse of Communism, many, many people remembered that first program. Unanimously they thought that it was a delightful moment in VOA history.

I began to think seriously about my mission in the Russian Service. After all, I was in a unique position and I wanted to do my best in this important role I now had. In fact, I came to several conclusions. These formed the basis for all my future work at the VOA. First of all, if the "product" we're selling is America, the best salesman is an American. Secondly, I must have balance in my programs, giving credence to all people regardless of whether or not I agree with them—in other words, giving both sides of any story. Thirdly, I realized that the best way to talk about America is through the eyes and mouths of other Americans. This is why throughout my career at VOA I did hundreds of interviews with people from all walks of life. Fourthly, Washington, DC is not the only America—nor is New York, Chicago or Los Angeles. Between these important and beautiful cities is the real America, the real Americans. To explain our country, we must talk about our differences as well as the beliefs that bind us.

It was very important to me to stress that you did not have to be born here to be an American. This is a country of native-born people, recent immigrants and older immigrants. Some of the most patriotic Americans were not born here. Each of us has an opinion. All of our opinions are worthy of note. Finally, I did not believe I was at VOA to belittle our listeners nor their political system. By reporting something positive about America, I was indirectly indicating a flaw in the Soviet system without insulting the victims of that regime. I tried very hard to talk "to" them, not "at" them. Above all, I must never lose my sense of humor nor my ability to make fun of myself. This, dear readers, was my credo.

As I noted many times, the VOA was jammed but not everywhere at every hour. Even within Moscow city limits, if one could not pick up VOA in downtown, one could take the metro a few stops and pick it up in a park or someplace else.

Reception was rather good in certain suburbs. Jamming was expensive for the Soviet government. It was not carried on throughout the entire country. We also came to realize that Russian-speakers in other countries could—and did—pick up our broadcasts. Throughout the years I received letters from Sweden, Germany, Greece, Japan and Cuba. We knew that the Soviet authorities intercepted most of the letters written to VOA. Actually, if all the letters we assumed were written reached us, we'd need another building just to house them. One day, after receiving a letter from a girl in Moscow, but postmarked Copenhagen, I announced that the girl did a very intelligent thing, that is, she gave her letter to a friend or tourist to be mailed from abroad. It seemed to work. I received many letters from listeners in the Soviet Union, but mailed from the Free World. I believe the Polish authorities were more liberal with mail as well, since I got several letters postmarked Warsaw.

After my initial "Night Owl" victory, I was ready for other ventures. By this time I was producing all our daily programs as well as doing a seventy-five minute rock and roll show, broadcast on Saturday evenings during prime time, as well as a show geared toward young people in the Soviet Union.

My very first "live" feedback was the result of a youth show I had done in the spring of '68. In July of that year we were visited by a young Soviet sailor who had defected in Japan a month earlier. He met with the entire Soviet Branch (the Ukrainians, Georgians, Armenians, etc.) to talk about life in the Soviet Navy and other matters of interest. Someone asked him what made him defect. He said that life in the Navy was rough, boring. At sea it was easy to pick up the VOA. The sailor recounted that earlier in the year he heard a program about young Americans who wanted to go to college but did not have the money. The man began to breed and sell tropical birds. He earned enough money to do that and study at the same time. "I thought to myself," said the sailor, "what a wonderful country it must be when a young guy, like myself, had such control and freedom to pursue his dreams. I want to be in America. So here I am." Well, it was my youth show that featured that story. I remembered the program well. With some humility I went up to him and introduced myself. He gave me a big bear hug and began to sob. "Thank you, Bill Vakguiir," he said. Few listeners ever learned to pronounce my last name.

SOME EXAMPLES OF MY VOA PROGRAMS

◆

[THE TAXPAYERS GOT THEIR MONEY'S WORTH!]

I want to make it very clear from the start that I never thought I was a William Faulkner, an Earnest Hemingway nor, above all, a Tolstoy or a Dostoyevsky. I never tried to impress anyone with my literary language. I was an American who spent years trying to learn the complicated Russian language, spent lots of time in the Soviet Union and, above all, knew and loved my native country. In my opinion, that qualified me as much as anyone to "tell America's story to the world." One of the major problems I encountered from day one in the Russian Service was the misconception that we were on the air to impress the listeners with our "flawless Russian language." In my entire life, in all my worldwide travels, I have never heard an Italian say about another Italian "He does not speak Italian." The same can be said for a Greek, a German, a Paraguayan, a Czech or a Somali. But in the Russian Service I heard—on a daily basis—so and so does not speak Russian. At first I considered it the "DP mentality." The only qualification some of my colleagues had going for them was their "native" Russian. Many of them—had they not been working at the VOA—would probably have to work as salesmen in a bargain basement or as unskilled laborers. It drove me crazy to hear Mr. R say that his editor Mr. D did not know Russian well. If Russians said that other Russians did not know their own language, what in the world were they saying about my fellow Americans and me? It did not take me long to learn that, excluding Mr. Mansvetov and the polished Alexei Tcherkassky (father of the ballerina Marianna Tcherkassky and born into a very noble Russian family in St. Petersburg), the other less educated and less self-assured Russian editors returned my scripts looking like a dog's breakfast. But they did the same to other Russians.

I usually had my scripts edited by these two men, so my frustration in that area was limited.

I will give only one example to prove my point. When I produced our Monday night Breakfast Show, which was broadcast from 10:00 pm to midnight (our time), it was my job to also write the billboard for the show. The billboard was read by the female announcer of the show. It consisted of a synopsis of the material to be broadcast after the news. For example: "After the news we will cover the President's appearance at the National Science Foundation. Then we shall describe the landing of the latest Apollo mission. In about fifteen minutes you will hear about the latest cancer-fighting drug. And now the news." Simple, right? I had an editor who had to change every second word. If I wrote "big," he changed it to "large." If I wrote "tomorrow," he wrote "Tuesday." In other cases he would simply say, "Sorry, Bill, you cannot say that in Russian." One evening I decided I had enough. I took the billboard wording directly from scripts written by our senior editor. The breakfast show editor, in his usual manner, changed every second word and even wrote on the page, "You cannot say it that way in Russian." The next day I handed my billboard to the senior editor. He became livid. From then on I insisted that our evening editor write the billboard.

I refused to allow these petty peons to stop me from doing my best to explain America through my cultural programs. It is obvious that I did something right, based on the people who recognize me to this day, who remember specific shows from years ago, and who to this day mention my name in letters to the VOA Russian Service. I attribute my success not to being some kind of genius but to my ability to reach out and to be honest and sincere.

As I said, I believed from day one that the best way to talk about America was through the eyes and mouths of my fellow Americans. It was time to set up my very first interview. It turned out to be not only the first, but one of the most popular, fun and informative programs. It was with the Beach Boys, who were giving a concert in the Washington area. They came down to our studios and spent nearly an hour with me. The Beach Boys were at the top of their popularity polls, had a string of hits and were continuing to put them out almost monthly. There was a lot of laughter during the interview. The Boys told jokes, clowned around and displayed their amazing ability to communicate in word as well as in song. They even sang a few bars at the mike. We took several pictures, which we sent out to everyone (there were many!) who wrote in after the show was broadcast. In fact, the Beach Boys later sent me a bunch of their records to be sent out to the first one hundred listeners that wrote in about the interview. The group spoke about their music, their home state of California, explained what surfing and surfing music was and talked about their concerts both in America and abroad. I learned an important lesson from this first interview. The more fame and fortune the person or group attained, the easier it was to deal with them. I found that to be true for the rest of my career in broadcasting.

The interviews continued, mainly with performing artists who I featured on my rock and roll show. These included: Bo Donaldson and the Haywoods, Mitch Ryder and the Detroit Wheels, the Three Degrees, Neil Diamond, Syreeta, Van McCoy, Gloria Gaynor, the Village People, Two Tons of Fun, Sylvester, and many more whom I shall mention later in the book.

A few interviews are especially memorable. For instance, long before I went to the VOA, I was a great fan of Martha and the Vandellas. When they were appearing in Washington I managed to get an interview with them after the show in their hotel room. We sat on the bed, drinking rum and coke, and chatted like we were old buddies. The girls were impressed that their voices and their music would be heard in the Soviet Union. The group showed an amazing ear for languages. At one point Martha Reeves asked me to teach them a few phrases in Russian. By the end of the interview they were actually introducing the songs I would play on the program in very passable Russian.

Not long after that, my buddy John Aldriedge and I traveled to Atlantic City to do an interview with another of my favorite groups, the Three Degrees. They were appearing at an all-black nightclub, NOT in the best neighborhood. John and I—the only white people in the club—sat so close to the stage that whenever the Degrees came to the front of the stage, their sweat dropped off on us!! How sweet that sweat was! The girls were delightful and gave me a very lively interview after the show.

One of the more touching interviews was with the duo Sonny and Cher. This time I had my dear friend Tamara Kit along to participate in the chat. The interview was held in their motel room of the Holiday Inn in Bethesda, Md. What made this interview so different was their baby daughter Chastity was sleeping in the adjoining bedroom. From time to time either Sonny or Cher had to look in on the baby to see that she was all right. Cher was magnificent! She sat on the couch, kicked off her shoes and went on and on, not only about her singing career but about her proud ancestry. She is part American-Indian and part Armenian. When I told her the program would also be heard in Armenia, Cher sent a special greeting to her fellow Armenians in the homeland. Once again, I felt gratified that our listeners were hearing how warm and down-to-earth these famous singing sensations really were.

For some years I also wrote and emceed a program called "Variety." There is so much more to American music than just rock and roll. In the Variety program I featured other categories of American music. One of the first to appear on this particular program was the famous pianist Liberace. He had been trained as a classical pianist but soon figured out that he could become richer and more popular as a pop performer. His concerts included everything from Tchaikovsky to merengue, to polka, to Country and Western. On stage Liberace wore the most outlandish costumes. His piano was always adorned with a huge candelabra, and on his right hand the pianist wore a huge diamond-studded ring in the shape of a candelabra. When I admired the ring during the interview, Liberace took it off and said, "Please, try it on." I thought how expensive it was. If I dropped it, I'd die. So I refused. But so kind and generous was Liberace that he at least made the offer. The pianist was extremely proud of his Italian-Polish heritage. He noted that Chopin was his favorite composer. Above all, during the chat Liberace became very emotional about growing up poor and abandoned by his father in Milwaukee. He expressed his deep gratitude to his mother for all her sacrifices. At the end he told young pianists in the Soviet Union never to give up their dreams. "The world needs musicians and artists to make it a bearable place to live" were his final words.

Neil Diamond appeared on one of my Variety shows. He mentioned that his grandparents were born in Tsarist Russia. In fact, Diamond was so anxious to perform in the "old country," he said, if invited, he would give a free concert. I passed on the word to our Cultural Section at the American Embassy in Moscow for future cultural exchange possibilities. I am sure it went in one ear and out the other. He was a delightful chap. Shortly after the interview, Neil Diamond gave a one-man show on Broadway. He offered to have me cover opening night "live" for a broadcast to the USSR. I tried my best, but union regulations prevented it from happening.

By the time disco became popular I began to broadcast a weekly program called Radio Discotheque USA. It went out Wednesday evenings; and, judging from the letters we received, it was extremely popular. I think I interviewed most of the popular disco stars, covered all the major concerts and even broadcast a few programs "live" from a discotheque. After the fall of Communism, I met a group of exchange students from Leningrad. They told me it was the most popular show in town. One of the girls held Radio Discotheque USA parties at her parents' dacha on the outskirts of town. I was amazed at the information she retained fourteen years after the show left the air.

I actually have an award, signed by President Jimmy Carter, for a program I broadcast during the 1976 celebration of the 200th birthday of the USA. There were many activities planned for the event, and I wanted to do something. But what? I came up with the idea of broadcasting my dance show "live" from the grounds behind the White House. The Park Service had set up tents for the visitors waiting to take the White House tour. There was plenty of room to organize a dance party for the visitors. With the encouragement and help of my dear friend and producer, Tamara Azarova Kit, (and, by the way, with so little encouragement from the VOA Public Relations office that it bordered on discouragement), we set up our loud speakers, our other equipment and did the program. I think people found the concept interesting. Between records I wandered among the crowds and interviewed the visitors. There were people from all over the world. It was one of the most fun things I ever did at VOA. The plaque of appreciation they sent me from the White House, signed by President Carter, is now probably in a closet in the Russian Service covered with dust.

The mention of the Bicentennial celebration leads me to describe the highest point in my career at the VOA. On July 4, 1976—the 200th Anniversary of the founding of our Nation—I had the unforgettable honor of emceeing a one hour special program called "American History Through Song." It was about the history of America as reflected by the music of the time, from early American music right up to the present day. As I sat behind the microphone that afternoon (with Tamara Kit once again in the producer's booth), I suddenly realized that here a guy who grew up in a small town in Pennsylvania was telling America's story to millions of people behind the Iron Curtain, and I became overwhelmed with emotion. As I was about to end the show with the words, "America is no utopia; we have a long way to go; we are not perfect, but America IS still the greatest place on Earth for the majority of us," I almost broke into tears. That was the best moment in my eighteen years, and it was worth all the sacrifices, the hard work and the indignities I suffered.

I do not want to give the impression my programs were only about music. On the contrary. I began my broadcasting career during the height of the war in Viet

Nam. I was often forced to go into the crowds during the many anti-war demonstrations to get interviews. On more than one occasion I was almost bodily harmed when the demonstrators learned I was working for the government radio station. As usual, I insisted on balance. If I did an interview with a protester, I had a second interview with a pro-government supporter. In 1994 I was at a dinner at the Freedom Forum where I met a Russian correspondent. He was anxious to tell me how impressed he was as a grad student in Moscow in 1969 to hear my Youth Show. In part one I interviewed a spokesman from the Young Americans for Freedom, followed by one with a Black Panther, followed by a feature on Angela Davis. Davis was in the USSR at the time, or shortly thereafter, and the grad student was surprised by the way I discussed Angela Davis, showing no opinion one way or another.

Throughout my VOA career, I was also able to acquaint our Soviet listeners with "the America beyond the Beltway." I called the series "Know Your American Cities." For this series I traveled to places like Atlanta, Portland, Tulsa, Philadelphia (of course!), Salt Lake City and others to give a feel for life with a different flavor. In every city, with the exception of Mayor Rizzo in Philly (much to my anger), I got an interview with the mayor and then with people from all walks of life: school teachers, construction workers, the wealthy and the unemployed, sports figures, people on the streets. I was extremely pleased with the responses I received everywhere. One question I often asked was, "What do you know or feel about people in the USSR?" When I was over there, Soviets always complained that they knew a lot about America, but Americans knew or cared little about them. These interviews showed that not to be the case. I was surprised by the number of interviewees who had been to the USSR (unlike the Soviets who had not visited the USA) and the ordinary people on the streets who said "Soviet people are just like us. All they want is a good life, as we do. We should be friends." Again, I NEVER prompted any kind of response from anyone.

In my efforts to show ethnic diversity I also spent time on an American Indian reservation in Sells, Arizona and conducted a number of very intense interviews with everyone from the chiefs to the chronically ill. I did not cover up the fact that medical care and economic opportunity were sadly lacking on the reservation.

I also attended and covered a Russian-American cultural week on the island of Kodiak, Alaska one year. It was not only an eye-opener for me, but obviously impressed our listeners, especially in Siberia. Many of the Russian-Americans living on the island traced their roots to that part of the USSR. My interview with 95 year old Anna Ivanovna Chichinova was nothing short of the entire history of Alaska in a capsule. She told the story with the clarity and grace of a young woman. When I asked Madame Chichinova what she wanted to do before God called her, she replied, "I've outlived four husbands. I would not mind adding a fifth!"

Among my journalistic souvenirs was a VOA first. The Voice did not have an office in Moscow nor was there much hope of opening one. For some reason, I long hoped to have the opportunity of ending an interview with the words, "This is Bill McGuire in Red Square." Well, in 1974 I happened to be in Moscow and so was Ray Conniff. I managed to set up an interview with the popular musical director of the Ray Conniff Singers. I believe he was married to a Russian-American. One cold evening I met Mr. Conniff in a Moscow hotel right off Red Square, conducted a lengthy, lively and informative interview with him about his musical career and got to say the words I had longed to say at the end of the chat.

Cultural exchange programs were becoming more popular and frequent between the USA and the USSR. Not all of them were government-sponsored. One year the first Soviet rock group, the Pesnyari, came to perform in the USA. When they appeared at James Madison University near Washington, DC, the Voice sent me to cover the event. Until that time, Soviet performing groups rarely gave interviews to the VOA and never to the Russian Service. I met the singers and musicians during a rehearsal the afternoon of the concert. Then I met their manager, their interpreter, their KGB nanny and the rest of the entourage. They all knew me from my Russian programs and seemed genuinely pleased to meet me. After the concert I filed a very positive report via phone to VOA Washington, which was broadcast on our Breakfast Show within the hour. The next afternoon their manager called me to say they would be happy to grant me a fifteen minute interview, a first for VOA Russian. Our Cultural Service Chief happened to be in Leningrad at the time. She reported very positive responses to the interview from her contacts in the city.

There are two more programs I would just like to mention in passing, because I worked very hard to make them interesting. The first was called "This Week in Washington." It was short and snappy and dealt with the multitudinous social, educational and cultural events in any given week in our nation's capital. I talked about art exhibitions, classical and popular musical concerts, plays, seminars on education, science and medicine and stressed any contact between Soviets and Americans. The program was a part of the Panorama show every Friday.

The second—and of no less importance—was my series on the Broadway musical world. Ever since I was eight years old I have been attending Broadway musicals. My first one was "South Pacific" in 1948. By the time I reached the VOA, I was completely immersed in the magnificent world of the American musical theater. In my opinion, to really know America, you have to know our musicals. I often had the opportunity to cover opening night either in New York or in Washington. Thanks to these programs, our audience got to hear the stories and the scores from such delights as The Wiz, My Fair Lady, South Pacific, Barnum, Sweeney Todd, Barefoot in the Park, Hello Dolly, Godspell, Cabaret, Dance, Hair, Ain't Misbehavin, Chorus Line, Funny Girl, Girl Crazy, The Ritz, On the Town, Pal Joey, Annie, Get Your Gun, Cage aux Folles and Mame, to name a few. But my very best program was the one I did on Chicago, the musical about life in a Chicago prison for women in the Twenties. With the help of another VOA writer, Kira Slavina, I translated several songs into Russian and had them read over music by some of the women of the Russian Service. I discovered that some of my female colleagues had great acting ability as well. It was a gem! On a sour note, however, one of my editors (Mr. Mansvetov had died by that time) and our Chief of Production thought the program was in poor taste ("We should not be singing about murder!!!, declared Osvalds Ursteins), or our new Cultural Chief (nameless because she does not deserve recognition by name), who decried: "Our listeners will not understand that it is a spoof." Well, I had more confidence in the sophistication of our audience than she and Mr. Ursteins did, and the show went on as was. One day I would love to see that wonderful musical performed in Russia in the Russian language.

For those, who might think that we government workers were grossly overpaid, I would like to say a few words about my salary. I was hired as a GS-5 to the tune of $5,000 a year. It was not bad money for the times, especially when many of my friends with PhDs in Russian were working as waiters or salesmen. I liked the job so much I probably would have worked for less! After two years Vladimir Mansvetov got me promoted to the GS-7 level. A year later I was emceeing all these programs I mentioned as well as producing at least one live air show per day. I felt I deserved a raise. When I met with our Service Chief in his office, he seemed surprised that I had the gall to ask for a raise. It bothered me that one of our producers had just been promoted to GS-11, although all she did was production work. She only had about four years of seniority over me, but, well, her father was the Chief of News and Commentary. Speaking of nepotism, it was rampant in the Russian Service (Mr. And Mrs. Mansvetov, Mr. and Mrs. Retivov, Mr. and Mrs. Fisher, Mr. and Mrs. Firsov, Mr. and Mrs. Antonoff, Mr. Barsky and daughter, Mr. Firsow and son. Enough?) I did not begrudge my colleague her promotion, as she was an excellent producer. Nevertheless, I did much more work. A GS-9 was not a fabulous salary. Our illustrious chief responded by saying, "After all, you ARE an American, and every word you write has to be edited." I responded, "Are the Russians also not edited, in some cases more than I?" It irritated him. What bothered me more was within the hour one of my colleagues also approached him (not knowing I had been there just before her). She was told, and I quote, "After all, you have been speaking Russian all your life, unlike Bill McGuire, who had to learn the language. He has accomplished something. You are just writing in your native tongue." End of conversation. Little did he know we would see each other in the cafeteria that noon and compare stories. Such was the hypocrisy in our office.

A short time later we got a new Service Chief. The day he arrived I had to laugh. It was none other than Bill Dickson, the diplomat who accompanied me to the airport in Moscow after I had lost my exit visa in 1967. After he had settled in a bit, I approached him with copies of what I had produced, written and emceed for one week ONLY. He was more than happy to begin proceedings to get a raise for me. It was my last raise for many years. Originally I came into the VOA (get this!)as a producer in the Yugoslav Service until a position in the Russian Service became vacant. On paper I was listed as a producer. Every time I asked our Production Chief for a raise, he would say, "Go ask the Cultural Section. You do more for them than for me." From the Cultural people I got the line that officially I was a producer; Production had to promote me. To be honest, money was not that important to me. I loved my job and had a daily feeling of accomplishment. Just before Bill Dickson left for another assignment, he called me into his office. He gave me what he thought was the best advice. "Bill, if you want to get ahead, you must begin to apply for a supervisory position. You can only go so far as a writer-producer-announcer. You deserve more. Think about it." I was deeply touched by Bill's comment but had to respond truthfully. I remember my exact words, "There isn't enough money in the U.S. Treasury for me to supervise the people in this office. In my current, lowly position I am a threat to nobody. People leave me alone. Once I am a supervisor begin the intrigues, the back-stabbing, the gossip, the misery, the insults. Thanks, but no thanks."

SCHLEPPIN' THE STATES WITH SOVS

✦

[ACCOMPANYING SOVIET DELEGATIONS IN THE USA]

One morning in early October 1969 Vladimir Mansvetov called me into his office and said he had received a call from the State Department asking if the Russian Service could provide them with an escort-interpreter for a Soviet delegation arriving for a two week period beginning October 15. Mr. Mansvetov thought it would be a good experience for me. He thought any contact VOA employees had with people from our target area would be beneficial. My first response was, "Would an official Soviet delegation accept a VOA employee as an escort-interpreter?" Mansvetov's answer was, "If he has a name like McGuire and not Mansvetov." I could see that my boss really wanted me to do it. It was difficult for me to say no to the man who gave me my big chance and who, I knew, always had my best interests at heart. Still, I had my fill of Soviet officials. If I never saw another Kremlin thug again, it would be too soon. However, a second aspect of the visit appealed to me greatly. The group would be visiting Philadelphia. I could see my family; and they, in turn, could meet a "live" Soviet representative. Little did I know at the time we would be appearing on Channel 6, and all my family, friends and neighbors would see Billy from Philly with high-ranking Soviets. Not a bad idea. I accepted. The part that I had not realized yet was my obligation to prepare programs for broadcast in my absence. More than once, while spending hours writing and recording my shows after work hours, I was ready to say I could not do it. But I had given Mr. Mansvetov my word.

And so on the evening of October 15, accompanied by some State Department officials, two diplomats from the Soviet Embassy and a few others (I wonder where THEY were from? Ha-ha), I went to National Airport to meet my delegation. It consisted of Petr Platonovich Udovichenko, the Minister of Education of the Ukrainian Soviet Socialist Republic, Andrei Yevgeniyevich Shirinsky, the Deputy Chief of the Administration of International Communications and Chief of the Section of Capitalist Countries and International Organizations of the Ministry of Education of the USSR, and Mr. Aleksandr Vasilyevich Peresypkin, a mere English teacher from School Number 11 in Kuybyshev. How in the heck did HE get on this delegation? He was the interpreter for the Soviet side, just in case the American interpreter did not do a good job of translating the wise words of his comrades.

It was easy to spot the three men as they deplaned. The Minister looked like he was on his fourth day of constipation. Shirinsky actually looked normal and not too exhausted from the flight from Moscow via New York. Peresypkin looked like a frightened guppy who had been out of the water too long. The usual welcoming remarks were made by State and the Soviet Embassy men, after which a sleek limousine whisked us off to the Embassy Row Hotel, one of Washington's finest. Nothing but the best for our Soviet visitors, I soon learned. The Minister was given a suite. The other two had beautiful rooms. After they were checked into the hotel, the big shots left; and I invited my delegation for a nightcap. I wanted to have a few minutes to go over our schedule for the following day. Above all, I wanted to say a few words to them about me, about the trip and to make sure we understood each other. I knew from the first moment I would have a problem with Peresypkin. I explained this was my first assignment and I would try my best. I admitted where I worked (they already knew). Shirinsky later admitted to me that he had heard me on the VOA. I said I was pleased to have them in my country. Then I told them what I have told every Soviet group ever since. "If you look for the positive, you'll find it. Same goes for the negative. America, like every other country, has a good and a bad side. I shall never deny our defects, nor shall I gloss over the things that make me proud to be an American. I hope by the end of this trip that we shall all be good friends and that you will have a better understanding of the USA." With those sweet words I bid them good night and left for home.

I often think that the term escort-interpreter is a glorified, euphemistic way of saying nursemaid or baby-sitter. In essence that is what I was. I had to be there in the morning to get them down to breakfast, translate the menu, and prepare them for the full day of activity. At night I did everything but tuck them into bed! One thing I must say about this first group, and every group after them, the Soviets knew what time meant. If I said 8:15 am, they were there at 8:15. I could see that they were suffering from a bit of jet lag, and I promised to see what I could do to get them a nap during the day. The limo took us for our first meeting at the US Department of Education. There were about twenty people seated around a huge, round conference table. Coffee and Danish pastry were served. When the Minister said he only drank tea, a secretary was immediately sent to fetch some hot tea. The American side rambled on and on about how wonderful the Soviet educational system was, how they put a man—and later a woman—in space, how education was free for all citizens of the country, etc.

In general, it was the typical liberal line of Americans who had never been to the USSR. The Minister began by expressing his gratitude for the visit and for the kind words of his hosts. He then proceeded to say that math and science are taught from the fourth grade on. While I was translating the words "from the fourth GRADE on," Mr. Peresypkin interrupted me by saying, "Excuse me, Mr. Bill, but Minister Udovichenko said from the fourth FORM on." The little mouse obviously thought he was in England where they say "form" instead of "grade." I knew if I let him get away with this, my life would be miserable for the entire trip. I had to put Peresypkin in his place. So, in the typical Nikita Khrushchev manner, I slammed my hand on the table, causing all to jump in surprise and told him not ever to DARE to correct my English again. The Americans were speechless, the Minister confused, and from the face of Andrei Shirinsky came a pleasant smile. I had figured out that Peresypkin was the KGB thug in charge of the troika. Shirinsky was obviously not too fond of his "nyanka" (baby-sitter) and was happy to see I could defend myself. "Shall we go on, gentlemen?" I asked.

The meeting was followed by a luncheon at the Soviet Embassy to which I was not invited. Did I cry? Of course not. My services were not needed. I went down to the VOA to tell my tale to Mr. Mansvetov and the crew down there. Mansvetov was generally pleased that I defended myself. Nevertheless, he reminded me that I should not make enemies of the boys from State ("creampuffs that they are," he added) nor of the other government officials who could block further assignments for me. Frankly, I could care less. If they take me off this assignment, I shall lose no sleep. If I never get another escort job, I still have my meager salary from the VOA. No, I was not going to take any crap from a Communist. I felt I was doing a good job. I was pleasant and respectful, but no English teacher from Kuybishev was going to correct MY English. That evening there was a lavish dinner in honor of our Soviet guests. Peresypkin was as quiet as a mouse. Udovichenko could hardly keep awake. Shirinsky was in a great mood, gave me several bear hugs during the course of the evening, even told me a few dirty jokes.

The following morning we visited some of the Washington, DC secondary schools and the University of Maryland. One of the schools taught Russian. The group asked to attend a Russian class. It was a disaster! The teacher spoke atrocious Russian, and the kids could not say the simplest things. This was an intermediate class, and they could not even conjugate simple, regular verbs. Worst of all, the teacher thought he was really impressing the Soviets with his excellent command of Russian. At the University of Maryland they organized a nice lunch for us. After coffee and dessert the faculty members asked Minister Udovichenko to say a few words about the Soviet Union and about Soviet education. He went on and on about the glorious life in his country, about free medical care, outstanding free education for all, equality for women, impressive housing construction, and so on. While we were walking out of the room, I whispered in his ear: "Petr Platonovich, you have completely confused me. I could not believe you were talking about the same country in which I just spent one year!" He raised his eyebrows and said: "My God, you did not tell me you had been to our country!!!!" I retorted: "You mean Peresypkin did not brief you?" No comment. After that, with a few exceptions, he toned down his description of the USSR, unless the trustworthy Mr. Peresypkin was translating.

From Washington we went on to Harrisburg, Pa. by plane. The reception there was nothing short of magnificent. It was probably the first time the residents of Harrisburg saw real, live Soviets. There was TV coverage, even a press conference in the airport. Accommodations were excellent. We had a limousine to take us everywhere. The delegation received gifts galore. However, the most impressive part of the Harrisburg trip was a visit to a local trade school, followed by a second visit to the Milton Hershey High School for Orphan Boys. We sat in on a beauty culture course at the trade school. The senior students were actually working as beauticians with local women for a small fee in the school. That day I saw—without doubt—the ugliest woman I had ever seen in my life. Even the Soviets could hardly refrain from reacting to this poor soul. She was having her hair done, a facial, manicure, the whole thing. At one point I looked at the woman, then turned to Minister Udovichenko and said, "Only God can help that woman! I hope she is not like you and does not believe in Him. He is her only hope." All three of the Soviets burst into uncontrollable laughter, even the mouse. Believe it or not, it was this remark that melted the ice between the Minister and me. After that he became very friendly toward me. He, too, shared a few jokes with me, not to mention a few drinks after his colleagues retired at night.

For me, of course, the high point of the trip was the stay in Philadelphia. We were housed in the beautiful Ben Franklin Hotel on Walnut Street. There was a lot of radio, TV and newspaper coverage. The first night when we appeared on the 11:00 local news, my folks were flooded with phone calls from family and friends. It was reported that "local boy makes good," and I laughed. The following morning my mother came down to meet us for breakfast. It is difficult to say who buttered whom up more. Mr. Udovichenko thought she looked more like my sister. (Indeed, Mother was very pretty and did not look her age.) She was delighted to meet a "Minister" who, she joked, was not wearing a cross. The conversation between my Mom and the Minister was so time-consuming, I was unable to eat anything. After breakfast he went up to his room and brought down a present for my mother from Kiev. There was only one unnerving part during the exchange. When the Minister said he was from Kiev, Mother responded, "Oh yes, we used to have lovely neighbors from Ukraine named Bulat. They had to flee Communist tyranny and did very well here in America." I knew if I did not translate her words, Peresypkin would. Petr Platonivich kissed her hand, and she smiled, "Please do come back to Philadelphia." Everywhere we went after that the Minister told all our hosts that I had a charming and beautiful mother.

Our final night in Philadelphia we were invited to a student dance at the University of Pennsylvania. Needless to say, the band was playing rock and roll. We sat watching the young kids dance for a while. Then I asked the group what they thought about what they were seeing. "I think it is decadent," replied my Minister. "You want to see decadence?" I asked. I grabbed a pretty, young girl and dragged her onto the dance floor. "Those men are Communists. Let's show them how we can shake our bods here in Philly." She was more than willing. In fact, we put on quite a show. One of the professors hosting us spoke Russian well. At one point I heard Udovichenko say to him: "Oh, my God, can you believe that epileptic snake is our interpreter?"

We left Philadelphia and traveled to Albany, NY and then to Boston. Albany was pleasant but not particularly memorable. I did not perform on the dance floor, and nothing of much importance happened. Well, actually, SUNY was trying to begin an exchange program with the USSR, and I believe progress was made during the visit. I was a bit tired and was losing my voice from so many hours of interpreting. In other words, I allowed Peresypkin to improve his American English. By this time I had become more tolerant of him, mostly out of pity. His English was not that bad, but he had absolutely no knowledge of modern American slang. Keeping in mind that Americans cannot talk very long without using slang words and expressions, it was confusing and frustrating for poor Peresypkin to keep up with his task. I was as helpful as I could be. We were all more comfortable with each other by this time. I think they began to see me as a human being rather than as an agent of the CIA. At the same time, the "troika" had to be impressed by the kindness, the openness and the generosity of the Americans they met. They were showered with gifts everywhere we went. We stayed in the finest hotels, flew first class, had limo service in every city, met with everyone they wished to see—unlike the way we were treated in the USSR.

Next stop—Boston. We arrived in late morning; and after checking into the hotel, we were taken to one of Boston's most elegant seafood restaurants. This is where I had my first embarrassing moment as an interpreter. The menu was extensive. There were fish that I had never heard of in Russian or English. I admitted to the Soviets that, first of all, I did not eat anything from the polluted seas; and, secondly, I did not know how to say shad and a few other fish in Russian. All three breathed a sigh of relief and admitted that they, too, did not like any fish or seafood. Was there Beef Stroganoff on the menu? Or Chicken Kiev? They said they trusted me to order what I thought they'd like. And so to the dismay of our hosts, I ordered good, old American prime rib, French fries, coleslaw and Boston bean soup for all four of us. They loved it. There was not a trace of food on their plates when they finished. In fact, they agreed it was the best meal thus far in the USA. That was saying something because we had not had even a mediocre meal. To add to their delight, the restaurant served Stolichnaya vodka from the Homeland. I could see that this visit, like many more in the future, was indeed the way to end the Cold War; that is, through people-to-people contact.

Boston will be remembered for another event that was not on the schedule. While we were still in Washington, I introduced Minister Udovichenko to Mike Terpak, the Chief of the Ukrainian Service of the VOA, who actually had the group to his home in Virginia. Mike told Petr Platonovich about the Ukrainian Institute at Harvard. Our second evening in Boston, the Minister and I were having our usual nightcap, sans the comrades, at the hotel. He remarked that he would like to see the Institute, but "perhaps, not being Ukrainian, the others would not find it interesting…or might not want to go…or not want him to go." I got the message. We agreed the following morning he would fake illness. I would send the others off with our Bostonian hosts and stay behind to "nurse him back to health." It worked. I called Mike Terpak; and he set up a luncheon, no publicity involved, at the Ukrainian Institute. For me it was the first time I was able to eat my lunch in peace without having to translate and chew at the same time. It also made me realize Ukrainian is different enough from Russian that I did not understand every word. There were a few moments of concern when the hosts expressed their views about the russification of Ukraine and the disintegration of the national tongue, but, in general, the meeting was conducted with grace and dignity. As we were leaving one of the professors came up to me and said, "You know, for a man that has been educated in the Soviet Union, his Ukrainian is not bad at all."

Our final stop was the Big Apple. We visited Columbia University, CCNY, a two year college in Brooklyn, an educational TV station and some other educational centers as well. All of us were pretty exhausted. The final evening in New York, a very wealthy New York stock broker had a lavish reception for us at his Fifth Avenue home. I have never seen so much champagne, caviar and jumbo shrimp (which we did not eat!) in my life. I could hardly believe that these capitalists, sworn enemies of the Soviet state, would devote so much energy and money to a reception for this group. It became quite clear to me that many of them were far to the left, bleeding-heart New York liberals who thought there was something to be learned from the "classless society" of the Soviet Union. One silly woman spent half an hour telling the group that "The Soviet Union meant the utopia of ballet. No other country, no other system could produce the perfection seen in Russian ballet." I suppose she was unaware that ballet was developed by the French and reached perfection in Russia long before the Communists took over." I refused to argue with her.

The most memorable moment of the evening—and perhaps of the trip—for me personally was an exchange between the good Minister and myself before the eyes of all. He walked up to me with champagne in hand and insisted on giving me a toast, which I was forced to translate. It went like this: "Mr. Bill, I want to raise a toast to your grandchildren. May they be Communists!" I drank reluctantly. Petr Platonovich smiled and began to walk away. I pulled him back by the elbow. Now it was my turn. "Dear Petr Platonovich. Thank you for your toast. And may I also drink to YOUR grandchildren? May they be Roman Catholics!"

The next day I accompanied my Soviet colleagues to Kennedy Airport. They were close to $1,000 in overweight luggage for the Aeroflot flight back to Moscow. The airline wanted me—that is, the State Department—to pay it. A man from the Soviet Consulate in New York was there as well. I suggested either the embassy or the consulate pay the excess baggage. It turned into an unpleasant screaming match with all concerned using undiplomatic language, to say the least. They would not budge. I would not budge. Fortunately, there was nobody from the State Department present, who probably would have coughed up the money. An agreement was finally reached with the manager of Aeroflot. It would be decided later who would pay. Sure.

The delegation boarded the plane for Moscow, but not before Andrei Shirinsky took me aside and expressed his sincere thanks for the trip. He said he considered me a friend. I remember his parting words, "Just think, Mr. Bill, if you were running the USA, and I the USSR, our countries would be the best of friends." I agreed.

I was exhausted. So I called Mr. Mansvetov in Washington to say I was as close to death from overwork as I have ever been. He said to take a few days off to rest. Then I went over to the American Airlines counter and asked where I could fly out WITHIN THE HOUR to rest and regain my sanity. Within the hour I was on my way to Puerto Rico where I lay on the beach, drank pina coladas and boogied all night in the discotheques of beautiful San Juan.

Three months later an officer at the American Embassy in Moscow sent me a copy of the first of the series about American education, written by none other than Petr Platonovich Udovichenko, based on his recent trip to the USA. It appeared in a newspaper for educators. The Minister stressed the fact that "American education is heavily influenced and dictated to by the Roman Catholic Church." We had not visited one parochial school, nor did we ever discuss religious education in the two weeks! He likewise went into great detail about the Russian classes in Washington, DC, taught by an incompetent with an inflated ego (that part was true!) and how poor, unattractive elderly women had to go to trade schools to try to get beauty care since they could not afford a regular beauty parlor. I read the article and was livid. I was slightly mollified when his first article ended with a very complimentary paragraph about his interpreter, "a dedicated capitalist and a believer in God, who danced shamelessly in front of the delegation atthe University of Pennsylvania, which organizes such decadent events for the students." He concluded with the words, "In spite of itall, Bill McGuire made our stay a delight."

THE KOMSOMOLS COME A' CALLIN'

✦

[THE "YOUNG" SOVIET POLITICAL LEADERS VISIT THE USA]

In September 1971 the American Council of Young Political Leaders, a bipartisan organization which promotes exchanges between young American political activists and their counterparts in other countries, invited the first group of Komsomols (Young Communist Youth League) to come to the USA to see how our political system works. Like all exchanges with the former Soviet Union, the program was coordinated by the Department of State, which had a fair amount of control over the exchange. My name was still fresh in their minds after my successful handling of the recent visit of Minister Udovichenko and his flunkies. I think a few kind words from Diana Moxhay on the Soviet Desk helped as well. Diana and I had met earlier that year in Siberia, where we had several mutual Soviet friends. The logic was it would be nice to have a young, Russian-speaking American act as the escort-interpreter. The VOA was more than happy to lend me to State. It was another good opportunity for me to have contact with the people in our broadcast target area. A slight problem arose when our chief wanted me to wear two hats. He wanted me to send in daily feeds by telephone about our activities to be broadcast on the Breakfast Show. State was opposed and so was I. It would be just too much extra work. The plan was scrapped, but I was still released to accompany our newest visitors from the USSR for about two weeks.

Late one afternoon I went to National Airport to meet my delegation. In addition to myself, there were people from the State Department, the Soviet Embassy, the American Council of Young Political Leaders and one or two of "questionable origin." I wore a pair of red, white and blue stripped trousers more or less as a joke. I knew the other "gentlemen" would be in their gray flannel suits (which they were), and I wanted to be different. By the way, the story of those pants comes in the next chapter. Eyebrows were raised when I arrived at the airport.

Finally my Komsomols walked through the exit. It was not difficult to recognize them. Soviets stood out in any crowd by their clothing, the way they smoked a cigarette, even the way they walked. But what confused me was their ages. The Americans they would be meeting were between eighteen and twenty five years old. These "young" Soviets looked like they were in their forties. I should have known the Kremlin would not send us a bunch of young kids. These were seasoned, diehard commies. As I approached the leader of the "column of ducks," I extended my hand and announced that I was Bill McGuire, their escort-interpreter. The senior member of the delegation, Aleksandr Kapto (age 38, looked older), displayed his sense of humor for the first and last time. He replied: "We saw you from the air," a reference to my pants, at which they were all staring.

The other members of the delegation included: Alla Smirnova, Raisa Lukyanova, Stanislav Kuzmenko, Felix Ovcharenko, Yuri Mayorov, Yuri Babich, Yuri Shaposhnikov. My remarks were followed by the usual words of welcome, peace, love, cooperation and what have you by my fellow Americans. After that we were immediately taken to a reception in Old Town Alexandria at the home of a local political figure from the Democratic Party. My Komsomoltsy seemed tired after the thirteen-hour flight from Moscow, but at the same time they thoroughly enjoyed the food (they went easy on the drink). It was indeed a lovely evening. Other than interpreting for others, I did not converse much with my group. I realized it would take a few days for them to warm up to me. They let it be known, however, that first night they knew who I was and where I worked. For instance, while answering a question from our Democratic host, Mr. Kapto prefaced his answer by saying, "In spite of what Bill and his colleagues at the Voice of America said...." Kapto was amazed to hear from the host that the VOA could not be picked up in the USA, so Americans did not know what VOA was saying. I insisted on making it an early evening. I knew my charges were tired. Besides, we had a full day ahead of us.

That full day began at the Democratic Headquarters at the Watergate (of all places) with a breakfast hosted by Chairman Larry O'Brien. The Soviets were still very careful about the questions they asked and the answers they gave. O'Brien was charming. He seemed sincerely happy to host these "young" political leaders. And, for an American, he did his homework on the role of the Komsomols, unlike many of our future hosts. That afternoon we were welcomed no less warmly (and with tastier food) at the Republican National Committee. As much as I tried to hide it, the delegation assumed I was more in my element with the "Elephant Party," as they called it. We also saw Washington by night, which had to impress them. The second dinner was hosted by a Republican. By the second evening, the Komsolols felt freer about having a few shots of vodka. They gently mixed our Smirnoff blend with the Soviet-made Stolichnaya. To me Stoli—as we called it and still do—had the smell and the taste of crude oil. The Sovs told us Smirnoff lost its "Russian soul" once it was brewed outside of the Motherland.

After our pleasant stay in Washington, DC we headed for North Carolina, where we were guests of Terry Sanford, the president of Duke University. He was the consummate host, who later went on to rise within the ranks of the Democratic Party. Dean Sanford, however, made sure we met with all political persuasions while we were at Duke. The Komsomoltsy were not yet "at home" in the USA. They were especially suspicious of anyone who spoke Russian well. This included, above all, Russian-Americans. One evening Dr. Vladimir Treml, a professor of economics at Duke, his wife, mother-in-law and two family friends, Dr. and Mrs. Evgeny Grivsky (whose son and daughter studied with me at Georgetown University) had a reception for us at their home. The Sovs were visibly ill at ease. Their conversations with the Russian-Americans were short but polite. Also present were a few students from Duke who did not speak Russian very well. Our Komsomoltsy seemed to enjoy hearing them murder the Russian language. I began to wonder why. Perhaps they felt a CIA spy would speak Russian perfectly. I noticed another interesting thing about my group. They seemed confused every time they were offered alcohol. Was there something in it, other than grain? Truth serum, maybe? Once again, they gravitated toward Stolichnaya vodka when available.

After we left Raleigh, we flew out to beautiful Denver, Colorado. They all admired the beauty of the mountains surrounding the city from the sky. (It was safe to admire Mother Nature, even in America.) As in all other places, we were given the finest accommodations, namely the Hilton Hotel. The next morning we were bussed up to a mountain resort to meet with various young politically active Denverites and to participate in a seminar about mutual Soviet-American concerns. You should have seen the faces of the locals when we walked into the hall. I was in front. The host immediately asked me, "Where are the 'young' Soviet political leaders?" It was difficult to keep from laughing, but I replied that these WERE the "young" Komsomols. However, due to the harsh climate, they age faster than we do! The English-speaking delegates looked at me in anger. This prompted the Soviet leader to say to me, "You know, when we saw you in those red, white and blue stripped pants in the airport, we thought we were dealing with a clown…" Before he could say any more, I interrupted him by saying, "You know, I was expecting 'young' political leaders. Let's just say we were all disappointed. Now let's make the most of the situation." In spite of the beauty surrounding us, the obvious disappointment of our hosts, my remark to Mr. Kapto and a few unkind words by some of the locals about the Captive Nations of Lithuania, Latvia and Estonia, the day was rather tense.

Things changed by the evening. We attended a political rally for a local Democrat running for office. I was losing my voice, so I asked Alla to interpret that evening. Her English was very good; but, unfortunately, like most of the English majors at Moscow State University, she had little or no access to American culture. Without knowledge of the culture, an interpreter can make some very funny errors. That evening Alla made the goof of the day, if not the trip. The candidate said, "Denver needs a change. The people have had enough Mickey Mouse politics." Suddenly I heard Alla's Russian translation: "The people of Denver are sick and tired of the politics of the candidate, Mickey Mouse." I laughed so hard, I almost fell off my chair. Alla turned tomato red and asked what was so funny? I said, "I'll explain later. Just continue the translation, please."

The following day we were guests at a real Colorado-style picnic given by the governor. It was full of the major political dignitaries, who were extremely polite and warm to the Soviet guests. They stuffed themselves on hot dogs, barbecue, French fries, corn, soda, beer, ice cream, etc. From there they took us to a local amusement park. Believe it or not, the Russian word for roller coaster is the "American Mountains." As soon as we entered the park, I said. "Okay, we must get on the roller coaster first." This caused my first fight with our representative from the State Department, whom from day one I referred to as the "Iron Arm of the State Department." This bureaucrat screamed at me, "I forbid you to put them on the roller coaster." I thought I was hearing things. "What did you say?" He repeated his command. I asked why. He said that, if I knew anything about Russians, I must know that they are not used to eating American junk food. A roller coaster ride would cause them to throw up. I saw that he was not kidding. "Look," I said. "First of all, you do not FORBID me to do anything! This is not the Soviet Union, and I do not take my orders from you! If I let you get away with this, you'll be telling me when I can use the bathroom. I stand firm." He threatened to call Washington and have me removed from the trip. This really infuriated me. My reply: "Listen, you brain-dead bureaucrat, if you try that, I'll call a local press conference and tell them how YOU are acting." "That is blackmail!" he said. "No," I laughed out loud. "It's RED mail!" Then I asked the Komsomols to vote—to ride the coaster or not. "All in favor, raise your right hand." They looked at Alla. Her hand went slowly up. Then the rest of the hands. As we approached the entrance, Yuri B. asked me: "Bill, what if by chance one of us does puke?" I smiled and said, "Be sure to aim it at the 'Iron Arm of the State Department'.

Our next destination—to the surprise of everyone, especially me—turned out to be the favorite stop of the trip for the young Soviet political leaders. It was Davenport, Iowa. When we were planning the itinerary I suggested that we show the Soviets a little bit of the "real America." All in Washington were in favor. I still do not remember why Davenport was chosen, but it was the ideal choice. On the plane from Denver the Sovs began talking enthusiastically about visiting, as they called it, the provinces. Felix Ovcharenko, one of the less pleasant delegates, asked me if the CIA had installed paved streets, running water and electricity just for their visit. Actually, the Soviets were the masters of building "Potemkin Villages." These "beautified" villages and towns go way back to tsarist times. Villages were spruced up if the tsar were going to pass through so that he would believe that all was well in the provinces. The Soviets, too, built special hospitals, collective farms, research institutes and other establishments to show to foreigners—in other words, a deliberate distortion of Soviet life. Therefore, these poor, brainwashed Komsomols actually believed they might be shown a "Potemkin Village."

The airport was small but certainly better-equipped than any small airport in the USSR. While we were waiting for our luggage, Alla Smirnova began to translate the billboards welcoming visitors to Davenport. I remember her saying, "Just imagine, Comrades, this town has thirty-one churches and three libraries! It ought to be the other way around." With great shock she also read the sign: "Home of the John Birch Society." The John Birchers were known by every man, woman and child in the USSR as the "most dangerous of all the American warmongers." I could hear the entire delegation whispering, "So, we are in John Birch country."

Davenport is a delightful city. To the amazement of our visitors, the city had electricity, running water, paved streets and much more. Our hotel was old but well-maintained with lovely furniture and bathrooms. Above all, warm, friendly people welcomed us. A tasty luncheon was served attended by the mayor and other political figures. More toasts were raised to Soviet-American friendship than in any other city. The Komsomols finally began to relax.

The following morning, however, was probably the most impressive day for the delegation. We were taken a few miles out of the city to a private family farm. Our Dairy Queen Raisa was finally in her element. She headed straight for the pig pens and began to admire the piglets. "Aren't they delightful, Bill?" she asked. I said I thought they stank. This upset Raya. The farmer gave them all a ride on his newest John Deere tractor. We saw the crops, the animals, the family home, the barn, the silos, the whole shebang! An unforgettable luncheon was served. The entire family attended. Hundreds of questions were asked, especially by our Raisa. Then the farmer asked her how many people worked on her collective farm in the USSR. She replied one hundred and thirty. She asked him the very same question. He said ten. All eight members of the delegation shouted in unison, "TEN!!!???" Needless to say, they did not believe him. In spite of it, they left the farm feeling full, happy and impressed.

That afternoon we finally had three hours to rest or do whatever we wished. Some wanted to sleep, but Alla reminded them that they could sleep back home. They were here to see America, above all, rural America. They asked me to take them to the department store directly across the street from out hotel. The department store (I wish I could remember the name) was no Macy's or Neiman Marcus, but it was far superior to any major store in Moscow. More than anything up to this point in the trip, this store blew the minds of our Komsomols. For some reason we wound up in the bridal salon first. The wide range of selections, as well as the prices, left the Sovs speechless. I was waiting for Felix or perhaps one of the Yuri's to remind the group that they had the same, if not better, at home. I did not have to wait long. Felix reminded them of the "high quality" of the dresses at GUM in Moscow (funny, but I never even saw a bridal section in GUM) and that the Moscow prices were more "within the budget of Soviet brides." I was forced to ask him if most Soviet brides rented the dresses rather than buy them. That was the opinion I got after my visits to the USSR. His answer was the typical Soviet manner of getting around an issue rather than answering the question. His response was that he was the groom, not the bride, and he was not involved in getting a wedding dress for the happy occasion. Once again, Yuri S.—the other "cheerleader"—felt it necessary to comment on the "outrageous" prices of goods in this store. I felt obligated to point out that, if he looked around, the store was not only full of customers, but that 99% of them were carrying bags with merchandise they bought there. "These are not rich people, Yuri (I remarked), nor are they standing in line to buy anything. Surely it must surprise you and the rest of your comrades that, even in this 'provincial town,' there are no lines for anything!" I could see that I made my point. I know these Komsomols were given a limited amount of hard currency before leaving Moscow, but—like all other Soviet visitors before and after—they always waited to buy things in New York City, assuming that there was more quantity and quality there at lower prices. I assured my group that was not the case. If they had anything special in mind to buy, they might as well buy it here. I concluded by saying many Soviets had merchandise from New York, but how many had a gift from Davenport, Iowa? Still, no purchases!

In the evening we were invited to a political meeting, followed by a tasty buffet, by none other than the John Birch Society. Our Iron Arm of the State Department was very apprehensive about the exchange. I was certain it would be fun for all (except him). In a way, the idea of coming face-to-face with members of the John Birch Society fascinated the Soviets. Not that they were also a bit suspicious of what might happen. Aleksandr Kapto asked me if there was any possibility the Birchers would "use violence" against them? Jokingly, I replied that only God knew, and they (the Sovs) could not ask HIM, because they did not believe in Him!! I could not have been made happier than by what was said by all that evening. The Soviets began by saying that the Birchers did not understand Communism. They did not realize that the policies of Lenin were the policies of peace, brotherhood and justice. Kapto spoke with fervor and conviction. As usual, when the other Komsomols were asked to speak, they parroted his words to the T. No deviation in the slightest. The Birchers were far more impressive. They had the facts as well as their own convictions. A very heated discussion followed. At times I thought things would get out of hand, especially when the Birchers spoke about the "rape of the Baltics" (using that term), the crushing of democratic uprisings in East Germany, Hungary, Czechoslovakia, human rights abuses in all 15 Soviet republics, the "guns instead of butter" politics of the Kremlin, lack of freedom of the press and other facts of life. For the first time I could see that these words were causing some of the Komsomols to think about was being said. The Birchers never came across as ideological nuts or violent warmongers. These were nicely dressed, educated and articulate. While criticizing the Communist system, they were also pouring drinks and offering more food to the "arch enemy." By the end of the evening more hands were shaken, more smiles exchanged than at any part of the trip.

By the way, when I was putting the Komsomols on the plane back to Moscow their last day in New York, I asked them which city impressed them the most? Without hesitation they all said in unison, "Davenport, Iowa." To them it was the real America. It is to me as well.

Next stop—Chicago. Chicago was memorable for several reasons. We probably did more cultural things there than in any city. This included visiting museums and art galleries. We were specially wined and dined by Mr. Eddie Rosewell, a prominent local Democrat. He gave a reception for us at his condo way up high at Marina Towers. Raisa and Alla remarked to me they had never been in living quarters that high up. It gave both of them a slight case of vertigo, but the view was spectacular. We met all kinds of interesting Chicagoans, many of whom had been to the Soviet Union and who spoke openly and freely about their impressions. The Sovs were always extremely interested in what Americans thought about the USSR. Unfortunately for them, their usual boasting about free education and medical care in the USSR did not resonate in Chicago. There were two medical doctors in attendance who considered the current state of Soviet medicine "abominable." One remarked that Soviet doctors would rather amputate an infected toe, for example, than treat it with antibiotics. The delegation head responded with the traditional Soviet answer, "We are still short on many items because of the war." The cocktail party resulted in a real accomplishment for me personally. We were going to New York next where the award-winning musical "Hair" was playing. I told Eddie Rosewell how much I wanted the group to see it, although no tickets were available. Our State Department leader criticized me for even suggesting such a thing. Rosewell contacted the producer, Michael Butler, who was in Chicago; and there were tickets waiting for us when we reached the Big Apple.

The following morning we had the distinct honor of being received by Chicago's illustrious Mayor, Richard Daley. I had never been intimidated by anyone in my life up to that day. But there was something about that man, as he walked into the chamber, that commanded attention and fear. He was a short man. I approached the Mayor and extended my hand, saying, "Good morning, Mr. Mayor. I am Bill McGuire, the escort-interpreter for the group." Without a smile (or any other expression), he looked at me from head to toe and replied, "What is an Irish boy named McGuire doing working for Russians?" I swear I could feel some warm liquid running down my right leg. "It's just a job," I said. The worst was yet to come. Mayor Daley sat with us at a round table and officially welcomed us to the Windy City, presenting each of us with a medallion bearing his image. Then came Aleksandr Kapto's turn to speak. I could not believe my ears. He began by saying: "Good morning, Mr. Mayor. It is a pleasure for all of us to be in your beautiful city and to accept this lovely present from you. We have some gifts for you as well. I want you to know that the Soviet people know Chicago very well. In fact, in the USSR it is known as the "City of Gangsters." (By this time, I was about to die.) "We know all about Al Capone, Dillinger and other Chicago heroes. We even know that you color the river green on St. Patrick's day. This is the same river that is full of dead bodies, murdered by the local gangsters. But, it is a city with great history and culture. Again, we are happy to be here." As I translated these words, I dared not look at the mayor. By the time I finished the last word, our host had already stood up and left the room. I was so angry at Kapto for his speech, I said to him, "I would not be surprised if YOU wind up at the bottom of the Chicago River after those words."

Later that day one of the Chicago TV stations wanted to do a half-hour special on the Komsomols emphasizing their trip to Chicago. The producer asked me what the delegation could do to "liven up the show." I suggested they sing a Russian song but NOT "Midnight in Moscow" or "Those Were the Days." We discussed it with the Soviets, who, in turn, asked me what Russian song I liked personally. I suggested "Ivushka" (about a weeping willow tree, based on the words of poet Sergei Yesenin). Not all of them knew the words. Suddenly, our beloved Dairy Queen Raisa, who had not spoken five words the entire trip, spoke out. "I know the words," she said sheepishly, and she began to sing them. She had the voice of a nightingale! Raya wrote the words down for all, and I suggested that they sing the first stanza followed by a solo from Raya. It worked. It worked so well, the TV crew—without even knowing Russian—were almost in tears from her voice. Our "Choir of Commies," as I began to call the group, repeated the song in other places. It was extremely well received wherever we went. The attention I gave her also made Raisa more relaxed around me. She began to talk more about her life, her children, the kolkhoz (collective farm)…but never in the presence of the others. I really became very fond of this Soviet peasant woman. But would she ever be a political leader? I would have guessed her age to be around 40, but her documents indicated she was 29 years of age. One ages fast on a kolkhoz!

By the time we arrived in New York City, the group (and their escort-interpreter) were rather exhausted. At least they got to eat. I had to gulp down large morsels of food while they were blabbing and then quickly interpret their words. The easy part of my work was their rote manner of speaking. I am sure Kapto was handed a script written by State Security in Moscow, which he memorized beautifully. By the time he was halfway through a sentence, I was already at the period. He never changed a word. The rest of the "young" political leaders did just that; i.e., they followed the "leader." Without exception, after Kapto made his speech, the others always followed with the words, "I would just like to agree with the words of Comrade Kapto and…." They repeated his exact words. No African gray parrot could have done better! The sad part of it all was they had no idea how it sounded to an American audience. Even the most pro-Soviet (of which there were many!) had to be confused by this behavior. Where was their originality? Did no one ever have a different opinion? Of course not! Their system was based on everybody agreeing on everything. When the Komsomols heard different points of view, let's say, even within the Republican party, they mistook it for chaos. Nothing was gray. It had to be black or white. As I mentioned earlier, Michael Butler had arranged to have tickets for all of us to see "Hair" the second evening in New York. The Soviets obviously had no idea about the subject, nor about the nudity. When they asked me, I simply said they would like the plot. It was anti-war, pro-love. My seat was next to the Dairy Queen Raisa. I offered to change with Alla so the two women could sit together. "No, please don't," said my kolkhoznitsa. "I want to sit next to you, Bill. This way you can translate for me." I reminded Raisa it was mostly singing. She'd understand. At the end of act one the entire cast appeared on stage naked as jay birds. The theater was dark, so I could only see Raisa's face (redder than a tomato). When the lights went on, Commander Kapto stood up, looked at me with a vengeance and in a very loud voice addressed his choir. "This is decadence, perversion, blasphemy"—was he serious?—"crude, disgusting, vile!" I replied: "In other words, you do not like it." No answer. "We are leaving now, Comrades." With that they all marched out of the theater. I remained. I saw the irony and the humor in the whole affair. In Russian "hair," (pronounced kher), is a slang word for the male organ.

Our visit to New York coincided with another visit by two Soviet Kosmonauts. We kept running into each other. My group was in awe of their compatriots, whom they had only seen on television. They had to go to America to actually meet the space heroes in person. Within one afternoon we had to attend two receptions at the United Nations, one given by the Soviet ambassador and the second by American Ambassador George Bush. It is difficult for me to say which of the two ambassadors impressed me less. They both looked and acted like they did not want to be there. In short, neither could wait for the reception to end.

We posed for photos with both dignitaries, exchanged meaningless chitchat and then blabbed some more with some other minor UN officials.

That evening proved to be the scariest for me personally. It was our final evening in the Big Apple. There was a big reception for the Kosmonauts and the Komsomols (the K&K evening, as I termed it…minus the third K). I was waiting for my group in the hotel lobby. And, by the way, as I wrote earlier, they were never late for anything! Only seven of the eight came down. When I asked about Mr. X, I was told that he was not feeling well and would remain in the hotel to rest. At first I thought nothing about it. We were all tired, maybe even a little weak from the trip. Nevertheless, it was highly unlikely for one of them to leave the group. I will not mention which of my Komsomols stayed behind. It is not that important today. We attended the reception and returned to the hotel around 11:00 pm. Before turning in for the night, I thought I should check in on my sick comrade. I knocked several times before he answered. Finally the door opened. Mr. X stood there in his boxer briefs. His eyes were red. "What's the matter?" I asked. "Have you been crying?"

At that point he sat down on the bed and began to weep like a baby. I froze in my tracks. What in the world was going on? Was he sick? About to defect? Did someone give him poison? I sat next to him. Mr. X put his arm around my shoulder as he continued to weep bitterly. I decided to allow him to do the talking. At last he spoke. "Bill, I am a ruined man, completely broken in mind and spirit. My life has been a lie. Everything I always believed in has been a farce, a distortion. My government has deceived all of us, and I was too dumb to see the truth. We are all slaves. I am a slave. Worst of all, there is no hope. This trip has opened my eyes, but I am not sure if that is good or bad." By that time I was sure he would ask for political asylum. "That is all I need," I thought to myself. I also thought that if he defected, that would be the end of the ACYPL exchanges. Too much work went into this trip. More were planned. So, I finally said to him, "You know it's not THAT bad. People like you see what the West is like. You have the power to make the necessary changes in the future. You are a future political leader. Go home and lead! Your country needs you. Mother Russia is depending on you. You must go back." To my great relief he said, "Of course, I'm going back. But I alone cannot change anything. I have lost the will to go on with my life." I gave him a hug, wished him pleasant dreams and left. I did not sleep a wink all night.

As expected, the Soviets were joined that last morning by two thugs from the Soviet Mission, who took them to the junk stores to buy transistor radios and other garbage from Hong Kong as presents for their loved ones. Speaking of loved ones, I wish to point out that every member of this and every Soviet delegation to the USA was married. The wives and children had to remain back in the USSR to deter any notion of defection.

While the Commie Choir shopped for bargains, I went out to lunch with one of the planners of the trip, Spencer Oliver. He and I had locked horns more than once. We were obviously on different sides of the political spectrum. When I disagreed with him about what would or would not appeal to the Soviets, I stood my ground. He had not yet been to the USSR. This was the first group of Soviets he had ever met. As a result, he was slightly "tilted to the left." At first, he thought I was just displaying my anti-Soviet feelings. However, as the trip progressed, he began to see the light. That day over lunch, Spencer—gentleman that he was—apologized for his actions. We agreed that my experience and handling of the Soviets saved the trip. We likewise agreed that these exchanges should continue. There was one exception, however. I asked not to be included in any further visits.

EDUCATION USA

◆

[MY THIRD AND FINAL EXHIBIT IN
THE USSR]

One hot summer afternoon in 1980 my mother and I were sitting on her patio in Philadelphia sipping iced tea and discussing unusual ways to celebrate a birthday. She was obviously preparing me for her upcoming birthday in September. During the conversation I remarked to her, "Other than myself, how many Americans do you know who celebrated their thirtieth birthday in the middle of Siberia?" In her quick and acerbic humor she answered, "How many Americans would WANT to? It's not something I would boast about, Bill!" Well, I was not boasting. It so happened that my thirtieth birthday was spent in Novosibirsk (actually a suburb called Akademgorodok), where I worked on my third and final American exhibition in the former Soviet Union.

"Education USA" I thought would be one of the best exhibitions USIA ever sent to the USSR under the cultural exchange agreement between our two countries. It was a subject dear to the hearts of most Soviets. They thought they had the best educational system in the world, mainly because it was free and available to all. I personally felt this particular exhibition would set the record straight about American education. Yes, higher education was not free in America, but it was attainable. Our pre-school and/or kindergarten classes were paid for by the parents; but the care, the food and the ambiance were far superior to those in the USSR. Well, in short, I was sadly disappointed. I would say all of us on the show were frustrated by the inaccurate and outdated depiction of American education. Let me point out that the Exhibits Division of USIA did not actually build the exhibit. They contracted all our exhibits out to firms that knew nothing about the target audience. USIA had a motion picture division as well. They could have produced a series of excellent videos on American education from kindergarten to the Ph.D. level. One of the films shown was obviously shot in the 1950's, judging by the long skirts and hairdos of the women and the baggy trousers and haircuts of the men. There was no mention of private nor religious schools, trade schools, correspondence courses (which were very popular in the USSR), work-study programs, scholarships, foreign students in the USA, (of which there were many!!). To add insult to injury, the exhibit panels were made in Italy, complete with the "Made in Italy" sign on the lower right corner. English-speaking visitors would comment daily: Can't you even build an exhibit in your own country? I admit some of the displays were impressive. As usual, the free brochure and exhibit pin were colorful and very popular. As for all previous American exhibits, people stood in line for hours—in rain, snow and sleet—just to get a glimpse of the show and to speak with a "real, live American." Perhaps we participants were too critical. A USIA official once remarked to me, "We could send an exhibition of American dogs eating cat food, and the Soviets would still come." Personally, I considered this attitude an insult to the many people who stood in those long lines for hours to see our exhibit.

The VOA did not want to release me for six months to work on this exhibition. However, I was beginning to complain more openly and often about all the work I was doing and for less money than some of our "dead wood" were making. I was actually thinking about leaving the VOA and the Government in general. When our chief asked what it would take for me to stay, I demanded—never thinking I'd get it—a raise and the exhibit where I could save money to buy a new car and furniture. How unfortunate that one had to threaten to get a well-deserved promotion.

Of the three USIA exhibits I worked on, I'd say the quality of the guides on "Education USA" almost made up for the lack of substance of the exhibit. The first day we all assembled at USIA headquarters, I looked around and decided this group would be a pleasure to work with. First of all, we had a real Russian prince (Sergej Schachowskoj) on the team. There were some school teachers, as well as some ex-guides like myself. We also had three other staff members of the Russian Service of VOA on board, which would have been unthinkable in the past. But the one who impressed me most that first day was a young lady whose father owned and operated a portable toilet business on construction sites, named Dolores "Dolly" Foley. While we were introducing ourselves to the group and telling a bit about our background, Dolly mentioned her father's business, recalling the words on his calling card: "It may be shit to you, but it's our bread and butter." I knew Ms. Foley would be an asset to the exhibit. She was. Her sense of humor helped her survive the daily trials and tribulations of working in the Soviet

Union. The three cities we would be visiting (Baku, Tashkent and Novosibirsk) would be three of the toughest in my exhibit history.

As a group we were also prone to having more parties and celebrations for birthdays, etc. We arrived in Baku, the capital of Soviet Azerbaidzhan, on December 29, 1970 just in time to celebrate New Year's in that provincial city on the Caspian, whose population was Muslim and non-Slavic. Our hotel was comfortable and the food was better than we had expected. Our administration managed to rent one small room in the basement of the hotel for our New Year's Eve party. We managed to have a good time in spite of where we were. As the evening progressed, some of us wandered about the hotel. The Azeris knew how to party and many of them invited us to join their celebrations.

One event in Baku stands out in my mind. I must share it with my readers. It was the night before our official opening in Baku. The Ambassador and his wife, as well as several Embassy functionaries, were in town for the big event. There was a restaurant high on a mountain overlooking the city and the sea, which could be accessed by a cable car. In spite of the view, there was nothing else good to be said about the place. The food was atrocious. Well, there we all were munching on our hors d'oeuvres when suddenly I noticed the Ambassador's wife almost jump out of her chair in fright. A huge rat ran from under her table. The rat had obviously run across her feet in passing. A waitress was exiting the kitchen. I walked up to her and said: "There is a huge rat running around the room. Can you do something?" She returned to the kitchen, completely unimpressed by my comment, and came back with an enormous, fat, old black cat in her arms. Then she literally threw the animal on the floor and said in Russian, "Go get it!" I laughed so hard I almost cried. The rest of the evening was spent quietly trying to eat the lousy food, hoping the rat would not return. As for the cat, he/she pranced about a few feet and then fell asleep.

Opening day was one of the better ones I can remember. The invited guests were friendly, unlike the surly Kremlin bureaucrats from Moscow (they were there too), and people actually seemed to enjoy themselves. We even had an orchestra. When they played Azeri music, the locals showed us how well they could shake their booties. Some of us (especially our gorgeous secretary, Masha Soukhanova, and myself) gladly joined in. The crowds in Baku were fewer than in other cities but were better behaved and less confrontational about the USA. Their level of Russian was lower than in the previous cities in which I served, but the change was refreshing. The annoying questions about Vietnam came later in Tashkent.

My favorite story about Baku deals with my infamous "red, white and blue" stripped pants, which made their debut in that city. These are the same pants I described in the last chapter, for which the Komsomols called me a clown. One day shortly before our opening, I was reading a supplement section of the New York Times. There was an add showing these "patriotic" pants, sponsored by the Cotton Industry of America with an address. I wrote them a letter explaining my position as an American guide in the USSR and said I felt these pants were just what I needed. I gave my size, address and credit card number. Much to my shock, two weeks later the pants arrived with a short note wishing me luck on the exhibit and informing me there was no charge. It was a gift from the company. (When visitors asked, "How much do your pants cost?" I would reply with a smile, "Nothing!") The first day I wore my pants, it caused a fury of excitement and comments. As I ascended my stand, an elderly Russian woman began to scream at me: "Look at you, look at you!!! This exhibit is supposed to be about education. What connection could a clown like you (again the word clown!!) possibly have with education?" I smiled sweetly and answered, "For your information, Madam, I teach esthetics."

People actually came to the exhibit asking for "the man with the pants." I did not wear them often; but when I did, they were the talk of the show. One day, my day off, I happened to be wearing the pants as I walked around the city by myself. Suddenly I turned around to find about ten people following me like a column of ducks. (I felt like the Pied Piper of Hamlin.) The man directly behind me began to ask how much I'd sell the pants for. Pointing out that they were my trademark, I said for no price would I sell them. He got up to 200 rubles. The answer remained "NO." Three hundred rubles. Still "NO." Finally he said, "Why don't you just give them to me as a present?" "Why should I?" He replied, "Because I'm Jewish." "What does that have to do with it?" I asked. "Well, actually I'm not Jewish, but we know that in America Jews get whatever they ask for. By saying I'm Jewish, I thought you'd give me the pants." "Now I've heard everything!" I responded.

When I got back to the hotel, I told the story to my roommate, the notorious John Aldriedge. We laughed for five minutes. This prompted me to compose one of the many limericks I wrote about my visits to the USSR. It goes like this:

"There once was a Jew from Baku,
Who liked pants that were red, white and blue,
But, he wasn't a Jew,

And I'm here to tell you,
If he was a Jew, I am too!

We were down by the Caspian sea,
Where huge rats run about rather free,
Where the food is divine,
But no meat from the swine,
And some Muslims won't even drink wine!"

We were warned not to walk along the boardwalk (Ulitsa Neftyannikov) late at night. One evening some of us were invited to the apartment of some local English teachers. I had a headache and decided to return to the hotel alone. It was about 11:30 pm. I was no more than three blocks from my hotel when the two men in front of me began to fight. They were speaking in Azeri, so I didn't know why they were arguing. One of them pulled out a knife and began to slash the other's hand. At this point the second man pulled out a larger knife and returned the slashes. Next thing I knew there was blood spurting out of both of them. I walked past them. They paid no attention to me, to my delight. I ran like hell the next few blocks back to the hotel. When I told the room clerk to call the police because two men were cutting each other up, she simply said it was "between them" and not to get upset over a "friendly brawl."

After Baku John Aldriedge, Sid and Gail Smith, George and Sharon Osmolovsky and I headed for the resort town of Sochi to bask in the sun and then cross the Black Sea to Odessa on the HMS Latvia. It was the one and only time in my life I have been seasick. I do not think there was a passenger on board who was not barfing his guts out. John and I shared what might loosely be called the "bridal suite," for lack of a better term. We got this suite because Intourist forgot to book us, even though we had the tickets in our hand. The boat was going to leave without us. But I, in my usual manner, began to scream profanities. As usual, it worked. Too bad John and I were so ill during the entire crossing. Otherwise it might have been a nice place to sleep. The room had a German-made short wave radio which received VOA broadcasts beautifully. It was Valentine's Day. We were able to hear songs dedicated to all of us by Tammy Dombrovsky on her dance show and more greetings on the Night Owl show from our colleague, Zhenya Nikiforov. Those programs really made us feel good in spite of the seasickness and some homesickness.

By the time we reached Odessa, all we wanted to do was take a bath and sleep. John and I argued over who would get the bathtub first. I fight dirtier than he, so I filled up the tub and soaked for fifteen minutes as he continued to yell: "Aren't you finished yet, McGuire?" Then a funny thing happened. I removed the stopper from the tub and began to dry myself. I heard a strange sound in the bathroom, but did not know from where. As I glanced at the toilet, I saw that my bath water was pouring out of it and flooding the floor. Ah, only in the Soviet Union!

That evening John and I bought tickets to a Polish variety show, which we thoroughly enjoyed. The theater was packed, but the audience was shocked by the shapely, scantily-clad Polish girls singing a song called "Sex Appeal" (in Polish and English). People looked at the loges where the Party people were sitting for guidance. To clap or not to clap? With some reluctance the Party people put their hands together, followed by the audience below. As we were exiting the theater, we overheard two women discussing the show. "Well, what do you think?" asked one woman. Her girlfriend responded, "You know Lyuba, we have to admit Poland is a WESTERN country!"

We stood outside the theater to meet the performers and congratulate them. When they appeared, they, too, greeted us warmly—after we said we were Americans. (By the way, Aldriedge spoke a few words of Polish.) They invited us to join them for drinks at a bar called Neptune, where we spent several hours discussing everything from the Katyn Forest massacre of Polish officers by the Red Army to Polish American relatives of the performers living in Chicago and Springfield, MA., as well as what the Poles called the "pitiful" state of pop music in the USSR. Above all, the Polish performers impressed us with their openness, frankness and friendliness.

And now I'd like to say a few words about what I call the "Cuban Connection." One afternoon just after lunch I returned to my stand where a bunch of people were waiting for the "man in the pants" with their questions. There were two young men in the crowd who looked neither Azeri nor Russian. Finally one began to ask me a question in rather broken Russian. At one point he turned to his buddy and said, "Cono, como se dice prestamo en ruso?" "Ah ha," I thought…"Latins!" So, I casually looked at him and said, "Me lo puedes preguntar en espanol, Chico. Hablo espanol." (You may ask me in Spanish; I speak it.) The looks of amazement on the boys' faces were nothing short of funny. However, when I began to answer the question in Spanish, the crowd became angry and yelled, "Russian, please, in Russian." Next day about ten Cubans (the boys were Cuban students) arrived looking for the "guy that speaks Spanish." We went over to a corner where we could talk in peace and had an interesting and frank exchange. They invited me to their dorm for a party that night. I was flying up to Moscow that evening on the Embassy run, so I had to delay my meeting with them. However, the delay gave me the chance to buy all kinds of goodies at the commissary for my meeting with the Cubans. One of them waited for me by the tower and took me to their rather miserable living quarters.

The room was full of Cubans (and a few other Latin Americans as well). I brought with me three bottles of Bacardi rum, Coca Cola, potato chips, pretzels, nuts and other American junk food. It was gone in about half an hour! Needless to say I was the center of attention. They asked me more questions in ten minutes than the exhibit visitors did in two hours. What impressed me most about the meeting was the lack of animosity toward the USA and their distaste for their Soviet hosts. They were all unhappy in the USSR. Their buddies in Moscow, Kiev and Leningrad were no better off. One chap remarked to me, "If I was a Communist before I came here, I am certainly NOT now! These people are bar-barians. They say we are lazy and look down on us. Imagine! Why, they do not even bathe!" One, very pretty, young brunette announced to me she was return-ing to Cuba for surgery the following week. In her own words, "It is simple sur-gery, but I would never allow these Soviet butchers to touch me." There was no doubt in my mind after this meeting that these young people were Cubans above all, Cuban patriots, not die-hard Communists. To be honest, two or three of them still felt they were Communists in their hearts, but that the Soviets dis-torted the system. One guy raised a toast to Fidel Castro. I had to drink. Then I toasted President Richard Nixon. Then they had to drink. Finally we made a compromise toast to Cuban-American friendship. As the evening progressed, the young people began to ask me about some Cuban singers who had left for the USA: Celia Cruz, Fernando Albuerne, Olga Guillot, Tito Puente and others. I asked if they had ever heard any songs by Cuban-Americans. Of course not. I saw a guitar in the corner, which I grabbed and began to sing (in my horrible voice) a few notes from "Cuando sali de Cuba" (When I left Cuba), "He perdido una Perla" (I have lost a pearl), and some other sentimental songs composed by refu-gees from Fidel's tyranny. Most of them wept bitterly. It was a very emotional evening for all. When I left, I was smothered with kisses from all present. They asked me to return again. I said we'd have to wait to see how these meetings were accepted or not accepted by the local KGB. Needless to say, no Cuban ever showed up again at our exhibit. I saw one on the street one evening, and he ran the other way.

Another evening I was in the apartment of a Russian couple. I asked them what they thought about Cuba, Soviet-Cuban relations and the Cuban students in the USSR. They said they had a negative impression of Cubans. "They are lazy and stupid. They will never make good Communists," said the wife. The couple also pointed out that "too much money was being diverted to the island of Cuba at the expense of the Soviet people. We resent that." I remember well how in 1966 Russians would often chant "Cuba-si, Yankee-no" in front of Americans. By 1971 I never heard the words. So, I asked this particular couple if the phrase was no longer in style. The man replied, "Nowadays, instead of 'Cuba-si, Yankee-no,' we say, 'Cuba-si, a ya v kino!'" (Cuba-yes, and I'm off to the movies.) It might be called apathy?

After a mini-vacation we headed for Tashkent, the capital of Soviet Uzbekistan. In my opinion, it was the most difficult city I had ever worked in, bar none. The harassment was constant. For the first time in my career on exhibits, I stormed off the stand more than once. Even the even-tempered John Aldriedge threw his microphone into the crowd one afternoon, calling them a "herd of buffalo." Although the Vietnam war was usually the primary reason for attacking the USA and our foreign policy, the visitors also brought up America's "racism," "unemployment" "exploitation of the working classes," "desire for world domination," "the brain drain," and, of course, "crime." Once, however, they brought up "narcotics." Fortunately for me, a few days before the comment, Leah "Mama" McClure and I had done some shopping at the local bazaar. At first we were impressed with the quantity—certainly NOT the quality—of fresh fruits and veggies we saw on display. By American standards the prices were astronomical, but at least the produce could be seen, if not had. It beat anything I'd ever seen in Moscow. Suddenly a fairly young Uzbek man walked up to me—assuming I was Russian (why??)—and said he had a high quality supply of hashish in his stand. I asked him to repeat the words for two reasons. First, his Russian was poor. Secondly, I thought I was hearing things. Sure enough, it was hashish. So when the question about drug abuse in America came up at the exhibit, "Why are so many of you Americans on drugs and where do you get your drugs?" I was able to answer. "Why? Because we live too well. From where? Right here at the Tashkent bazaar, where hashish is sold openly." The man left my stand.

I must say, in all fairness, the harassment and annoying comments came from the Russian residents of Tashkent. Perhaps the KGB did not consider the Uzbeks worthy of being trained to taunt Americans. By nature they were quiet, peaceful and docile people, as a whole. The hotel food was bad, to say the least, but the dining room staff could not have been more pleasant. The first night I watched the waitress serve what we would call spaghetti to a table of Uzbeks. I asked what it was called. Something "logman" was the answer, but it had no sauce on top. Next night I asked for the "logman" with tomato sauce on top. The waitress asked: "Why tomato sauce on top?" I explained that is how we eat it in the USA. When she served the "American version of logman" two Uzbek men at the next table approached me with their forks and asked for a taste. They liked it. In short, after that episode the waitresses always told foreigners that spaghetti with tomato sauce was available but not on the menu.

I would like to briefly talk about a few of the people I knew well in Tashkent. First of all, there was a pretty Uzbek girl named Saiida, who was a dancer with the National Ballet of Uzbekistan. She had piercing brown eyes, high cheekbones and beautiful long, black hair. There was something very sexy about this woman and at the same time childlike. She spoke Russian excellently, having studied in Leningrad for many years. What surprised me about Saiida was how she swallowed the Soviet line completely about Communism, Russian intellectual superiority, a better Uzbekistan under Communist rule. She was correct about one area. Before the Red Army came in, the country was devastated by local wars among the various tribes and families. Now there was peace. Well, peace by Soviet standards. The dancer could not understand why America did not accept Communism and live in peace like all the Socialist countries. She had a 20 year-old brother who was about to be inducted into the army. One evening the three of us were sipping tea at a local outdoor cafe. When Saiida mentioned peace among the Socialist countries, her brother asked her—in the most vulgar terms—if she weren't a bit confused. "What about relations between the USSR and the People's Republic of China? There are border clashes daily…and you know it, little sister." He offered to take me in her car one day to the border with China, where I could see with my own eyes—in his words—"thousands of fresh graves of young Soviet soldiers." I did not go because we were not allowed to travel more than twenty-five kilometers from the center of the city. Rashid told me another funny story. I had no reason not to believe him. He said that whenever the daily Trans-Siberian Express passed near the Chinese border with Uzbekistan,   the   local   Chinese   peasants—under   instructions   from

Beijing—dropped their pants and "mooned" the passengers. When Moscow had enough of this harassment, according to Rashid, the passengers were issued large portraits of Chairman Mao. When the pants were dropped, and the Chinese buttocks up high, the passengers posted the Mao pictures in the windows of the train. The "mooning" stopped after a short period.

Rashid told me another story that happened a month before we arrived in Tashkent with our exhibit. There was a major soccer game between the Moscow team and the Uzbek National team. The stadium was filled to capacity. Moscow won. The locals were so incensed they began to beat up the Muscovites, as well as Russians in the crowd. There was blood everywhere. The Red Army had to be brought in to quell the disturbance, according to Rashid. Unlike his sister, he felt no love for the "Russian liberators." In fact, he was disgusted about entering the Red Army. Rashid pointed out that Uzbeks were sent far from home to serve, as were Latvians, Georgians and other minorities. He explained that, everyone knew, in case of a local revolt, the Uzbeks would never fight against their brothers. In fact, I asked Latvians, Georgians and some others if Rashid was correct. They all agreed. So much for mutual trust among the Socialist brothers.

Sergej and Nellie Schachowskoj, Yura and Sharon Osmolovsky, Masha Soukhanova and I became close friends with a young, Russian couple Sergej and Nina. Nina was the daughter of a Soviet general. In fact, I believe he was in command of the forces in Uzbekistan. Assuming that were true, Nina had the privilege of meeting with us Americans with no serious repercussions. Without doubt, Nina was from the most privileged class, the military. She had Western clothes, records, a transistor radio from Japan. She adored American music, especially jazz. She and her family even got to travel beyond the borders of the USSR on vacation, but NOT to Western countries. It was Nina that taught me a cute phrase in Russian: "Kuritsa nye ptitsa, Pol'sha nye zagranitsa," meaning "a chicken isn't a bird any more than Poland is 'abroad.'" I believe the family also lived in East Germany. One would think that this young woman would be happy with her life. Far from it. She actually began to hate her father (as did her mother) Nina claimed that "power ruins an individual." She said, "Before he rose to the rank of general, he was a happy, family-oriented man of good humor. Now he spends his time thinking about whom to do in, whose rear to kiss for the next assignment and whom to bribe for some French wines." Nina saw another revolution in the future but not necessarily within her lifetime. Strangely, this delightful couple had nothing but contempt for the Soviet masses, who were—in their words—"too stupid to realize they are being deprived of the most basic freedoms in life." Nina also criticized her fellow children of high Party officials for their "hypocritical acceptance of the status quo."

Finally, I wish to relate the story of a young professor of French named Cieshelski (his parents immigrated to France from Poland), who was in Tashkent on a teacher exchange between the Sorbonne and Tashkent University. The poor professor was disgusted. He was not allowed to bring in the teaching materials he needed for the position, not even a non-Communist French newspaper for the students to read. He and his wife (who did not speak a word of Russian or Uzbek) lived at the Hotel Tashkent with us. We often ate dinner together. Dr. Cieshelski could not wait to get back to Paris to do his best to terminate this—as he called it—"farce in educational exchange." He was also amazed at how the Russian professors looked down on their Uzbek colleagues, not to mention on the students. The French professor admitted that before coming to the USSR, he was very much to the left (to the horror of his Polish-born parents) and believed the "Soviets were humans like the rest of us." During my last meal with the Cieshelskis, he went so far as to say that if a war broke out between the USSR and Red China, he'd volunteer to fight for the Chinese. One evening he related to me a toast he had heard in Warsaw: "May Red China invade Poland three times!" One was supposed to ask, "Why three times?" Answer: "In order to invade Poland three times, the Chinese have to invade the Soviet Union SIX times!" One has to appreciate Polish humor, right?

After Tashkent, we took off for Akademgorodok, the pride and joy of the Soviet science community, just outside of the major city of Novosibirsk. It housed the Siberian Academy of Sciences and very important research centers. The residents had the best of whatever was available in the USSR. There were even small, private homes in addition to the usual ugly Soviet high-rises. The day after we arrived was Lenin's birthday, a major holiday in the USSR. On TV we saw a huge balloon in the shape of Lenin floating above Red Square. It was April 22, 1971. The temperature was well below zero; but the Siberian birch forests, the ground covered with fresh snow and the quaint, little houses (built long before the Revolution) made all seem like a fairyland. John Aldriedge and I went down for breakfast around 8:30 am. When the waitress approached our table, I gleefully exclaimed, "Good morning. Happy Holiday!" She looked at me in disgust. "What do you want to eat?" she snarled. I replied, "Isn't today Lenin's birthday? I said 'Happy Holiday.'" Then she said, "And I said, what do you want to eat?" So much for her enthusiasm. There was a parade. (I guess you'd call it that.) But, it was cold, windy and snowy. Some Party hacks were shouting, "Long live Lenin!

Long live the teachings of Lenin! Long live the peace-loving policies of the Soviet Union! Long live the friendship among our Socialist brotherhood! Long live the directives of the Twenty-sixth Party Congress!" and so on and so forth. I have never seen a less interested, less fired-up crowd in my life. But, then there was the good news. There was a meat market/bakery across from our hotel. The bakery had tasty chocolate mini-cakes called "yozhiki" (little hedgehogs) all the time. They had bread, if one arrived before 8:00 am. But, there had not been meat in ages. This historical day, however, the market had a sign in the window: "Meat Today." The lines were as far as the eye could see. On my way back from the parade I asked one woman what meat was for sale. She replied, "Horse meat" (konina).

I remember another funny story that same day on my way back from the parade. There were two middle-aged women walking in front of me. One was asking her girlfriend, "How is your brother Valeri doing these days?" The reply: "Oh, Valeri is doing very well now. His health is improving daily since he gave up meat." "Oh, is your brother a vegetarian?" "Oh no, he's Russian," replied her less sophisticated friend. I laughed so hard the women turned around to see why I was alone and laughing so loudly.

Once again, our pavilion was quite far from Novosibirsk. One had to take the train—a thirty minute trip—to reach us. The "Science City" was small compared to the population of Novosibirsk. Nonetheless, the Siberians are a hearty and determined bunch. The trains carried a good number of visitors, although not the record crowds we were used to. Many of the scientists living in Akademgorodok attended our special by invitation only seminars on Mondays, but otherwise it was risky for Russians to be seen even attending the American exhibition, much less talking to an American. The third day of our show I witnessed a scene I shall never forget. I was standing outside the pavilion taking a break. What seemed to me a very old man (a typical Siberian with a long beard, rubber boots up to the knees, no teeth, a heavy, bulky, black coat) was holding a three year old boy by the hand; he walked up to me and asked, "Is this the American exhibition?" "Yes," I replied. "Do you have a man named Prince Sergej Schachowskoj working here?" "We do." "Ah, then it was worth the trip. We have come from the village of (_), and I want my three year old grandson to see a REAL RUSSIAN PRINCE before I die." The child extended his little hand to me (by this time I was almost in tears) and said, "Good morning, Uncle. My name is also Seryozha. Pleased to meet you." I took the visitors in to the hall, gave them their pins and brochures and called Sergej from his stand to meet them. The old man fell to his knees, kissed Sergej's hand and said, "What an honor to meet you, your Highness." Sergej told me later this was also the shining moment of the trip for him.

After work we often took the elektrichka (local train) into Novosibirsk, where we discovered a neat youth cafe called EVRIKA (Eureka). There we met dozens of delightful, young Soviets, anxious to exchange opinions and information with us Americans. They seemed to have no fear of the authorities. One evening I asked two of our friends, Lalya and Mila if they were not risking their scholarships by meeting with us Yankee Imperialists? They assured me that "the farther one travels from Moscow, the more freedom one has. Remember, most of us Siberians were sent here in the first place, because we did not conform to Moscow and her rules." We had many a wonderful evening listening to Lalya playing the piano in her parents' apartment. When one of us would travel weekly to the Embassy in Moscow, we would bring back all kinds of goodies for our parties at Lalya's…

Novosibirsk was the home of some excellent artists. Masha Soukhanova and I spent an evening in the home of one of the most talented artists I had ever seen anywhere. The entire small, private house was covered with his paintings. We wanted to purchase several of his works, but which ones? Suddenly Masha screamed to me, "My God, it's almost time for the last train back to Akademgorodok. We must run." We ran like hell to the station and jumped on the train as it was already moving. Masha remarked that we were the only passengers. How strange! There were always other Americans on that last train. Turned out we boarded the wrong train. It was on its way to an onion field for the night. We came as close to freezing to death that night as ever. How we survived that cold (not to mention the smell of onions everywhere!) I'll never know. We never even found the engineer. By dawn the train returned to the city, where we boarded the next train to our destination, arriving at 7:00 am. We just had time to shower, change clothes and get to the exhibit. Even more amazing, no one noticed we were missing!

The last night in Siberia was memorable for two reasons. Our friends Mila and Lalya organized a touching good-bye party for us. It lasted so late we had to take a taxi (actually three taxi's) back to Akademgorodok. When I reached my room, one of our guides knocked on my door and asked for my help in "burying some Bibles." "What?" I asked. He was a devout Christian. Through some Christian organization he had received about fifty pocket-size Bibles in the Russian language. He had distributed many of them, but had about a dozen left. The fellow did not want to throw them away nor be caught with them at Soviet Customs leaving the country. Somehow he managed to find a shovel and off we went to the forest behind our hotel. And there, under the bright Siberian moon, in a birch forest at 2:00 am, we planted our Russian Bibles in the earth. I like to joke with friends that, somewhere in deep Siberia, there grows a white birch tree covered with Bibles.

While in Akademgorodok, Masha Soukhanova and I met a young chap named Oleg. He was in his early twenties and lived in one of the special 'bachelor" apartment houses for unmarried workers. We did not have a lot in common with Oleg, except he impressed us with his sincerity and naivete. He was an orphan, who was working and taking a correspondence course to one day improve his lot and perhaps find a job in Moscow. He and I were about the same suit size. As I mentioned earlier, I usually left all my clothing behind with friends whenever I'd leave the USSR. The night Masha and I arrived to leave the clothes, he insisted on treating us to a bottle of wine. As we sat sipping the wine, he began to stare at the Russian Orthodox cross Masha wore around her neck. Finally he said the following: "I really appreciate the beautiful clothes you gave me, Bill; but there is something I would prefer to have." "What is that, Oleg?" exclaimed Masha. "Your cross!" He told us that "on his own" he was coming to the conclusion that there is a God. He planned on taking private, underground lessons in Orthodoxy in the near future. Oleg voiced the opinion that more and more young Russians realized that Communism did not satisfy their spiritual needs and were beginning to look to religion in their lives. Masha reluctantly gave the boy her cross. He began to weep. Without saying goodbye, young Oleg ran toward the forest. We knew we would never see him again.

Next day we headed for the West via Moscow. Our pretty, blonde guide, Robin Pratt and I went first to Amsterdam, where she was joining her fiance a few days later. Then I went on to my beloved Spain, where Masha Soukhanova joined me a few days later. The two wonderful weeks in the South of Spain, mainly in Torremolinos, then Granada and Seville, brought us back to reality and normalcy. Once again, we sadly remembered the wonderful friends we made in the USSR, friends, who would never (we thought) see this beautiful country, eat this delicious paella, dance in these wild discotheques. We both agreed if we never saw the Soviet Union again, it would be too soon!

TOURING THE USSR WITH
THE JOFFREY BALLET

◆

[IF THAT DIDN'T TURN ME OFF,
NOTHING WILL!]

The State Department was more than delighted when final word came from Moscow that Goskontsert would accept a tour of the City Center Joffrey Ballet. Other classical American ballet companies had performed in the USSR (American Ballet Theater, New York City Ballet and others), but the Joffrey was unique and quite different from other American companies. In order to get approval for the tour, State invited Sofya Nikolayevna Golovkina to New York to preview the repertory. She was wined and dined like a queen, much to her delight. For a die-hard Communist Golovkina had very bourgeois tastes. She demanded—and got—the best hotels, restaurants as well as gifts. Golovkina was the Director of the prestigious Moscow Bolshoi School of Ballet. She ran the school with an iron fist (accepting mainly the children of Party officials) and had the ear of the Minister of Culture, Ekaterina Furtseva, as well as all the Kremlin leaders.

In private conversation Golovkina never hid her love and respect for Josef Stalin. In her youth she was a ballerina of some note. Unlike most Russian women her age, she obviously had better access to fine creams and other cosmetics. In short, she did not look her age. Above all, Golovkina was very open to flattery. She and I hit it off from day one. Perhaps because I knew a bit about her career as a ballerina or perhaps because I knew so much about ballet, Sofya Nikolayevna and I were never at a loss for conversation. She immediately switched to the informal form of "you" with me in Russian but seemed pleased that I continued to use the formal "you" when addressing her. One of the most informative conversations I had with her was an exchange about the possible repercussions of the Joffrey performances in the USSR. I asked her what if Minister of Culture (an oxymoron)

Furtseva did not like what she saw? Furtseva had disbanded more than one Soviet dance company for being "too Western" in orientation. "Ah, Furtseva is going to die soon anyway" replied Madame Golovkina. Indeed shortly after our talk, Furtseva went on to her eternal reward. Was Golovkina a mind reader, a soothsayer…or did Furtseva not die a natural death? Golovkina spread a few gossipy stories about the Minister to me as well, but I deem them unworthy to print. Gossip is just that. Besides,the old hag is dead!

Once the deal was signed, State's wonder worker Irene Carstones was given the task of putting the program together. Irene was one of these women, who lived for the "Department" (as she always referred to it). She never took a vacation nor a sick day. I liked and admired Irene without closing my eyes to her negative side. One day shortly after I left USIA, I saw Irene on the street. She was eighty years old and still working. I asked her when she was going to retire. "There is a whole new world out there," I told her. I'll never forget her response, "If I retire, I'll die." Well, she retired a year later and died within three days of her retirement. Scary! Irene knew all the nuts and bolts of putting together a cultural exchange program to the USSR, although she had never been there and spoke no Russian. She was a tough-talker, a no-nonsense woman and took no crap from anybody. I would imagine that most of the people involved with Soviet cultural exchange would have given anything to be selected for the Joffrey trip. Irene interviewed them all and selected me for several reasons: I had established a reputation as a "take no crap from Soviets" person; I had Soviet experience; I spoke Russian; and mainly, I knew a lot about ballet. Irene was certain that Robert Joffrey would approve of me. He did. After meeting Mr. Joffrey, I knew he and I would make a good team. He was very naive about the Soviet Union as well as the realities of Soviet life. But then, most of our artists were oblivious to that world. Joffrey cared little about politics. This trip, however, convinced him that political control of the arts was far more tight there than in the USA.

The troupe was performing at the Kennedy Center in Washington a few weeks after I had been selected as the escort-officer. This was my first meeting with them as a whole. It was supposed to be a briefing. One of the dancers later told me they were surprised to find a young, excited and knowledgeable escort with a sense of humor. I talked TO them, not AT them. Yet, my message was not well received that first time. Without trying to scare them, I informed them they would be watched, followed and discouraged from contact with Soviet citizens, even dancers. I could see the look of disbelief in their faces. Then I was obligated to give the list of do's and dont's. No drugs, no sexual contact with Soviets, no buying nor selling on the black market, no unofficial currency exchange, no taking pictures of train stations, airports, men in uniform, shabby buildings, etc. I understood their reaction as I recollected my skepticism during my first security briefing at USIA almost ten years earlier. I thought, "They might think I'm nuts now, but they'll soon find out I'm telling the truth."

Two chartered Pan Am planes carried us to our destination (we were on one plane and the second carried our props). We left Kennedy airport one cold evening in November 1974. The planes stopped for refueling at Shannon airport around 2:00 am their time. The Duty Free shop was closed, but the Irish gladly opened it for us to stock up on some last minute things like cigarettes, perfume, etc. They also opened the bar for us to have our last Irish coffee for a few weeks. The Irish security guards were quite impressed with our lovely, young ballerinas. As we sat sipping our drinks in the bar one of them asked where we were going. "The Soviet Union." "Do any of you speak Russian?" asked a guard. The PR man, Bob Larkin, replied, "No, but we have our interpreter, Bill McGuire, with us." "Bill McGuire? That's an Irish name!" I answered, "Yes, can you imagine such a thing? Only in America!" Then off to Leningrad.

Just as we were about to cross into Soviet airspace, I got on the loud speaker and reminded my group for the second and last time, that if they had any drugs of any kind, now is the time to dispose of them. I passed around my Pan Am flight bag and said I was accepting "all donations" to be flushed down the toilet, no questions asked. I was surprised at the amount of pretty, multi-colored "vitamin" pills returned to me. They all went down the toilet and are probably planted in some remote field in the Northwest corner of the USSR.

We were met at the airport by Diana Moxhay, a friend from the Embassy, members of the US Consulate in Leningrad and representatives of Goskontsert, our official hosts. Keep in mind that within the past two years I had accompanied two Soviet delegations in the USA. We stayed in first class hotels, ate in the best restaurants, had the finest means of transportation and were treated like royalty wherever we went. I was not surprised, however, that the exact opposite was true when dealing with the other side. Our hotel in Leningrad was cold, drafty, lousy food, surly service. What surprised me more was the lack of courtesy and professionalism on the part of our Consulate. I will not dwell on those guilty of rudeness and incompetence on our side (they know who they are and what they did) nor will I give them the honor of mentioning their names in this book. Let me just say in passing that at least one of our diplomats, an ex-marine, thought the Joffrey dancers were not of "Marine quality."

Actually, I should cite at least one example. The Consulate had organized a reception for the Joffrey following the opening in Leningrad. Because dancers never eat before a performance, I asked my colleague to make sure there would be plenty of food, as they would be hungry. In addition, I expressed the hope that there would be food for the vegetarians in the group. I also requested a one hour break between the show and the reception for them to shower and relax. The bus was waiting for us at the theater with an American diplomat, who informed me that we "had to get to the consulate immediately" as the Soviet guests were there waiting for us. Somehow I convinced the troupe to go. When we got there the food was in short supply and completely inadequate for the dancers. They became furious at me. What could I do? The consulate lied to me. I must also point out that—although everyone from the Leningrad ballet world had been invited to the reception not one big name showed up. Mikhail Baryshnikov had recently defected to the West, and we were told in conversations much later that the entire Soviet ballet world had a bad case of Baryshnikov-itis. The evening was a disaster to say the least. From that dreadful reception we returned to our cold, drafty rooms at the flea bag they called a hotel.

The very first night in Leningrad—even before the reception—my Joffrey crew got their first experience about Soviet reality in regard to contact with foreigners. We were eating dinner in the hotel dining room. A young Soviet band was playing. During their breaks they sat with us. We had a group of musicians as well. The two groups of musicians hit it off beautifully. In fact, they were to meet the following day on Nevsky Prospekt to have coffee and see a bit of the city. Needless to see, the Soviets did not show up. The following day Tom Gambino and some others were walking down Nevsky and saw one of the musicians. His face was badly beaten. When he saw our guys, he ran away, motioning NOT to follow him. I remember how depressed and shocked our musicians were as they recounted the story to me. Tom said, "God, Mr. McGuire, I think you WERE telling us the truth back in Washington." "You ain't seen nothin' yet!" was my response.

We were invited to visit the Kirov Ballet the next day. It was obvious that the instructors and the pupils were ill at ease to see us. Even the directors, Konstantin Sergeyev and Natalia Dudinskaya, whom I knew (and to whom I brought greetings from our mutual friend, Tanya Kamendrowskaya) never looked me in the eye. We were treated to a tour of the Kirov Alumni Museum. It did not shock me, but Robert Joffrey and his dancers were amazed to see all traces of Rudolf Nureyev, Natalia Makarova and Mikhail Baryshnikov had been removed, even from the yearbooks! They were non-people; they never existed. That is how the Soviets dealt with defectors.

In an almost James Bond-like manner, we managed to have a few short meetings with some of the Russian dancers. Among them was Aleksander Godunov, who assured us he would defect the first chance he got. It was Godunov who related to us the fate of many of Baryshnikov's close friends, many of whom were inducted into the army or sent to Siberia…or worse. Little by little I could see the Joffrey-ites beginning to understand why these dancers had defected.

As far as the performances went, Leningrad was and is one of the more sophisticated cities in that country. The audience that first night was tightly controlled by Goskontsert, but even what I call the "die-hard Commies" appreciate good, innovative dancing. Nevertheless, the evening was marred—at least for me—by my attempted act of kindness. I had one extra ticket. So, an hour before the performance I went outside the theater, where hundreds of young Leningraders were scrambling to get a ticket to the sold-out performance. After chatting with several young students, I decided to give the ticket to a pretty blonde named Ksenya. She hugged me, kissed me and thanked me from the bottom of her heart. Then I returned to the theater. As they were closing the doors, I happened to be standing nearby. As I looked ut on the street, I could see little Ksenya being beaten by the police and crying for help. Unfortunately I could not remember which seat she had, or I would have done something, had a KGB thug been sitting in her seat. No good deed ever went unpunished in the USSR! That's for sure.

As we were leaving the theater, these same young students (who had not even seen the show) were waiting to get autographs from the dancers. Our ballerinas were thrilled to oblige when out of nowhere came several policemen, who literally pushed us on to the bus and physically removed the well wishers, in some cases brutally. I can still hear one of our girls scream: "Mr. McGuire, do something!!!!!!"

None of us was unhappy to leave Leningrad. We boarded the overnight train to Riga, our next stop. According to the contract, we were to fly or have first class train compartments within the USSR. There were 73 of us and only 18 first-class tickets on the train to Riga. The majority had to go in second-class. For the second time, I almost had a revolt on my hands. Once again, it was not my fault. The Joffreyites bedded down as best they could while "yours truly" began to walk through the cars out of frustration. As I was approaching the back of one of the cars, I could hear American music. Bunched around a tape recorder was a group of young men—ranging from ages 18 to 22, I'd say—listening to a taped VOA dance show emceed by my friend Lisa Borissowa. I listened a bit to be sure it was VOA and then I asked, "Is that the Voice of America?" They nodded. "Is that Lisa Borissowa?" "Yes...do you like her, too?" "I know her." "Yeah, sure." "Seriously, Guys, I am an American from Washington and I know Lisa and some others at the VOA." Suddenly they turned off the machine and began to ask me questions. I was not expecting the answer I got when I asked if they knew Bill McGuire. "Oh yes," said one lad. "We like him just fine. He plays great music, all the hits. And he speaks excellent Russian...for a black man." I thought my hearing was failing me. "Bill McGuire is NOT black. I know that for certain." "Oh yes he is!" replied one guy. "Look, he announced on the air recently he is in love with Aretha Franklin. He even dedicated an entire program to her. He plays a lot of Black music. In America white boys are not allowed to date or fall in love with black girls." The others chimed in. "He is one of our favorites, but he IS black. Usually we do not like blacks in our country; but, as long as he stays in America, we like him." Did I dare tell them who I was? Of course not.

The Hotel Riga in that quaint, Latvian capital was the best we had during our tour. It was also the best food. In addition, we had more young people in the audience—after the first night for the Party people—than in other cities. The Latvians showed great appreciation for the "Cakewalk" and the "Green Table" ballets to the delight of our Resident Choreographer Jerry Arpino. In short, it was a welcome change after our stay in Leningrad.

We were in Riga for Thanksgiving. I sensed a great deal of frustration on the part of the dancers, the musicians and the crew. Although I tried to get several turkeys from the Embassy Commissary, it was impossible. I had to do something to boost morale, especially my own. So, I booked a private room in the hotel, an orchestra and the best food and wine in Riga to celebrate our national holiday. It worked, if only temporarily. Some of the waitresses asked me just what is "Thanksgiving." I said it is a day in which we thank the Almighty God for the blessings He has bestowed on our country. "Isn't that wonderful?" exclaimed one of the waitresses in rather poor Russian. "You know, we Latvians believe in God, although we are not supposed to since the 'liberation.' Unfortunately there is little to be thankful for these days."

Our first free evening I decided to just walk along the quaint, narrow streets of Riga by myself. I did not get far when two young Latvians approached me for a cigarette. After I said I do not smoke, they realized I was a foreigner. "Was I with the Joffrey Ballet?" "Yes." "A dancer?" "Hardly!" They were going to a local jazz club and asked me to join them. We got a table near the bandstand and ordered a drink. The band played so well, including some American melodies ("Take the A Train") that I went up to the stage during intermission to compliment the musicians. One of them looked at me strangely and remarked, "You have a very familiar voice. Do I know you?" I replied, "Well, I am escorting the Joffrey Ballet here in Riga, but in my country I work at the Voice of America. My name is Bill McGuire." "BILL MCGUIRE!!!! No, it can't be! Our authorities would never give YOU a visa, you're too popular! Are you really Bill McGuire?" I showed them my passport. The musician grabbed the mike and announced, "Comrades, you are not going to believe this, but this man is Bill McGuire from the Voice of America." The room burst into applause. Next thing I was surrounded by people asking for my autograph. What a pleasure to meet my listeners in Latvia. Once again, they remembered things I had said years ago that impressed them. What memories they had. I had to ask the question: "Did any of you think Bill McGuire was black?" All heads shook a "no." Then I related the story on the train to Riga a few nights ago. One girl responded, "Oh, pay no attention to them. They were Russians. They do not know black from white." My hand was sore from signing autographs, and I stayed there until the place closed. The kids listened to both the Russian and Latvian broadcasts on the VOA (with some heavy jamming to deal with). They felt the Latvian shows were better, with the exception of the Bill McGuire shows. Actually I agreed. The Latvian Service had an excellent chief named Irina Karullis, whom I knew and respected. She had a lot of American-born Latvians on her staff, giving their programs a definite American flavor.

Our final performance in Riga ended with a forty-three minute ovation (I counted it). The rock band began to play some hits of the day and we turned the stage into an American discotheque. The audience went wild. Our Goskontsert manager Nikolai Martyshevsky ran up to me and screamed: "This has turned into a circus. For the sake of my weak heart, stop this nonsense immediately." After the way he and Goskontsert treated us, I could have cared less about his weak heart. It took me twenty minutes to get the crew off the stage.

Vilnius, the capital of the so-called Lithuanian Soviet Socialist Republic, was our third stop on the tour. Keep in mind I had visited the city twice before and felt a great love for Lithuania. Unfortunately, this trip was not impressive. Once again, Goskontsert screwed us royally. They and the Soviet musicians stayed at a fine hotel near the theater. They put us in a flea bag, and we had to be bussed to the theater. By the time we reached Vilnius, many of us had come down with colds, the flu and a disease not yet recorded in the medical books. Our leader, Robert Joffrey, became so ill he did not make one performance in Vilnius. At one time five of the dancers were in the hospital. The first victim became ill on the bus going to a rehearsal. The disease resembled severe epilepsy. In fact, it took five men to hold him down. Worse, the hospital did not want to let me in to see the patients. I went there one evening and demanded to speak with the doctor in charge. If the woman that met with me was a physician, I am a nuclear scientist. "Can you please tell me what is wrong with my people?" I asked politely. She replied, "Spasms." I was at my wits' end, with no help nor cooperation from the Embassy. Moscow would not go along with my plans to cancel the tour after calling a press conference to explain what a sham this cultural exchange had become. Among my other complaints, I actually saw Soviet workers throw our washing machine out of a third floor window.

Maybe it's time to inject a bit of humor into this sob story. In each city we hired a few local women to help the wardrobe mistress with washing and ironing the costumes, etc. She was a typical New Yorker with a spicy tongue and a penchant for four-letter words. We had two charming, elderly Lithuanian women working with us. The first afternoon, our wardrobe mistress came into my office and asked me to translate for her. I asked what the problem was. She said the women continually came up to her with a needle and thread in hand. "Please tell them I have nothing for them to sew…and to stop shoving a needle and thread in my f——n face!" I approached the ladies with the message there was nothing to sew. They replied that the American woman was constantly using the verb to sew. Finally it dawned on me that the word for "sew" in Russian is "shit"—a word used a lot by our Dorothy.

Although we were ill, frustrated and disgusted by the time we reached Moscow, the dancers seemed to acquire a second breath, knowing that the end was near. They danced better than ever. In addition, they began to learn more about my personal problems trying to get things done, to protect them from the disturbing issues I faced daily, and to keep myself from having a nervous breakdown. By Moscow once again I had a wonderful rapport with everyone in the company. I found it sad to watch their previously good impressions of the USSR turn into shock and disgust. But, they were real pro's. Opening night in Moscow was an enormous hit, a triumph for American choreography. The embassy had invited the entire Bolshoi Ballet company, as well as all other leading figures of the Soviet dance world to a reception following the performance. I personally looked forward to meeting Galina Ulanova and Maya Plesetskaya. No one from the Bolshoi showed up. Only Kremlin officials and Goskontsert flunkies attended. I asked the Ambassador, "How many times do the Soviets have to show us they could care less about cultural exchange? Who really benefits from it?" I suggested next time the Bolshoi comes to the USA, we put them up in flea bags, give them lousy food, give them no publicity, boycott their receptions. Unfortunately for us, these matters in the USA were in private hands. The Government could do no such things. As a matter of fact, we agreed to almost every group the Soviets endorsed for cultural exchange. Most of the people we suggested were rejected by the Soviet Ministry of Culture. Cultural exchange was definitely a one-way street, negotiated by spineless bureaucrats on our side.

By the way, after we returned home our musician Tom Gambino wrote a book about his impressions of the Joffrey tour in the Soviet Union. He titled the book "Nyet" (a word he heard hourly in the USSR). Our beloved State Department tried its best to prevent the book from being published. However, the persistent Tom won with a little help from legal organizations. It's a book worth reading.

As long as I am venting my spleen about the exchange, I must say that the female interpreters Goskontsert gave us in Moscow were olympic-class bitches. One of them named Natasha had a habit of approaching the dancers just before a performance and bringing up issues like racism, drugs and unemployment in the USA. It upset them greatly, and they finally complained to me. I had to forbid her to go backstage before a performance. One evening one of our musicians was dining in a Moscow restaurant with another Joffrey employee. A man approached his table and asked if he were with the Joffrey. The man said to be "especially careful" around the interpreter Natasha, who was his exwife and a KGB employee. The musician seemed surprised when I informed him almost EVERYBODY that had contact with us either worked for the KGB or reported to them. There was one exception to what I just wrote. We had one delightful, elderly interpreter named Henrietta Belyaieva. She was obviously from good, Russian stock (before the Revolution) and spoke English beautifully. She did her work well and avoided her coworkers as much as possible. One evening I asked Henrietta if she had ever been abroad, especially to England or America, to use her English. She smiled sadly and indicated that she was not trusted enough to travel abroad.

Perhaps the lowest kick in the groin came the day I met with Soviet Customs officials, representatives of Goskontsert and our beloved interpreter Natasha to inspect the crates for shipment back to the USA. The Sovs were extremely careful that whatever we brought in to the country (up to the last light bulb) went out with us. For this reason I was unable to fulfill a request made by dancer Rudolf Nureyev, who asked me to bring in some films of his performances, together with a movie projector, for his sister Roza in Leningrad. I know the temperamental Rudik (as sister Roza called him) was unhappy with my refusal, but I had to stick to the rules. At any rate, we were all gathered for the "selective" inspection of the crates. All of a sudden Natasha pointed to one particular box and said, "Let's open this one." They did. In one of the drawers she found an icon. "Contraband!" she shouted. This was the straw that broke this camel's back. Out of over 100 crates, she knew which one to open to cause a scandal. It had obviously been planted there—probably by her—and she thought I'd fall for this charade. At this point "yours truly" burst into a string of profanities, screaming at all of them and, obviously shocking them with my words. I told Natasha she was the lowest form of humanity, a stupid robot, a skunk (yes, she had body odor too!) and a disgrace to womanhood. I assured her and her comrades this event would appear in the New York Times for the world to read. I already had her name. I began to ask the names and patronymics of the others, who refused to give the information. They all looked at Natasha in disgust, as if to say, "This time it didn't work, Bitch."

While all this was going on in Moscow, President Gerald Ford and Leonid Brezhnev were meeting in Vladivostok to discuss matters of mutual concern and better relations between our two countries.

The day I accompanied the Joffrey dancers to the airport was a bittersweet event for me. I was happy to see all of them leave for home, better patriots than when they left. But I was sad to see the hopes and illusions of young, innocent Americans shattered by what they had witnessed over the past two weeks. I embraced them all. Some of the girls cried. Above all, we parted friends.

Robert Joffrey, Gerald Arpino, Bob Larkin and I stayed a few extra days in Moscow to take care of some matters of protocol, see a bit of the city and try to meet with some Soviet ballet people we knew from their trips to the USA. Joffrey and I finally had a very short and uncomfortable meeting with prima ballerina Maya Plesetskaya. Aleksander Godunov managed to meet secretly with Bob Larkin one evening long enough to tell him how he had been chastised after meeting with us in Leningrad.

According to the terms of the US-USSR Cultural Agreement, the US provided transportation to the USSR, and the Soviet government brought us home. That meant I flew back to Washington via Paris on Aeroflot. In those days it was usually more pleasant to walk home, but the flight—especially the food we picked up in Paris—was not bad at all. My friends, Tamara Kit and John Aldriedge, met me at Dulles airport. They insisted on taking me out to dinner that evening to hear the news before anyone else. I insisted on going home, taking a shower and a nap first. When I entered my apartment on Tunlaw Road NW, I sat on my suitcase and burst into tears. I must have cried for half an hour. That day I made up my mind I would never return to the Soviet Union as long as the Communists were in power. I kept that promise.

MY FINAL YEARS AT
THE VOA

◆

[MOSCOW ON THE POTOMAC]

Before I get to the sad saga of my last years in the Russian Service of the Voice of America and why I left, I feel obligated to say a few unkind words about VOA's string of mediocre directors. "Mediocre" is the kindest word I can find to describe them. Some were worse than others. Some were dedicated and at least tried to run a professional radio station. But, let's face it, any government organization, corporation or small business is only as good as the person on top. The chief can either hinder or help, or the chief can simply do nothing and collect a high salary. Unfortunately for all concerned, VOA directorship has always been a political appointee. In addition, this person has never been at the top of the president's political paybacks. One VOA Director's claim to fame is that she is the one who had Monica Lewinsky transferred from the White House to the Pentagon, after rumors of hanky panky in the Oval Office began to spread. With few exceptions the director has had little or no knowledge or experience in international broadcasting, journalism and foreign affairs.

My very first shocking experience with a "mediocre" VOA director was many, many years ago. A group of women journalists, including two women from the Soviet Union, came to visit the station. They had a one hour meeting with the director. Someone in the PR office thought it would be nice for a Russian-speaking American broadcaster to meet the Russian women. That's how I got invited to the reception. In all fairness, the director was extremely personable. He shook the hand of every woman (about 25) and made them feel welcome. Coffee was served, VOA ball-point pens, etc were presented to the journalists. Then the chit-chat began. At one point he asked a lady from which country she came. She replied, "Liberia." "Oh, that's one Latin American country I have not visited yet, but I hope to some day." Some years later our newly appointed director announced that—since many of our studios had glass windows and we gave regular VOA tours—it would add "flavor" if the broadcasters wore their national costume to work. The Voice of AMERICA? It almost prompted me to contact the Philadelphia Mummers Society and obtain one of their fancy, feathered costumes to wear in Studio 4. But, the headdress might be too wide to get through the studio door!

Perhaps my favorite director was Mary Bitterman, who came in under Jimmy Carter. She summoned me to her office one afternoon to get the "American perspective" of what was going on in the Russian Service. Ms. Bitterman was also a Georgetown graduate and was associated with radio over in Hawaii. She truly wanted to make a contribution, but was so overwhelmed by what she saw at VOA that she was completely confused about how to help. I had already met with several VOA administrators in the past, and my patience was wearing thin. Perhaps I was a bit sarcastic with her, but at least I was telling the truth. I was not certain any one person could bring about the changes needed, but I compared her to a shrink to whom I could vent my frustrations without paying $100 an hour. First of all I pointed out that even though this nuthouse was called the "Voice of 'America', the forty-some services, except for the English Service, were controlled and staffed by immigrants. That in itself was NOT bad, I pointed out. We are all the children, grandchildren, etc., of immigrants. In many cases immigrants love and appreciate America more than the native born. My point was that America is a country made up of people born here, people that came many years ago, and people who arrived recently. The VOA should reflect this wonderful diversity of opinions and conceptions. No "one" group should be considered superior nor inferior. However, our Government should give native-born Americans the opportunity to learn foreign languages and work at the VOA. I suggested there should be a program sponsored by the VOA, the Department of Education, and an American university (such as Georgetown University, known for language teaching), which would offer not only scholarships but also study in foreign countries. The program should include a work-study portion to allow students to work at the VOA a few hours a day to get the needed experience. Above all, candidates should be selected to include ALL races, religions or non-religious, and ALL parts of the USA. I felt and strongly feel today that Americans are no less able to learn foreign languages than any other group on Earth. The Voice of America must develop cadre composed of the native-born, past and present immigrants, working together to really and truthfully "tell America's story to the world." Mary Bitterman seemed impressed. She asked me to put my proposal in writing, which I did. A few weeks later she was gone. (Few of the VOA directors lasted very long.) When I asked her replacement what happened to my proposal, the answer was, "Who knows?" The sad truth was, "Who cared?"

Let me take this idea one step farther. In the summer of 1998 I wrote a letter to Father Leo O'Donovan, the President of Georgetown University, requesting that Georgetown establish an International School of Broadcasting and Journalism, where Americans could combine language study with unbiased journalism and where students from other countries could also receive a degree, for instance, in international broadcasting in the major languages of the United Nations. It was a project I wanted to establish and help Georgetown get funded. Although I was not afforded the courtesy of a reply, I have not given up on the idea. So, let's get back to my final years at the VOA. If I have to name a specific event that I consider the "beginning of the end of the Americanization of the Russian Service," I guess I would mention the death of Vladimir Mansvetov in April 1974. It was a terrible loss. Between 1974 and 1976 things were beginning to decline, but not at autobahn speed.

In general, the other Americans (John Aldriedge, Tamara Kit, Marina Levitzky, Marie Ciliberti, Tammy Dombrovsky, Liza Borissow, Mary Patzer, Jack Murphy, Brant and Charty Basset, Carolyn Smith, Zora Safir, Jill Dougherty, Gary Wackernah, Mary Kruger, to name a few) and I continued to do our dance shows, youth shows, programs on education, economics, performing arts, women's issues, special events and holidays. There was feeling, innovation, admiration, respect, dedication and unlimited cooperation among us. The programs retained a distinct, friendly American flavor. The letters that got through to us reflected this.

In 1976 the first of the emigres—a man from the Soviet Union—came on board. He spoke English and was a hard-working, dedicated employee. I remember his first day on the job. A bunch of us took him for coffee to welcome him to the staff. Within a few months seven more recent arrivals from the USSR began working one Monday. On Wednesday of the same week, three of the seven began taking "Beginning English" classes (at the expense of the American taxpayers!!!!) during work hours. Was it unreasonable for us to ask how these people passed the entrance exam, if their English wasn't good? No doubt there was some political pressure to hire these people. Needless to day, not one of them was an American citizen. So, for the first time we saw a complete disregard for the VOA Rules. The Rules clearly state that, if an American citizen is available for a position, it must go to him or her before it can be given to a non-citizen. In other words, in a country of 250 million people, there were NO American citizens that VOA could have hired?

Moreover, we "citizens" had to have a security clearance to work at VOA. How was it possible to "clear" a recent arrival from the Soviet Union? Would the KGB really cooperate with our Security people on background checks? Hardly! I am not one who sees a spy behind every post, but logic dictates that it would benefit the KGB to infiltrate an agent or two into the VOA. Correct? Whether it was intentional or a coincidence, the Service was soon afflicted with low morale and afire with turmoil and anger between the emigres and American-born employees. Even more revolting, despite the fact that most of us American-born employees had Masters degrees, spoke English and Russian, had security clearances and experience working in the USSR, we were hired at the GS-5 level. However, these newcomers, whose sole qualification, for the most part, was that they spoke native Russian, were offered jobs at the GS-11 level. In contrast, VOA had hired Dr. Ludmila Foster, a Russian-American who for years wrote one of the finest and most popular programs on the air ("Books and People"), and who was a published author with a Ph.D. from Harvard, at the GS-9 level! Something was clearly not even-handed in the VOA Personnel's hiring policy regarding citizens and non-citizens.

Before anyone starts throwing daggers at me and calling me "anti-immigrant," I would like to point out that I personally brought one woman from the former Soviet Union to VOA Personnel. She spoke flawless English and Russian, had a degree from an American university, knew the USA, and had a lovely voice. She was hired on my recommendation and became one of our most productive employees. Furthermore, at first, we American-born welcomed the idea of new blood into the Service. We were convinced that we could help the recent arrivals with their English, and they could help us keep abreast of current Russian expressions, etc. It did not turn out that way. Unfortunately some of the emigres chose to use their native Russian expertise as a club with which to belittle the Russian skills of the American-born staff. History was repeating itself. Remember in an earlier chapter about my first days at VOA, I mentioned that many emigre broadcasters kept trying to impress the listeners with their literary Russian? Our job at VOA was not then and is not now to be Russian poets or grammarians! Our job is to present our country to the world—to talk about America and American political, cultural and social institutions.

Let me add that the new arrivals were not satisfied with their highly paid jobs as translators, news readers or producers. They demanded—and got—to be emcees of their own programs!! The number of mistakes, some silly, some disastrous that went on the air to Russia was overwhelming. I could probably write a second book devotedto the hideous misinformation about America that went on the air. But, my purpose is not to belittle the non-citizens. After all, they did not walk in off the street and grab the microphone. I blame the spineless administration and clueless USIA Security for their failure to protect the Service's mission—a failure that, in my opinion, was anti-American. If their actions were not anti-American, what are? Here we were telling people in the Soviet Union how wonderful America was, while what was happening right there in the Russian Service was as anti-American, anti-democratic, illegal, discriminatory and illogical as anything that happened in manipulative Soviet bureaucracies. Rules that were strictly enforced in regards to U.S. citizens were ignored in regards to non-citizens!

Since this book is about me, I will cite examples from my own story. Between 1967 and 1976 I was the regular emcee of the Wednesday "Night Owl" program. As I said earlier, the show was jammed less than others because it was broadcast at midnight in Moscow. In short, most of the show got through to the listeners. I knew the new arrivals were casting greedy eyes on my program. After Mr. Mansvetov's death, his position was given to a woman who was extremely talented as a writer-emcee. As an administrator, however, she was a disaster with a capital D and a coward with a capital C. I suspected she was looking for an excuse to take me off my show. Finally one Wednesday I broadcast an interview I had conducted with movie critic Rex Reed, who had recently visited the Soviet Union. Reed ended his remarks with the comment that the "people in the USSR deserve a better form of government." She was listening. The next day she wrote a memorandum to the Division Chief (whom she later married) absolving herself of all responsibility for Rex Reed's "offensive remarks to our listeners" even though the script had been edited, as was everything that went on the air. Then she removed me from the program and handed it over to Mr. W, one of the recent emigres, who was still studying "Beginning English" at VOA expense.

This new shining star on the VOA horizon was also given my New Years Eve show. When I used to emcee the program (actually we took turns), I would invite the entire staff to the studio to give their greetings to the listeners and, if they wished, to dedicate a favorite song of the year to them. I invited everyone, although not everyone chose to participate. The show was lively and funny. At midnight (4:00 pm our time) we had the sound effects of champagne popping,

Auld Lang Syne playing, etc. When Mr. W took over, he invited only his close emigre colleagues (not one American-born!) on the show to send greetings exclusively to their RELATIVES and FRIENDS in the USSR—not to the listening audience. When an editor criticized his show's narrow focus, he claimed that he had emceed the show exactly the way Bill McGuire used to. This infuriated me so that I sought him out and reminded him that Bill McGuire did not say hello to personal friends or relatives in Moscow, Leningrad, nor Odessa, and that I had given the "whole" Russian Service the opportunity to send greetings to the "whole" USSR. Years earlier I created a weekly music show called "On Broadway," because I thought Broadway musicals told more about American life than many other sources.

A few weeks before I left the Russian Service, I was asked to revive the program; however, this time I was obligated to co-host the show with one of the new arrivals, who had no familiarity with or comprehension of Broadway musicals. To add insult to injury, she insisted on writing "my" lines for the show, many of which were factually incorrect. I finally removed myself from the program. Our Cultural Chief lied to me more than once. We were on very good terms until one evening when I was producing the Breakfast Show. The show's emcee (one of her favorites) arrived drunk at the studio and read drunkenly on the air. The next morning I related the matter to her. She vehemently rejected such a a possibility and called in the emcee, editors and supervisors to inquire into my "allegations." Naturally, the man denied the charge. She glared at me. I left the room and returned with a tape of the show, which I played for all to hear. Listening to the incoherent rambling, everyone was embarrassed to tears. I demanded an apology for my having been accused of inventing the incident. No apology was forthcoming. She could not forgive me for having publicly challenged her authority but easily dismissed the unprofessional behavior of her favorite. After this, her goal was to get me out of her shop.

Shortly after that, I requested to cover a Russian-American festival in Kodiak, Alaska. One morning she called me into her office to say she was sorry, but our finance officer said there were no funds for the trip. I accepted it and went about my work. Later that day I saw him in the corridor. When I remarked that it was too bad there were no funds for this trip, which would be of great interest to our audience, he looked at me in sheer amazement and said, "What are you talking about? Of course there's money. I am surprised Ms. L didn't ask for it." It became increasingly obvious that this spiteful, incompetent administrator was seeking to find fault with everything I did. I knew her aim was to remove me from her section. (My job was listed under the Production Staff, and that's where she hoped to send me.) I decided to do some short interviews with members of our Russian staff, who had interesting lives before they came to the VOA. For the pilot program I selected Aleksei Nikolayevich Tcherkassky (father of ballerina Marianna Tcherkassky), whose family was well-known in old St. Petersburg, and who knew well and associated with some of the greats of the ballet world (Tamara Karsavina, Alicia Alonso, Suzanne Farrell, George Ballanchine and others). He told fascinating stories. The second part of the show featured our colleague, Kira Slavina, whose father Mark Joffe was a painter. There is a museum in Israel of his works. Kira was a poetess in her own right, having published books in English and Russian. I thought the show was lively and interesting; but the Chief informed me, "Who in the Soviet Union wants to hear the boring tales of old emigres?" That was the end of the program. She squashed it.

One more story about her. While I was in New York City on VOA business, I managed to conduct an extremely interesting interview with ballerina and teacher Alexandra Danilova. First, of course, I had to get Madam G's permission. She was very much against the idea, because, in her opinion, Danilova was too old and frail, spoke Russian mixed with French, and, therefore, was not a good subject for an interview. I insisted. To my delight, the interview was first-class. (Danilova had forgotten more Russian than this woman ever learned!) What was so disturbing to me was that although my interviews with old emigres were being frowned on by Madam G (NOT her real name, by the way), she was encouraging the new arrivals to interview new emigres in Washington, Los Angeles, and New York. Her pets were unable to do an interview in English. Not one of them ever conducted an interview in English while I was at the VOA; they had to rely exclusively on their fellow Russian-speaking émigrés for program material. They couldn't read The Washington Post, the New York Times or Los Angeles Times as news sources and relied, instead, on the New York Russian immigrant newspaper Novoye Russkoye Slovo.

Not only was the Russian Service replacing American-born employees with emigres, but also it was rejecting the applications of aspiring American-born candidates. I found out about this the year I was invited by Georgetown University to participate in a seminar for Russian-language majors at the school. Representatives of Government and the private sector were there. Dr. Valentina Brougher invited me not only because I was a Georgetown graduate but also because, in her opinion, I was an "American" success model for her language students. I accepted with the permission of our Division Chief. The seminar went very well. I was impressed with the fluent Russian of Dr. Brougher's students and distributed several employment applications given me by the VOA Personnel Office. As a result, several of the students applied for jobs. One day a disturbed Dr. Brougher called me to inform me that VOA Personnel was telling her students there were NO positions available in the Russian Service. I flew into our Division Chief's office and demanded to know why I was told to distribute applications for positions when apparently there weren't any jobs. He shrugged and said, "I thought there were." There were—just not for Americans. Emigres from the USSR continued to be hired.

I want to describe two particularly disturbing stories about the dire consequences of bureaucratic deceit on two young Americans. The first story is about John Bordeaux. The day he came to take the VOA test I happened to be on duty to record the voice tests of new applicants. Applicants read on tape what they had translated from English to Russian in their exam. Bordeaux passed with flying colors. He also had an excellent radio voice. A week later he received a letter from Personnel saying he had "not passed" the test. Interestingly, a few days later he took the State Department's interpreters' exam—which was far more difficult than the VOA test—and passed with flying colors. For a time John was interpreting in Geneva at the SALT talks. After he received the VOA rejection notice, he called me to ask my opinion. I assured him that there must have been a mistake and told him to inquire. He did. He also sent a letter to his state senator. A week later he received a second letter informing him he had "passed" the exam. John then applied for a security clearance, which usually takes three to six months (unless, of course, you just arrived from the USSR and your background CANNOT be checked!).

Eight months later, he still had no clearance. He came to the VOA to speak with our Service Chief (NOT the infamous Madame G). I could hear John's voice and the Chief's rising. Bordeaux left the office red in the face and extremely agitated. He walked over to me and said, "That son of a bitch told me that as long as he is Service Chief, I will never work in this office." That happened on a Friday. On Saturday morning John Bordeaux suffered a massive heart attack at age 25 and died. On Monday morning I told the news to the Service Chief. He shrugged, "Well, you know that boy was mentally unbalanced." (Indeed, deceit and discrimination are destabilizing.)

The second case I call the "M Massacre." It involved a young American, who was already on staff. He was one of the most talented employees ever to work in our

Service. Things at work were going from bad to worse. Morale was low. Several of us demanded a meeting with the Service Chiefs and administrators. We expressed our grievances in detail and insisted that they hire citizens as well as non-citizens, that we not be discriminated against, that we get our programs back, that we receive salaries commensurate with our duties and performances and that we not be castigated for pointing out mistakes made on air by the new emigres. The most vociferous among us was the man I'll call Mr. M. It is true that he lost his cool several times and loudly stated facts the bosses did not want to hear, although they were truths they could not deny. The grievance meeting took place on Friday before Labor Day, 1976. Monday was the holiday. Tuesday morning two USIA Security men picked M up from work, interrogated him for three hours, and accused him of being a homosexual and smoking marijuana. They told Mr. M that he was a security risk to the VOA; and they threatened that if he did not resign, he would be fired and disgraced. This unfortunate, naive, 24-year-old American and award-winning member of the Russian Service, resigned out of fear.

This, in my opinion, was the darkest, most shameful page in the history of the Russian Service. Needless to say, this KGB/Gestapo tactic had a chilling effect on the rest of us. Many of us scrambled to read OUR security files under the Freedom of Information Act. Above all it also made us aware that the USIA was capable of using the Security pit bulls to silence dissension. However, if anyone was a threat to American security, it was THEY. How could they justify having handed security clearances to recent arrivals from the Soviet Union while withholding one from a loyal, talented and educated American citizen? (These are the same buffoons who allowed the Soviets to bug our new US Embassy in Moscow from top to bottom costing US taxpayers billions of dollars for reconstruction.) In addition, USIA Security as well as our incompetent administrators had the gall to say the "M massacre" was not in any way instigated by the grievance meeting held the Friday before. And the Pope is NOT Catholic!

This particular story has a happy ending thanks to the perseverance of those not yet disposed to funnel jobs only to non-citizens. One evening six of us American-born met in my apartment to discuss the situation. We invited The Washington Post writer Robert Kaiser to hear our stories. I had met him once in Moscow and felt he would write fairly about the situation for the world to read. He took copious notes that evening, but he never wrote one word later. I wonder who or what silenced him? Nevertheless, we accomplished something very important that evening. We helped Mr. M find and fund a good lawyer to sue the Agency. We decided we would fight to the finish and had no qualms about going public. If The Washington Post was not interested in publishing the shocking truth of events at the VOA, we were sure another paper would be. I must also point out that neither the VOA Employees Union nor the ACLU would have anything to do with this explosive case. The Cultural Service Chief Madame G was heard to say, "Mr. M will return over my dead body." Nevertheless, after 23 months Mr. M was finally reinstated. Publicity and a court battle were avoided. In retrospect, I think we should have called a press conference and exposed this bureaucratic travesty to the world.

Between 1976 and 1982 VOA Personnel mysteriously lost or misplaced the employment applications of over 50 Americans. Most of the thirty American-born staffers in the Russian Service found the discrimination so unbearable that they left. For those of us who remained, it was one disaster after another. As the number of newly arrived, "akt"-writing émigrés grew, so did the number of law-suits against the VOA, all of which cost the taxpayers a lot of money. One emigre sued over sixty times!! Another emigre was planning to sue a supervisor for anti-Semitism, until he found out his supervisor was Jewish. Fistfights broke out in the studio. During one of them, the words "I'll leave your children orphans," went out on the airwaves. An entire book could be written, maybe two, about what happened in that place and is happening UP TO AND INCLUDING TODAY!

In addition to complaints from our listeners that the Russian broadcasts had lost their American focus and feel, we received complaints from listeners in the USSR that the station was spending much too much time dwelling on the plight of Soviet political dissidents. Of course, many dissidents deserved VOA's attention and support—but not to the extent made inevitable by the "emigre-clogged" Russian Service. The VOA also focused too heavily on the stories of successful Soviet emigres living in the USA. Several Russian listeners told me how bored they became listening to the repetitive droning of disgruntled dissidents and the prattling of prosperous emigres. Our listeners wanted to learn more about Amer-icans and the American way of life. What did the new emigres know about the American view of life? It is no wonder that the numbers of Soviet listeners dropped off sharply after 1976. Interestingly enough, the names most Russians remembered and still cite today are the names of those of us who gave the broad-casts an American flavor.

Another constant subject for programs was Alexander Solzhenitsyn, the political icon of the day, who began his exile in the United States by "graciously" lambasting the "moral fiber of American youth." (By the way, how many young Americans had he ever met? I met him once at an AFL-CIO dinner held in his honor when he first arrived in Washington. The man looked and spoke like a crazed hermit.) After the collapse of Communism, his irrational ranting and raving deprived him of any credibility in the new, democratic Russia. Given his authoritarian bent, had he ever become president of the USSR, the jamming of the VOA no doubt would have continued!! He announced that jazz was decadent and useless, but the VOA's jazz programs were among the most popular!

I'll conclude by describing the straw that broke "this" camel's back. It was a Saturday in January 1984, and I was working the early shift. There was a woman—a Soviet emigree, by the way—of whom I was very fond. She and I had the kind of relationship I had hoped we native-born would have with all the emigres: If she had a question on proper English, she came to me with it. If I had a question on Russian, I went to her. That morning she came to my desk and asked me to translate an "akt" (remember that charming word from my days in the USSR?) against Mrs. T from Russian into English. Usually I made it a rule not to get involved in disputes among my emigre co-workers; but in her case, I made an exception. I was sitting at the typewriter translating the "akt," when I felt a hand on my shoulder. Then a woman's voice said, "Bill, let's go have a cup of coffee." replied, "I can't right now. I am translating an "akt" against Mrs. T." When I looked up, it WAS Mrs. T inviting me for coffee. Right then I made up my mind that I had to get out of the Voice to save my sanity.

Within two months I applied for and got the position I held my last ten years in Government service—a job I loved. Contrary to what one might think after reading this chapter, my good-bye party in the Russian Service was attended by all. In spite of my inner feelings, I always treated everyone in our office with courtesy and respect. It was a wonderful tribute to me to hear the new Chief Natalie Clarkson say, "You are welcome to come back here at any time. We shall miss you." I was presented with a beautiful wristwatch. My farewell speech was the shortest in VOA's history. "Thank you for coming today. Now let's enjoy this magnificent buffet." Most memorable, however, was a plaque given to me that day by my dear friend of so many years, Tamara Kit. It was inscribed with the immortal words of Dr. Martin Luther King, Jr: "FREE AT LAST, FREE AT LAST. THANK GOD ALMIGHTY, I'M FREE AT LAST!"

MY FINAL YEARS AT USIA

◆

[WORKING WITH SPAIN AND
LATIN AMERICA]

My new position, my final one with the U.S. Information Agency, began on March 4, 1984. I entered the Office of Satellite Speakers on Monday at 8:00 am. Although the USIA building is located only across the street from the VOA, I felt like I had landed on another planet. My new colleague, Judith Trunzo, was sitting at the secretary's desk reading cables. She looked up, smiled at me and said civilly, "Good morning. You must be Bill McGuire from across the street. Welcome aboard." The first day I sat quietly in my office reading about the types of programs I would be organizing. Our office chief, the lovely, kind and intelligent Carol Wilder, took me around to meet the rest of the staff, one of whom (the hilarious Wendy Beaver) I already knew. Everyone seemed so normal and friendly. I kept waiting for one employee to scream at another or for a fight to break out. The silence was almost frightening. My God, people were even speaking English and in polite tones!

Before describing my new position, I want to say a few words about the USIA Director, Charles Z. Wick. In my last chapter I mentioned that the Voice of America had a string of mediocre directors. So did USIA. It, too, was a spot reserved for political patronage. However, Mr. Wick was an exceptional leader, who had an excellent understanding of what we were all about. He also happened to be a close friend of President Reagan. As a result, USIA got the money needed to accomplish its mission. In my opinion, he was the best director USIA ever had. Wick "dragged" the Agency—against its wishes—into the 20th century! Under his directorship the Worldnet (USIA TV) and my new office, which was independent from Worldnet but used its TV facilities, were inaugurated. Among Charles Z. Wick's talents was his ability to sing our praises before Congress when we did something especially impressive. Leadership declined woefully after his departure. More fatally, the Agency was devoured by that lack Hole of spontaneity and creativity—the State Department.

A few words about the Satellite Speakers Bureau. By the way, they later changed the name, because it sounded too "techy" and "spacey." We answered requests from American embassies around the globe, which, in turn, received requests from local journalists, politicians, cultural or scientific figures for electronic contact with specialists in the USA. There were four major program categories. The first type was the "Telepress Conference." That was simply a telephone hookup between an expert in the USA and the interlocutor in the host country. Sometimes a local journalist did a one-on-one interview with an American. Let's say the American was in Los Angeles, California, and the journalist in Bangkok. We called California and called Bangkok and bridged the lines for the verbal exchange.

The average program lasted one hour. A second type program was the "Electronic Dialogue." For this exchange we pre-recorded a scene-setting video with an American expert on the subject matter, which was shown in the embassy and followed by a question and answer session by telephone. This gave the audience a chance to see what the expert looked like in person. Again, the video could go into the embassy library and could be used again and again in the future. We also kept a copy of the program in our library for future use. The third program was called the "Televised Electronic Dialogue." This was an exchange between an American guest and a foreign host recorded for future showing on TV. Our guest was in the USIA studio or in another American studio. A telephone hookup was established for the Q and A. The foreign studio videotaped the questions on their end, and we taped the American answers later. We sent our video to the embassy, where the two tapes were spliced together to create a seamless American and foreign dialogue for broadcast on local TV. This type of show was very useful and effective in countries where the cost of a live satellite transmission was far too expensive. The fourth type of program was an actual satellite transmission to the country.

To my delight, from day one I dealt mainly with Spain and Latin America, in other words, with the Spanish-speaking world. I was able to compile an extensive list of Spanish-speaking experts throughout the USA for my programs. When our expert did not speak the language, we used interpreters. As time passed, and I became more at ease in the job, I began to originate some programs. For instance, we did programs commemorating historical events, such as Black History

Month, the end of World War II, etc. Many times the embassy would call me to suggest a particular program. When I arrived at P/DS, I noticed a lack of cultural programs. This was my golden opportunity to showcase American culture. In spite of some resistance, I managed to organize some excellent exchanges between leading American figures and audiences abroad, about which I shall proudly speak shortly. My theory was: If you ask an American or anybody overseas, "Who was Secretary of State ten years ago?" the answer would probably be, "I don't know." However, if you ask anybody, anywhere, "Who is Ray Charles? Who is Tommy Lasorta? Who is Gregory Peck?" They know!

My first assignment was to find a Spanish-speaking American expert to discuss heart transplant surgery with a group of doctors in Caracas, Venezuela. When Carol Wilder gave me the project, she was concerned it would be too difficult a task. It was my first assignment, and I was determined to find the right person for the job. I remembered the first heart transplant was performed at Brigham Young hospital. I called the PR office there. Guess what? The expert had served in the Peace Corps and spoke Spanish very well. First success! I was elated.

I realized early on in my new job that we were actually in a position to be of some help during a crisis. Shortly after arriving at my new job, I got a call from the U.S. Embassy in La Paz, Bolivia. The Bolivian press had quoted an American senator who said that the Bolivian government was run by a bunch of drug dealers. Our USIS man felt at any moment a crowd would burn down the embassy unless we had a rebuttal of this statement for immediate placement in the local media. They wanted a White House spokesman. I made a few frantic calls and managed to get a spokesperson to do the program. Within the hour we were on Bolivian radio. The situation in La Paz remained calm hopefully in part because we managed to do the program.

After reviewing our past programs I became aware that many of the requests were political in nature and involved a State Department spokesperson. I wondered how long I could avoid dealing with that department for which I had so little respect. Then one day Carol dropped a request on my desk from the embassy in—(who cares?)? It involved a State Department expert on arms control. The program would be in English. Without going through too much red tape I managed to get Mr. X to do the Telepress Conference. He was in his office at State and I in our USIA studio, doing the bridging. Finally the hookup was established, and I said, "Go ahead with the questions." The interviewer on the other end began by asking the expert to say a few introductory words on the topic. My

State Department "mate" intoned, "Americans are basically interested in three important subjects...." Before he said another word, I murmured to myself laughingly, "Sex, drugs, and rock and roll." Suddenly a voice asked, "Who the hell said THAT?" The blood rushed to my head. I had forgotten to turn off my microphone! "This is curtains for me," I thought. I remained silent. Our expert went on with his introduction, and no more was ever said about my gaffe.

I am not going to go into any great detail about the politically oriented programs I did, especially the ones with US Government spokespersons. In some ways they reminded me of the Communists I had dealt with, that is, they rarely gave a straight answer. Instead, they were masters on how to talk around an issue rather than addressing it. I can recall one of the worst programs I ever organized involving a State Department official. The topic was the US position and policy on Nicaragua, and the journalists were in Madrid, Spain. This jerk agreed to do the program in Spanish for one hour. He insisted that I be present in his office for the exchange, rather than bridge the lines from USIA. When I got there he announced that he would not speak in Spanish. I pointed out it was too late to get an interpreter. "That's YOUR problem," he informed me. Then the whiz kid said he would devote only a half hour to the program. Again I reminded him he had agreed to an hour. "My time is too precious to give them an hour," was his retort. When I informed USIA Madrid of all the good news from my end, they were fit to be tied. Immediately I said that if they had a complaint, they should address it to the man (sitting next to me as I said this) who was causing all our woes. Our USIA officer in Madrid offered to translate. Our expert's response to the very first question was, "That is a very stupid question. If you can't ask more intelligent questions than that, I'm going to end the program."

To my amazement and delight, one of the Spanish journalists who spoke English took the mike and said, "As far as we're concerned, that WAS the last question. We're not here to be insulted by you." I always admired the Spanish for their spunk and ability to defend themselves against some low-level, pompous American flunky. Unfortunately this flunky was a rising star at State—no doubt the chief stimulus to his pomposity. A few months later I read that this narcissist was made the American ambassador to a Central American country. Ah, the rewards for rudeness!

I am convinced that in the area of drug prevention, education and treatment my new office made impressive progress in the following years. I organized a weekly call-in for Radio Caracol in Bogota, Colombia with experts from all over the

USA. Colombians could call in with their questions from all parts of that country as well. Later I produced a video with the help of Dr. Jose Szapocznik and other experts on drug-related issues. It was shown throughout Latin America. The video featured two Spanish-speaking teenagers, one still using drugs and one who had given them up. Their message was strong and impressive. Another participant was the president of a local "Parents Against Drugs" organization. He stressed what parents could and should do. I will never be able to thank Dr. Szapocznik enough for the hours and hours he devoted to our transmissions. He not only helped many in the USA but in Latin America as well.

In my early years at USIA, the Agency policy was to avoid the subject of AIDS. We simply did not comment publicly about the disease that was killing people like flies around the world. Then I had the distinct honor of meeting Dr. Mathilde Krim, Director of AMFAR in New York. She was attending the AIDS Conference in Atlanta but took two hours from her schedule to participate in a call-in via satellite to Libreville (not my area, but I found the request a challenge). That one program was the cause of a complete change of policy on the part of the Gabonese government about the epidemic. The embassy cables and assessment of that program helped me to organize many more electronic exchanges with countries around the world. The multi-lingual Dr. Krim was always there when I needed her. In addition to the Telepress Conferences, she made videos for me in English and French. She was one of the brightest stars ever to shine on our programs. A million thanks to you, Dr. Krim!

Some of the very best programs I did in my ten years at Satellite Speakers were the ones with our cultural representatives. But, let me mention the two worst programs I ever produced. The first was with author Joyce Carol Oates. She proved to be an insufferable prima donna. Her show was scheduled to transmit at the same time as another live program. So I had to arrange for her phone exchange to be transmitted via a commercial bridging station. Unfortunately, the commercial phone company piped "Muzak" in the background, while arranging the foreign connection. This music annoyed Ms. Oates, but she did not ask the company to turn it off. She held her fire until I checked in on her to be sure all was well before the program. She began screaming at me for subjecting her to "torture." By the time she was asked the first question, her sour mood was evident; she was angry and could not have been more sullen. The audience on the other end was so offended by her attitude that they curtailed the exchange. Her parting remarks to me were, "Don't you ever ask me to be on your program again!" To which I replied, "I'd rather die than deal with you again."

The second disaster (considering all the shows I did, two disasters are not bad, eh?) was less of a disaster than an embarrassment. It was with beatnik poet of the 60's Alan Ginsburg. A group of literary experts and journalists were gathered at the US Consulate in Rio de Janeiro to interview the poet about his life and works. Rio was one of my best customers, and they requested and got some of the best writers in the USA. I warned our USIA Officer that Ginsburg had a rather foul mouth. That did not matter to the Brazilians. Several people from USIA came to my studio to hear the program. Ginsburg was speaking from Chicago. When he was asked about a particular poem, Ginsburg recounted what inspired him to write it. According to him, he was standing in a second story window in New York City, masturbating and looking at a handsome Puerto Rican boy on the street. The boy was buying two cantaloupes from a vendor. That was the inspiration! All of us in the studio were aghast; however, according to USIA's Fred Emmert in Rio, the Cariocas did not even bat an eyelash.

I had a third close-call. I was doing a program from New York City for Madrid with a very famous American fiction writer. He arrived in the studio high on something other than Jesus. I could see the man was on some drug. I suggested we cancel the program, but he insisted he was in control enough to do the dialogue. I opened the program with the words, "I am happy to present to you the world-famous, American writer, XX. He will be speaking to you from the 26th floor of a building here in New York City." Mr. X took the mike and said, "Mr. McGuire said we are on the 26th floor. Well, I'm a helluva lot higher than that!" I wanted to jump out the window! Or, maybe I wanted to push him out!

No doubt my favorite programs were with America's finest stars of song and cinema. The one time in my life I was speechless was the day I walked into the office of Ray Charles to record a video about his life and music for worldwide distribution. He was sitting at his desk and rose when I walked in. "Good morning, Mr. Charles," I said, "I am happy to see you." His reply: "Well, I am happy too…although I can NOT see you." Charles sat at the piano, played a few notes and in his charming, easy way, talked for over thirty minutes about his fantastic life. It was a meeting I shall never forget.

Stevie Wonder was another unforgettable musician. I had to fly out to Portland, Oregon to catch him in one spot long enough to do a video. Before the camera began to roll, Stevie chatted with me like an old friend all the while he was busy composing a little melody to play for the beginning of the program! If ever there was a musical genius, it was and is Stevie Wonder.

When it comes to charm, grace, talent and warmth, I have to give the prize to the late Pearl Bailey. A few nights before her taping at USIA TV, she invited me to her concert in Washington DC. After the show, she and I went to her dressing room. Pearl kicked off her shoes and began to tell me about all the famous people she had met, who did NOT impress her. She had a wonderful personality, a great sense of humor. I brought our secretary, Sheila Savoy, with me to the taping. Pearl gave her a hug and even posed for a picture with Sheila. A few months later, Miss Bailey published another book. She sent me an autographed copy. Her untimely death brought a tear to my eye.

I had the honor to do several programs from Hollywood with Egyptian film director and critic Yusef Mohammed Rizkallah. Rizkallah organized special tributes to American actors whose films were top box office hits in Egypt. He arranged very special ceremonies to which he invited English-speaking Egyptian actors, actresses, critics and directors to interview an American star. Film clips were shown between questions. After the event was shown on Egyptian TV, it was passed on to other TV stations throughout the Arab world. I admit I was a bit surprised to hear that one of the most popular American actresses in Egypt was Ali McGraw and that "Love Story" was one of the most popular American films ever shown in that country. Ms. McGraw was delighted to accept the honor. She was nothing short of magnificent on and off camera. After the exchange she and I had a cup of coffee with her agent in the Los Angeles studio. I felt like I had known her all my life.

The program with Gregory Peck was no less outstanding. He, too, was a delight to work with. I realized the more famous the person, the easier it was to deal with him or her. There is an interesting postscript to the Peck program. A few months after the show he was returning from Rome in first-class, and an Arab sheik was seated next to him. The sheik told Mr. Peck how much he enjoyed the program on TV in his country (Qatar, I think). As a good friend of our Director Wick, Peck told him the story. This was proof to me the programs were really shown in other Arab countries, although I never doubted Mr. Rizkallah's word.

I do not want to turn these programs into a competition. Nonetheless, when I discuss the Hollywood series of programs, I am often asked who was the "sweetest"? (Angie Dickinson), the most "intelligent"? (Meryl Streep), the most "introverted?" (Julia Roberts), the "nastiest" (guess!). We also had programs with Robert Wagner, Jack Lemon, Richard Dreyfus and others. There can be no doubt that these programs made more friends for America than all the diplomats ever did. Having these actors on our programs helped to point out that, in addition to being movie stars, they were engaged in all kinds of social and charitable work. Many were very active in the fight to preserve the environment, to cure cancer, AIDS, Alzheimers' disease, childhood diseases, to combat human rights abuses, etc. These are the people who make foreigners fond of America.

I must also mention the multitudinous programs our office organized on teaching the English language and American studies for use around the world. We did not neglect science, technology, sports, medicine, journalism or human rights either. When democracy came to several Latin American countries during my time as Program Development Officer, we created programs on privatization, personal property rights, effective journalism, the electoral process, human rights, transition of power, rule of law and others.

I am especially proud of an initiative I took in 1988 and 1992 during the presidential elections. I produced major videos with representatives from the Democratic National Committee and the Republican National Committee to discuss their party platforms. I gave equal time to both views. These programs were put into several languages and shown around the world. For my viewers in Spain and Latin America I made two videos in Spanish with emphasis on how the election outcome might affect Latin America. The first was moderated by the gracious and talented Christine Emery. Although the program content was of utmost importance, several Latin American journalists called me to ask where I found that "beautiful blonde" to moderate the program? It was the first USIA-produced program to be shown in Cuba.

On election evening I gathered a bunch of political affairs experts in our studio to give hourly wrap-ups on the outcome, beginning at 8:00 pm Washington time until we knew who was elected president. The studio lines were hooked up to several embassies around the globe, where election parties were being held. The updates lasted about two to three minutes. The schedule was something like this: 8:00 pm in English, 8:05 pm in Spanish, 8:10 pm in Portuguese, 8:15 pm in Arabic, 8:20 pm in Russian, 8:25 pm in French. At the top of each hour we began again. It was a great honor to be part of such an important event in American history. This is what USIA was originally set up to do. I feel we did it well.

By early 1994 we heard there were plans to install a Compressed Digital Video studio in our office with links to the major capitals of the world. We finally had it in working order by March. Each of us took turns learning this newest form of communication, which was indeed impressive. It was like a video-telephone (to make it sound simple!). My final program with USIA—which also capped my thirty year career in Government was a series with Moscow! How befitting that I should begin and end this interesting, fascinating and rewarding career in Moscow.

I failed to mention that during these years I was also assigned to work on the Reagan-Gorbachev and Bush-Gorbachev summits as an escort for the Russian delegation at the Arab-Israeli Peace Signing at the White House and also as a participant in Vice-President Al Gore's trip to St. Petersburg in December 1993. In other words, I was somehow eternally connected to the Russian world!

In April 1994 the Government announced its first "buy-out," that is, the Government offered to pay employees with twenty or more years of service an incentive of up to $25,000 to leave service or retire as part of an effort to reduce the size of Government. At that time I became aware that my remaining family in Philadelphia was in poor health and needed me. If I was not the first to apply, I was among the first. Our Chief, Jon Silverman, for whom I still have the greatest love and respect, was not happy about my decision to leave. Since we were a small but very productive and cost-efficient office, he felt the reduction in force would not affect us. He was wrong. Shortly after I left, USIA closed the entire office. Apparently "brilliant" upper management minds had decided that America was safe and no longer needed to tell its true story to the world.

My retirement party was the most impressive I have ever attended. My buddy Dennis Raver videotaped the festivities, which were very much to my liking. My co-workers wrote and even sang a song about me to the tune of "You make me feel so young." However, their version was, "He makes Us feel so young." There was laughter, music, gifts, awards for service, great food, tributes, including several telegrams from the embassies I worked with, wishing me the best, recorded messages from several of the experts I recruited, even a greeting from Dick Clark, host of the American Bandstand, a beloved idol of my teenage years. My closest friends of many years: Tamara Kit, Nick and Carol Moravsky, Marie Ciliberti, Marina Oeltjen, Jack Murphy, Bob Lee and many others were in attendance. In short, it was a memorable ending to a memorable career.

CONCLUSION

There are a few things that I wanted to accomplish by writing this book. Obviously I wanted to tell my own story. I wanted to point out that I had the distinct honor of having worked on three different fronts, which played a significant role in "lifting" the Iron Curtain. The first was the Voice of America. In spite of all the nonsense and turmoil, the VOA managed to be effective—and it still has not received all the credit due it. During the golden days of VOA, I believe that we got our message across very well. We talked about America—the good side of our country and the bad.

The second area was the yearly American exhibits to the USSR, which, since 1959, gave the peoples of the former Soviet Union an opportunity to speak with real, live Americans and hear basic truths about our country, our system and our philosophy. Finally there were the people-to-people exchanges. While each of these areas had their problems—and they certainly could have been better—they were good enough to accomplish their goals. I failed to mention the International Visitors program of the U.S. Information Agency, which organized trips to the USA for hundreds of Soviet citizens as well as countless numbers of privately funded citizen exchanges. We can and should be very proud of these efforts.

In my opinion, however, the real credit for saving the USA, the USSR and, in fact, the world from the Communist menace goes to President Ronald Reagan. It was his faith in the American system and his determination that destroyed the "Evil Empire." He was the first to call a "spade a spade." It was President Reagan who had the courage to stand before the Berlin Wall and make his famous remark, "Tear this Wall down, Mr. Gorbachev." He charmed President Gorbachev into doing the right thing. Anti-Reaganites criticize the financial "excesses" of the Reagan years, while failing to acknowledge the millions spent under their own administrations to develop weapons of mass destruction, nuclear arms and spying satellites. Ever since Nikita Khrushchev visited the USA in the early Sixties, American presidents and their "advisors and Sovietologists" tried in vain to reach agreements with the USSR. These sincere but terribly naive negotiators sat as "equals" with their Soviet counterparts. SOVIETS WERE NOT

EQUALS! The Soviet side came to the table with their hands covered with the blood of innocent people. They were responsible for the massacre of their own citizens and the subjugation of other nations as well as for being the catalysts in bloody conflicts around the world. They were the ones who built walls, jammed foreign broadcasts, prevented the reunification of families, told blatant lies in their state-controlled media, crushed innovation in the arts, tortured dissidents, suppressed religion. Were THEY our equals?

I have met some of the finest people in my life in the former USSR. It is my fervent hope and prayer that this new, democratic era will bring the peace and prosperity they so deserve. They are long overdue to join the international brotherhood of nations. My second hope is that greed and corruption will not destroy the future of a nation so rich in human and natural resources.

Most important of all, I would like to point out that—at least in my opinion—the future of the United States of America does not lie in Russia. Nor does it lie in Europe, Japan, China, nor the Middle East. We are "Americans" from Canada to Tierra del Fuego. Our future and our destiny are here in the Americas. We have everything we need to survive and prosper right here within the Americas. We must develop this hemisphere—and live and work as a team. Cuba must join the American brotherhood of nations. If we achieve this, once again the label "Made in America" will have meaning.

AUTHOR'S BIOGRAPHICAL INFORMATION

Bill McGuire, a native of Pennsylvania, studied Russian at Georgetown University. He never intended to make a career in Russian; but fate and destiny changed his mind, when in 1966 he took a position on a US Information Agency cultural exchange exhibition to the former Soviet Union. His admiration of Russian culture and repugnance at Communist ideology led him to work on other exhibitions. In 1967 he was invited to work in the Russian Service of the Voice of America, when VOA was attempting to give their programs a more "American"

sound. He was trained to write, broadcast (a rock and roll show among other things) and to produce other Russian language programs. On several occasions he was on loan to the State Department and other US Government agencies to accompany American delegations to the Soviet Union and Soviet delegations visiting the USA. He was the Escort Officer for the Joffrey Ballet on their successful tour of the USSR in 1975. He is now semi-retired and lives in a suburb of Washington, DC.

0-595-27097-2